Commercializing SDI Technologies

This is one of a series of books on technology and entrepreneurship sponsored by the IC² Institute at the University of Texas at Austin, under the general editorship of Raymond W. Smilor and Robert L. Kuhn. The series provides materials from practical and scholarly perspectives that can in turn assist leaders in policy and decision making. It ties practice to theory. Each book in the series is designed to build on the one before it so that an extensive foundation of research and practical insight are available to leaders in business, government and academia. In the process, the series provides foresight into complex topics. It offers an opportunity to introduce relevant topics in technology and entrepreneurship as well as allow for important contributions to established lines of research and practice.

OTHER TITLES IN THE SERIES

Commercializing Defense-Related Technology edited by Robert L. Kuhn

Corporate Creativity: Robust Companies and the Entrepreneurial Spirit, edited by Raymond W. Smilor and Robert L. Kuhn

Technology Venturing: American Innovation and Risk Taking, edited by Eugene B. Konecci and Robert L. Kuhn

Managing Take-off in Fast Growth Companies, edited by Raymond W. Smilor and Robert L. Kuhn

Supercomputers: A Key to U.S. Scientific, Technological, and Industrial Preeminence, edited by J. R. Kirkland and J. H. Poore

Commercializing SDI Technologies

• • •

Edited by Stewart Nozette &
Robert Lawrence Kuhn

PRAEGER

New York
Westport, Connecticut
London

Library of Congress Cataloging-in-Publication Data

Commercializing SDI technologies.

Includes index.
1. High technology industries—United States.
2. Strategic Defense Initiative. I. Nozette,
Stewart, 1957–   . II. Kuhn, Robert Lawrence.
HC110.H53C65   1987   338.4′762   87–18333
ISBN 0-275-92332-0 (alk. paper)

Library of Congress Catalog Card Number: 87-18333
ISBN: 0–275–92332–0

First published in 1987

Praeger Publishers, One Madison Avenue, New York, NY 10010
A division of Greenwood Press, Inc.

Printed in the United States of America

The paper used in this book complies with the Permanent Paper Standard issued
by the National Information Standards Organization (Z39.48–1984).

10 9 8 7 6 5 4 3 2 1

CONTENTS

A Point of Departure
  Robert Lawrence Kuhn   ix

Foreword
  Hans Mark   xi

Acknowledgments   xiii

Introduction
  Stewart Nozette   xv

Part I: The Strategic Defense Initiative Program

1
Defense R&D and National Competitiveness: Past, Present,
  and Future Prospects
  John McTague   3

2
The Strategic Defense Initiative Research Program: Conception
  and Execution
  Gerold Yonas   9

3
The Strategic Defense Initiative: What, Why, and How
  Major General Robert R. Rankine, Jr., USAF   23

PART II: The Commercialization of Technology: Present Public Policy

4
Technology and World Leadership
    D. Bruce Merrifield   39

5
The Department of Defense Policy Environment on
    Technology Transfer
    Gerald D. Sullivan   45

6
Perspectives on Technology Transfer
    George Gamota   55

PART III: Private-Sector Requirements for Successful Commercialization

7
Collaborative Research and Development
    Admiral Bobby R. Inman (Retired)   63

8
Investment Banking Requirements
    Wayne G. Fox   69

9
Innovative Financing for Emerging Technology Companies
    Mark Lancaster   85

PART IV: SDI Technologies and Spin-Offs

10
Telecommunications Markets
    Colonel Gilbert Rye, USAF (Retired)   95

11
Automation and Expert Systems
    Bruce Bullock   99

12
Space Robotics: Commercial Opportunities and Challenges
Ronald L. Larsen   113

13
Supercomputer Systems Markets
Lloyd M. Thorndyke   137

14
Kinetic Energy Technology
William F. Weldon   143

15
Optical Technology
Robert R. Shannon   149

16
Advanced Materials for SDI: Promises and Prospects
Stanley I. Weiss   155

17
Biotechnology, Bioprocessing Research, and Space:
  Ingredients for New Health Care Products
Baldwin H. Tom   161

PART V: Perspectives on Commercialization

18
Views on SDI Commercial Potential
William Gregory   171

19
Legal Perspectives of Commercialization
Richard A. Givens   177

20
Collaborative Aspects of Commercialization
Eugene E. Stark, Jr.   185

21
Case Examples of Commercialization
Robert P. Stromberg   193

22
International Technology Transfer Issues: The SDI and Eureka
Rodney W. Jones   197

23
Comprehensive National Security: The Power of American
Science
Robert Lawrence Kuhn   211

Summing Up
Initiatives for Commercializing SDI Technologies
George Kozmetsky   217

Appendix
The SDI Office of Educational and Civil Applications
Colonel Joseph Rougeau, USAF (Retired)   223

Index   225

About the Contributors   239

About the Editors   243

About the Sponsors   245

A POINT OF DEPARTURE

ROBERT LAWRENCE KUHN

The commercial benefits of the Strategic Defense Initiative (SDI) can be explored only within the broader context of science and society. Although SDI is a program to research the feasibility of an effective defense against ballistic missiles and is not primarily an engine of industrial technological advance, one cannot ignore its potential to augment American economic power. For whereas the defensive impenetrability of SDI's systems may be open to debate, the economic endowment of its hypermodern technology is not. The fascinating, wild-card contribution of SDI is its amplification of American mercantile competitiveness, with commercial spin-off of the predictable product. This is a real benefit to the United States (and a subtle threat to our national competitors). SDI will catalyze great progress in computing power, directed energy, electronics, electro-optics, automation and robotics, artificial intelligence and knowledge systems, advanced materials, and telecommunications; moreover, space technology of such progress will inevitably circle back to build the civilian sector, generating competitive advantage to American business by developing innovative products, processes, and services. Thus, by the natural force of the market, SDI will enhance America's *comprehensive* national security, which embeds the economy and society as well as the military and defense.

This volume, we trust, is an important argument in the national debate. Conflicting claims provide the impetus for public inquiry in a free society. Truth will eventually emerge, regardless of current constraints or values imposed, so long as diverse viewpoints are expressed freely and exposed widely. The criticism that scientists argue vehemently both sides from the same facts is confirmation of the gravity of the SDI issue, not the comedy of scientific endeavor. Form is as important as content. By allowing opposing opinions to clash in controversy, we enrich substance and ensure continuance. All too often, however, the pendulum swings too far. Motives are questioned, names are called. Hard debate is stifled, real choice choked off. When parochial position masquerades as a priori assumption, when politics and personality take charge, honesty and momentum are sacrificed on the altar of political advantage and personal ambition, SDI objectives and spin-off are too important for that.

Commercializing SDI Technologies should be read in the spirit of free inquiry. One should ask throughout, "Is it 'correct'?" and, if so, "Is it 'right'?" If propositions espoused are controversial, even offensive, that's good. If positions are founded on faulty data, or constructed with illogical reasoning, that's bad. The reader shall be judge.

FOREWORD

HANS MARK

One of the great strengths of the United States is the ability to conceive and develop new technology. This fact is not lost to the rest of the world and has greatly impacted our ability to influence world events. The present strategic defense research effort is no exception. A broadly based research program to expand the strategic defense capabilities of the free world is both timely and sensible. Through such basic and applied research into the technologies required, new options may be uncovered that will greatly enhance our security.

The history of science and technology has shown that pushing back the frontiers of knowledge to meet the needs of national defense can also have major impact on the economy of a society. Through history the requirements of national defense have spawned many valuable products and processes. This has been true since the early days of the American Republic with the introduction of manufacturing based on standardized interchangeable parts for firearms, to the modern commercial jet airplane, to the exploration and development of space.

The Strategic Defense Initiative will almost certainly do the same. This volume explores the problems and opportunities of transforming the knowledge acquired into economically productive activities, thus contributing to our security and our future as a technologically preeminent nation. It represents the first step in the process.

ACKNOWLEDGMENTS

The editors and authors would like to extend thanks to the many individuals and organizations who contributed to this volume. Specifically, we wish to thank Dr. Gerold Yonas of the Titan Corporation (formally Chief Scientist of the Strategic Defense Initiative Organization, SDIO); Dr. Louis Marquet, Deputy for Technology SDIO; Maj. General Robert R. Rankine USAF; Col. James Ball USAF, Director Educational and Civil Applications SDIO; Col. Joseph Rougeau USAF Retired, former Director, Educational and Civil Applications, SDIO. Also providing helpful input were Dr. James Ionson, Director, Innovative Science and Technology, SDIO; and Lt. Col. S. P. Worden USAF, Office of Science and Technology Policy, The White House.

The conference and volume would not have been possible without the dedicated support of the Large Scale Programs Institute, IC^2 Institute, University of Texas at Austin, and RGK Foundation, as well as industrial and academic supporters of the Large Scale Programs Institute. Specific thanks are extended to the IC^2 Institute and RGK Foundation staff, Mr. John Yochelson of the Center for Strategic and International Studies at Georgetown University, and Texas Commerce Bank.

Finally, deepest appreciation is extended to Dr. George Kozmetsky, President of Large Scale Programs Institute and Director IC^2 Institute; Dr. Hans Mark, Chancellor, University of Texas System and Chairman, Large Scale Programs Institute; and Dr. Eugene Konecci, Vice President of Large Scale Programs Institute. Their inspiration and support were essential to the success of the conference and volume.

INTRODUCTION

STEWART NOZETTE

Understanding the process by which we transform our national, scientific, and technological resources into commercially productive activities is of vital importance to our future. This volume examines key issues regarding the potential impact of the Strategic Defense Initiative research program upon the technology base of the United States and the transformation of this body of knowledge into new economic wealth for the people of the United States.

Since March 23, 1983, when President Ronald Reagan committed the nation to undertake a research program aimed at determining the feasibility of "rendering nuclear ballistic missiles impotent and obsolete," many words have been devoted to the Strategic Defense Initiative. The pros and cons of altering the present national strategy of deterrence based on offensive ballistic missiles, and the technical feasibility of the SDI concepts themselves, have been discussed and debated by many learned experts in the United States and overseas without resolution of the questions that SDI was formulated to answer.

This volume examines SDI from a different perspective. The SDI research program is the most technically challenging research effort yet undertaken by the United States and as such is uniquely valuable, irrespective of whether defensive systems are ever built and deployed. The time scale of this effort—five years for research and perhaps half a century for transition to defense-based deterrence—represents a major long-term challenge to American institutions. The results of this research may provide even greater challenges to American industry in exploiting these technologies for commercial purposes than in deploying the operational defensive systems themselves. Because of its stringent requirements, SDI provides the paramount national stimulus to expand the American technological base into the twenty-first century.

The volume examines these issues from many sides and poses the question, "Can our previous experience with large-scale programs (e.g.,

Manhattan Project or Apollo) provide guidance on how to capitalize efficiently and effectively on the investment in defensive research so as to achieve *comprehensive* security for the United States and its allies?" Comprehensive security necessitates both military and economic security,[1] requiring detailed examination of how the fruits of cutting-edge research may be most effectively transformed into economic wealth. It can be argued that it does little good to have first-rate defense of a declining, noncompetitive economy.

These and other pertinent ideas are examined on the following pages by experienced and learned experts from government, industry, and the academic community. Included are descriptions of the objectives of the SDI research effort, the policies governing the transfer and diffusion of technology, how the private sector can capitalize on advanced technology, and analyses of the markets for advanced technology that may be developed through SDI research. The volume concludes with a set of initiatives that may increase the likelihood that SDI research can indeed provide *comprehensive* as well as purely military national security.

The comprehensive security of the United States requires new mechanisms that will provide incentive for government, industry, and academia to work together as colleagues, not as adversaries. Only then may we realize the true potential of the Strategic Defense Initiative to mold a more secure future.

NOTE

1. See Robert Lawrence Kuhn, *Commercializing Defense-Related Technology* (New York: Praeger, 1984).

PART I
THE STRATEGIC DEFENSE INITIATIVE PROGRAM

1

DEFENSE R&D AND NATIONAL COMPETITIVENESS: PAST, PRESENT, AND FUTURE PROSPECTS

JOHN McTAGUE

One interesting aspect of a position in the Office of Science and Technology Policy is being afforded the opportunity of addressing important subjects from a larger perspective. In Washington, D.C., there are three topics in the newspapers, all of them bad. The first is that the United States is going down the tubes because of huge trade deficits and lack of competitiveness in international markets. The second is that our expenditures on defense enhancement are wasteful and even counterproductive, since they displace higher leveraged investments in the civilian economy. The third is that the Strategic Defense Initiative is, *at one and the same time*, dangerous to world security, fatally flawed technically, and harmful to our economic competitiveness because it is draining talent away from productive R&D to efforts that are irrelevant to our commercial technology base.

Underlying the issues of economic competitiveness, and the relationship of defense enhancements to the overall national well-being, including economic strength, is the effectiveness of our technological lever. Are we using our technology and our technological talent well enough to assume our future?

This nation spends an enormous amount of money on research and development (R&D), approximately $120 billion in 1985. Of that amount, almost half is federal government investment, and of that half about two-thirds is allocated to national security enhancement. That $34 billion defense R&D investment certainly dominates the commercial sector, like it or not. Is its impact positive or negative? Is there adequate transfer of defense-generated technologies into the commercial sector? Is this transfer becoming more or less relevant, more or less effective? Few questions are more important.

While the desire to remain competitive—whether in the realm of defense or in the realm of business—is of course the obvious motivation for technology transfer, the synergism of this link is at times so familiar as to breed indifference. To neglect this more general tie between defense research and national competitiveness is to neglect not only the stunning technological and industrial achievements born of this relationship, but also to overlook ways of ensuring that the relationship grows more beneficially over time.

Yet, what we propose as an intimate connection may not be so recognized by the country at large, or, more importantly, by those who influence society. To paraphrase Lincoln, because those who mold public opinion ultimately decide how our society will be governed, we must consciously articulate the relationship between defense R&D and national competitiveness, lest others succeed in curtailing the one, thereby ensuring the decline of the other.

When we step back, no longer focusing on the specifics of the defense R&D-commercial sector interface, but rather looking at the larger environment in which that interface exists, we note that the two sides form a remarkably healthy relationship considering the growing hostility of the surrounding environment. To be more exact, we are exploring the assumption that the commercialization of strategic defense technologies is a going concern, that our topic is a viable one, that, in short, our economy derives benefits from military R&D. However, far too many of the molders of public opinion—in our schools and universities, in various interest groups, indeed in positions of public service—are sowing the notion that defense research serves only defense concerns. They contend that defense research is a drain on our economic vitality, and that it is getting worse, not better.

The preferred method these days for preaching this dogma is to set research expenditures within a zero-sum theoretical framework that maintains that a dollar spent on defense is a dollar not spent on social welfare. Defense, it is held, adds nothing to the gross national product (GNP). History, however, begs to differ. Quite aside from the fact that defense research provides for the social welfare in the most fundamental of ways by maintaining continuance of society itself, defense research, as past records illustrate and future prospects indicate, has and will continue to bring forth economically beneficial commercial applications and to assure that the United States is competitively preeminent.

Thus, while my main purpose is to elucidate the many civilian economic benefits stemming from defense research, with general emphasis on the consequences for our global competitive stance resulting from such research, an admittedly ancillary intention is to refute the false and often ideologically motivated notion to which I have alluded. This analysis proposes to demonstrate that the famous "guns or butter" dichotomy is a false one (or more precisely put, gun "development" versus butter "development").

Undertaken to preserve and enhance the security of our nation, defense research has provided the ingredients for superior weapons, munitions, communications equipment, combat vehicles, and various other support material for a modern military force. At the same time, the same research has generated profound and positive effects on civilian life. Utilizing all the basic sciences, defense research naturally has been a fertile ground for scores of products and ideas that have made life more interesting and more convenient. The transfer of technology arising from military R&D has found widespread civilian application. All around us are products that are spin-offs of defense R&D.

World War II research gave us, among other things, the jet—a contribution of monumental proportions that changed the way Americans conduct business and spend their leisure time.

One can recall *Score* and *Courier*. Those were the first two satellites to prove the feasibility of communications from orbiting vehicles. They were the products of defense R&D. Today, we take for granted the idea of seeing the Olympics live from halfway around the world, or transmitting reams of data to a foreign corporate office.

Miniaturized electronic circuitry, which gives us inexpensive, reliable, high-quality stereo systems, television sets, and many other commercial electronics products, owes a great deal to the military's post-World War II effort to reduce the size and weight of electronic parts.

The goggles used to aid victims of retinitis pigmentosa, or "night blindness," came from the goggles employed by soldiers on night patrol and air rescue teams in Southeast Asia. Laser range finders used by engineers, indeed the laser itself, titanium metals used in building virtually everything, jeeps used by those who feel carefree, and hand-held laser speed indicators used by police to detect those who become a bit too carefree are all in existence because of defense R&D.

If one were to measure, in terms of jobs created alone, the effects on the U.S. economy of these fruits of defense R&D, one could only conclude that defense research has had high leverage on the U.S. competitive position in the world.

But what about today? Is defense R&D giving us anything new and useful for a better life? What commercial spin-offs have resulted from defense R&D recently? Some examples follow.

Magnetrons are key components of radar developed by military R&D in the 1940s and further developed and made available to industry, at a cost of about $2,000, in the late 1950s. Today a typical magentron costs around $25. The commercial application is located in the kitchen: the microwave oven.

Carbon-carbon composites are a newly developed high-temperature structural material currently being brought on line in a number of critical aerospace applications, such as nose tips for missile reentry systems and the leading edges and nose cap of the Space Shuttle. Carbon-carbon's largest current civilian application to date is in aircraft brakes, where its use significantly expands the breaks' life span while reducing weight by 50 percent over the typical steel brake system. Practically all new aircraft, including the Space Shuttle, also make use of a new aluminum alloy, which provides improved stress corrosion resistance in combination with high strength.

In the medical field, numerous developments by the Department of Defense (DOD) are finding life-enhancing applications. Navy research in ocean acoustic tomography, a technique for describing a region by multiple sampling of wave fields traversing a given region, led directly to the CAT scan. Civilian medical practice makes use of a host of defense developments in the area of acute trauma care, including blood preservation techniques, creams for burns, and surgical techniques for maxillofacial injuries, to name just a few.

Perhaps the most unusual defense R&D application comes from, believe it or not, antisubmarine warfare (ASW) technology. ASW research today is enabling paraplegics to sit, stand, and walk under their own control. By capturing and interpreting myoelectric signals from above the level of the spinal cord injury and transmitting them to the paralyzed muscles below, a detour around the lesion is created and the seemingly impossible becomes possible.[1]

Finally, in the last phase of development in defense labs is a malaria vaccine that makes use of recombinant DNA.

Thus the intimate linkages between defense R&D and commercial applications catalyze better lives. World War II and postwar economic growth are testimony to this guns and butter synergism. Defense R&D constantly opens up new technological horizons that American industry can exploit, thereby overcoming our inherent disadvantages, such as higher labor and capital costs, compared to foreign competitors.

Throughout the history of science and technology, there have been times when particular areas of knowledge were in a stage of revolution, such as physics at the beginning of this century. But never before has there been a time when virtually every discipline in science and engineering has been undergoing such rapid change. We now see the downstream effects of our large postwar investment in basic research   basic research very often founded by DOD and now finding wide application in the civilian sector.

Today's defense research is laying the groundwork for assuring America's unquestioned leadership in science and technology. Such research should be fostered not only to perpetuate our national security, but to leverage our economic future as a competitive nation.

For instance, a collaboration between the Air Force, NASA, and the Defense Advanced Research Projects Agency (DARPA) provides an excellent example of defense research that will have a natural commercial application and will help leverage America's economic *and* military competitiveness in the future. I speak of the transatmospheric vehicle, or TAV, the so-called aerospace plane. This plane will make use of the most advanced materials. It will cruise at hypersonic speeds and even insert itself into orbit, and it will take off and land at conventional runways. It will take you anywhere around the globe in a couple of hours. The TAV is born of defense research and development; it will strengthen our national security substantially and it will provide enormous economic leverage for America's future as well.[2]

The research being conducted under the Strategic Defense Initiative is right now rolling back the frontiers for continued economic growth. Just since 1983, we have seen breakthroughs in laser technology that we had thought a full decade away. At the heart of any effective ballistic missile defense system will be a computerized battle management system capable of analyzing millions of pieces of data every second. The concentrated research effort into supercomputers, artificial intelligence, and computer software being conducted under SDI will incalculably benefit a society that finds more helpful uses of computers every day. New composite materials and new optical concepts are being created.

When we assess the past and present impact of defense R&D upon the economic competitiveness of the United States, especially as it is reflected in direct spin-offs with commercial application, a healthy synergistic relationship becomes evident. Far from being antagonistic or mutually exclusive, the relationship between defense research and national competitiveness is close and constructive. Even a cursory glance at future prospects for commercial applications of the defense research now being conducted underscores this thesis.

In fact, the effectiveness of defense and industrial research have the same origin: a well-defined, important goal. When one needs an accurate missile, a rapidly firing laser that can hit a distant target, or a computer capable of performing 100 gigaflops, both the success of the main goal and the excellence of the spin-offs are more likely to reach fruition. As far as the connection between defense R&D and economic competitiveness is concerned, it is not a matter of guns or butter; rather the technology of swords and the technology of plowshares have much in common, and much to share with each other as they both remain sharp.[3]

NOTES

1. NASA Spinoffs, NASA Educational Publications 1977–1985, NASA Office of Educational Publications; and George A. Keyworth, "The President's Strategic Defense Initiative," Testimony to Committee on Foreign Relations, U.S. Senate, April 25, 1984.
2. Jerry Grey, "The New Orient Express," *Discover*, January, 1985.
3. "Will Star Wars Advance or Retard Science," *The Economist* 296, no. 7410 (September 7, 1985), 95–96.

2

THE STRATEGIC DEFENSE INITIATIVE RESEARCH PROGRAM: CONCEPTION AND EXECUTION

GEROLD YONAS

The concept of a Strategic Defense Initiative was first broached by President Reagan in March 1983, during a televised speech to the nation. He called for a concerted effort to study "the feasibility of a ballistic missile defense capability that would enhance the security of the United States and its allies. . . ." What the president's speech called for precisely was a study, with these objectives: investigate the previous work, future proposals, and prepare a program plan.

This study, referred to as the Fletcher Study (1984), defined a set of technologies that could approach the problem of defense against ballistic missiles—not just long-range ballistic missiles, but short-range missiles as well. The overall approach taken was to examine a multitier system that could provide an effective defense. The term "effective" is not very well defined even today. It means a high level of effectiveness through multiple attempts to intercept a ballistic missile on its flight. The one thing this Fletcher Study called for was a comprehensive research program—not a development program, not a deployment program, but a *research* program. This program is to provide a basis for a decision—the decision on whether to proceed beyond the research phase into development and deployment.

The SDI is different from many other advanced technology programs, because its goal is a function of other strong factors that may change. Specifically, we face a determined opponent. The nature of the technologies can be effected to a great degree by the countermeasures the opponent may follow. We are faced with the responsibility at the very outset of not only studying the measures that can defend against ballistic missiles, but also examining at the same time, and with equal vigor, the expected countermeasures. There are many countermeasures that can be carried out, and these govern the nature of the technology. We are

Table 2.1
Strategic Defense Requirements

---

1. Survivable
   - Defense suppression must not be appealing
   - Defensive systems must be "harder" than targets
   - "Cost" to negate defensive components must be greater than the number/cost of targets these components can handle
   - No "Achilles heels"—i.e., battle management systems
2. Robust
   - Simple growth path for defenses to negate "responsive" offense
   - Visible existence of advanced defense possibilities deters offensive responses
3. Cost-effective
   - Must "cost" less to proliferate defense than to proliferate offense
   - Leads to offensive arms control possibilities

Source: All of the tables and figures in this chapter are from the Strategic Defense Initiative Organization, U.S. Department of Defense, Washington, D.C.

competing with a resolute opponent. It will not be enough to look upon SDI as a technological venture that seeks solution to a natural problem. At the beginning of the program, criteria had to be developed to examine the possibility of a set of countermeasures that may change with time, and for making decisions within the program to deal with them (see Table 2.1).

The first criterion to satisfy was the requirement of arms race stability. We do not want a technology that creates a desire in the minds of our opponents to build more offensive weapons, to engage in ever-increasing preparation. The approach being explored is a defensive system that is cheaper and more effective than the countermeasures. This requirement of cost-effectiveness may be necessary to generate arms race stability.

The second issue is crisis stability. This criterion requires the system to be highly effective. The approach to high effectiveness is the previously mentioned multitier system, which will be able to maintain effectiveness in light of countermeasures. Effectiveness also requires the survivability of all the system's components. One can not have components that themselves invite attack, as this could lead to instability in a crisis. A research program must determine the countermeasures, and the requirements of being stable, cost-effective, and survivable. Through the interaction among countermeasures, requirements of cost-effectiveness, and survivability, an architectural process was initiated to define

Table 2.2
Major Technical Issues

- Midcourse discrimination
- Cheap intercept in all phases (particularly low-cost kinetic energy weapons [KEW])
- Boost-phase intercept
- Lethality against responsive threat
- Survivability
- Battle management software

the technological requirements. The technological issues are summarized in Table 2.2.

To achieve the multitier defense one must have the ability to intercept during all phases in a very cost-effective manner, particularly in the boost phase when the rockets are just rising off the pad. Very high leverage exists at this point, as the reentry vehicles and decoys have not been deployed. Boost phase intercept is critical to the cost-effectiveness criteria. If the Soviet Union decides to change its attack structure, to have either faster or harder boosters, systems must exist that are lethal against these different approaches. If the Soviets decide not to change their actual attack, but rather to attack our sensors in space or our predeployed systems, these systems must be survivable. Finally, coordinating the entire system is a very complex set of very rapid decision-making actions. This requires dramatic development of computer hardware along with new software techniques to handle these complex problem.

When people examine the SDI programs, they are often confused by the complexity, since there are so many different attributes. It is a program layering architectures at every stage, with a total architecture linking together the various components: surveillance, interceptors, various support technologies, and battle management and software managing the entire program. At every point in time there must be a total backbone—a spine holding together these various components of the program, all of which must evolve in time.

It is not too feasible to start off with the most mature technologies that could be easily countermeasured. The postulated responses the Soviet Union may carry out must be examined. Therefore, we must have advanced technologies that could be successful against responses. In addition, we have to look even further out into the long term, and define technologies that have such enormous growth potential that the Soviet

Figure 2.1
Meeting the SDI Goal

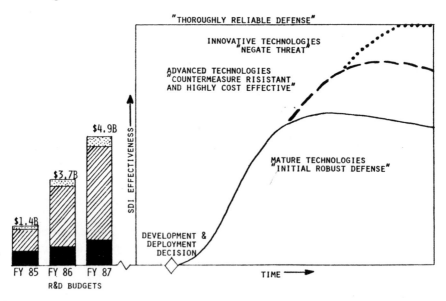

Union could not countermeasure at all. Thus the Soviets would see that it would be to their advantage to engage in a joint offensive builddown. A mutually managed transition might involve reducing the offensive weapons threatening both sides, and engaging in a natural defensive buildup that would give all greater safety and security.

Following this strategy the SDI has defined three kinds of program activities: the more mature, the advanced, and finally the ultimate technology for the future. We must define our investment strategy within SDI and look at these various components. The approach is summarized in Figure 2.1. Although the mature technologies could provide a great deal of capability, they would degrade with time as countermeasures began to be added to the picture. There might be only a temporary advantage of defense over offense. There would be no basis to make the fundamental transition away from deterrence based on offense to deterrence based on defense. For this reason we believe exploring a set of advanced technologies is critical to making a decision five years from now. Today we are not putting our total investment in the most mature technology where we could go beyond the research phase and into an engineering and integration phase. The decision has been made to put a minor share of our investment strategy into the advanced technologies that can head off countermeasures, and that may be workable.

SURVEILLANCE

The single biggest element of the SDI program is surveillance. There are many ways to intercept ballistic missiles, postboost vehicles, and reentry vehicles in their flight. The first critical issue is not attacking those objects, but finding them: knowing that an attack has been launched, acquiring the target, tracking the target with great precision, pointing the weapon systems, and assessing whether the targets have been destroyed. The surveillance, acquisition, tracking, and kill assessment is about 35 to 40 percent of the SDI program.

We are exploring sensors in space, in the air, and on the ground. Approaches being investigated include precision radar imaging where the data are reduced in a second—or even in less than a second. Even in the classical area of radar imaging we find requirements for extremely rapid data processing. Various sensors are being investigated that can be placed on an aircraft: optical, infrared, and radar sensors. These have the advantage of high position and additional mobility. Finally, representing the epitome of mobility are sensors based in space (Figure 2.2). Radars, infrared sensors, and optical sensors are all being examined. In all of these cases we are looking at collecting high-precision data, and reducing and interpreting that data in a matter of seconds. Again, one sees the connection between sensors and very rapid data processing.

The most important element is the first warning, the first information that boosters have been launched. In order to manage the battle, we not only require warning that missiles have been launched but also precision information, on where they have been launched, knowledge about their track, where they are going, and the nature of the boosters. We require an advanced infrared sensor platform called a BPSS (the booster phase surveillance system).

The next element of surveillance is the midcourse of the flight. Here we may have to track hundreds of thousands of objects because the Soviets would deploy very lightweight decoys. This chaff (or junk) generates large amounts of traffic and confusion, thus thwarting intercept. The midcourse phase is a relatively long time, 15 to 20 minutes. We must put together information to determine which are the targets and which are the decoys. We are investigating various kinds of midcourse discrimination techniques. Highly precise active information may be obtained by bouncing a laser beam off an object and, because of the very high band width of the coherent light, we can discriminate the real from the decoy by observing the vibrations. (We may even introduce a mechanism to perturb the objects in order to enhance the discrimination procedure.) Again there is the problem of the flood of information. Collecting information about hundreds of thousands of objects in a few minutes and reducing that data is a data analysis nightmare.

Figure 2.2
**Defense Architecture Utilizing Space-Based Sensors and Ground-Based
Interception**

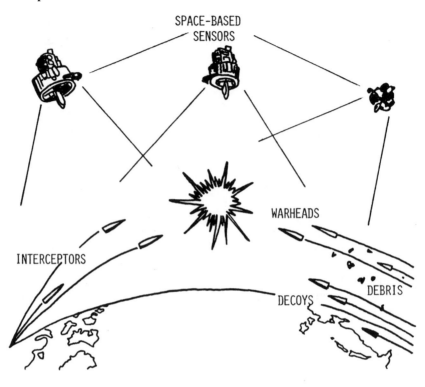

Critical to midcourse discrimination is infrared data. Over the last few years, infrared technology has expanded rapidly, with sensors, optics, and cryogenic coolers. In all of these cases we have seen a dramatic evolution of that technology. In the past we have relied on focal point arrays containing thousands of infrared detectors, allowing detection of a cold object against the background of space. Now we require extremely high resolution and so millions of detectors are needed. This necessitates the invention of new ways to produce infrared elements in such huge numbers. Semiconductor production must be revolutionized.

If the SDI had never begun, the sensor aspect (radar, optical, and infrared) would probably have developed with "normal" speed. But SDI requirements sweep up many technologies in a storm of technical revolution. (Other examples include the surveillance and early warning systems.)

Figure 2.3
Kinetic Energy Technology

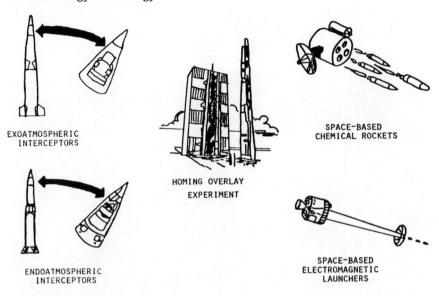

EXOATMOSPHERIC
INTERCEPTORS

HOMING OVERLAY
EXPERIMENT

SPACE-BASED
CHEMICAL ROCKETS

ENDOATMOSPHERIC
INTERCEPTORS

SPACE-BASED
ELECTROMAGNETIC
LAUNCHERS

INTERCEPTION

Interception with kinetic energy (smart conventional weapons at very high velocity) or directed energy each absorb about 20 percent of the SDI budget. Kinetic energy technology is illustrated in Figure 2.3.

Over a year ago, the SDI carried out an experiment over the Pacific, launching a reentry vehicle on a booster from Vandenberg Air Force Base and an interceptor that used an infrared detector to maneuver itself in front of the incoming reentry vehicle, colliding with it and destroying it, convincingly. This test proved the principle of being able to "hit a bullet with a bullet."

In the kinetic energy field we have already shown proof of principle. The challenge is to get to the right point in space at the right time, in a cost-effective manner. Although an experiment showed the proof of principle, it used a component that was large and expensive, as shown in Figure 2.4. The approach currently being investigated involves very small missiles that can be launched from the ground to destroy an incoming reentry vehicle. This follows midcourse discrimination. Cost-effectiveness requires being able to produce a missile for about $1 million. A very smart projectile weighing a few kilograms must be produced. It must maneuver in front of and collide with a reentry vehicle. These objects must be produced in very large numbers—thousands or tens of

Figure 2.4
Interceptor Comparison (U)

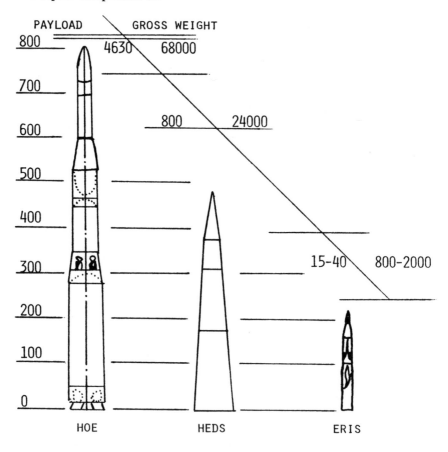

thousands. Production and affordability are extremely important factors in this approach. The challenge is whether one can mass produce this technology effectively. Kinetic energy weapons, small rockets deployed in space, are vehicles roughly 2 meters tall and 30 centimeters in diameter (Figure 2.5). Can these rockets be produced in numbers of 10,000 or more, at very low cost (roughly $1 million)? This question must be answered by the SDI research program.

The Soviets could choose to discard their existing booster fleet, an enormously costly path, and build an entirely different kind of attack modus, one based on fast burn boosters. This hypothetical threat is discussed often. Yet it is not enough just to invent the countermeasure, one has to go through a detailed analysis of the entire weapon system and define the total architecture. There are responses that can lower the

Figure 2.5
Space-Based Kinetic-Energy Weapon Concept

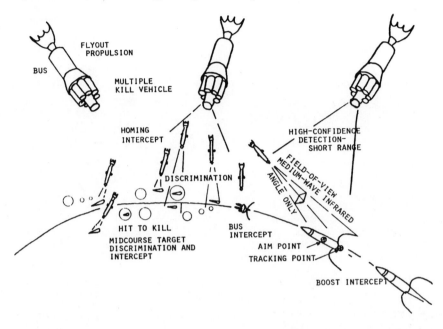

boost phase time. We do not know how fast, how precise, or what the impacts on cost may be. But we must always have interceptors that can go faster than rockets. How fast we have to go we do not know, but we are investigating technologies using extremely high-velocity guns that can exceed the velocity of any chemical rocket.

Chemical rockets can propel a projectile to 10–12 kilometers per second. In principle, if you have an electrical energy supply and a gun driven by electrical energy, a projectile velocity of 20 or 30 kilometers per second could be achieved. The most innovative ideas suggest projectiles going 100 kilometers per second. These projectiles can cover thousands of kilometers of space in a period of tens of seconds to a minute. The critical issues in these systems are being able to produce a gun barrel that can withstand extremely high pressures, the requirements of being able to produce a power supply that can generate not millions or tens of millions of watts, but *hundreds of millions* of watts for a very short time. A sensor or brain must be packaged into the projectile, along with a propulsion unit that can tolerate an acceleration force of several hundred thousand Gs (see Figure 2.6).

The advantage of directed energy is the ability to point at something in your sights and then shoot. Because the projectile moves at the speed

Figure 2.6
Space-Based Hypervelocity Launcher

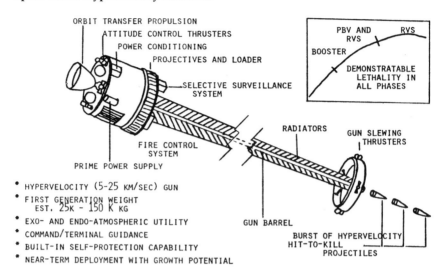

of light, the object can be targeted easily. There is no brainpower required to be on board the projectile itself. The SDI is looking at lasers and particle beams, on the ground or in space. Space-based lasers are the most mature aspect of directed energy weapons (Figure 2.7).

Quite a few years ago we began to look at chemically powered lasers, which have the advantage of having very high efficiency conversion of chemical energy into light energy. They are in fact simple; the chemical supply can be placed in space with the laser. The problem with chemical lasers, however, is that the wavelength of their light happens to be long, with an infrared output instead of a visible output. (This is due to the nature of the chemical reactions employed.) The long wavelength necessitates large optics. A cost-effective chemical laser can not have a single aperture covering tens of meters. Many small apertures is the only solution. Thus methods to phase lock the multiple apertures must be developed so that they act as if it were one large aperture (Figure 2.8). The technological requirements are rapid production of large numbers of optical components, very precise optics, and techniques for phasing together these small elements into the equivalent of one large element. Problems of structures, controls, computers, glass, and lightweight optics must be solved together to make practical a large optical system in space.

The other approach is to put the laser on the ground and beam the light through the atmosphere to a relay mirror, then down through a

Figure 2.7
Space-Based Laser Concept

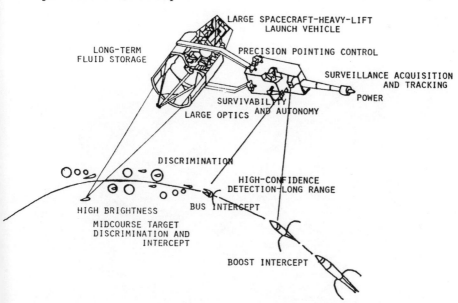

sighting mirror to the booster. Here the issues of developing the lasers are simpler. The laser and its power supply (Hoover Dam, for example) are all there on the ground. The problems to overcome involve transporting the beams through the atmosphere to mirrors in space. This is one area where SDI has had some truly substantial breakthroughs in the last couple of years. It is feasible to transport the light, correct for atmospheric turbulence, and produce a beam of very high quality that can be transported from the ground to space and then back down.

Another directed energy approach is to use particle beams. These have the advantage of being able to penetrate through the outer skin of missiles or reentry vehicles. Lasers engage the outside of materials; they either have to blast or burn their way through the outer skin. But it is practically impossible to shield against a particle beam, since they can go through tens of centimeters of skin. The technology issues have to do with making these particle beam systems lightweight, efficient, and very reliable. There have been many years of high-energy physics research that is based on the creation of these kinds of atomic accelerators. But until SDI no technology has been developed to take these accelerators into the space environment.

The above-mentioned areas encompass 80 to 90 percent of the entire SDI program. The additional remaining technologies are extremely important to the issue of cost-effectiveness. There is a relationship between

Figure 2.8
Single Primary System and Synthetic Aperture Counterpart

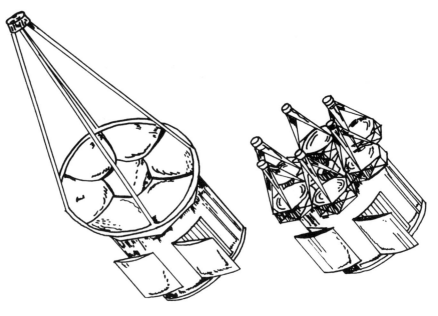

survivability and space logistics. There are many countermeasure technologies our adversaries may develop that could neutralize our predeployed assets; but if we can lower the cost of lift from thousands of
dollars per pound to hundreds of dollars per pound, then we could
envision and deploy low-cost shielding that could solve the survivability
problem.

SYSTEMS SUPPORT

Many of these system elements require an inexhaustible power supply
that must run continuously at low levels, hundreds of kilowatts for
example, and then be turned on in a crisis and run at hundreds of
megawatts. One approach to the problem is to develop a very lightweight, very reliable nuclear reactor that runs continuously for years at
a level of a hundred or hundreds of kilowatts. This energy could then
be stored in capacitors, batteries, or flywheels. When the energy had to
be used, that energy could be switched on. These, remember, are entirely
new technologies: reliable, lightweight nuclear energy; techniques for
storage, handling, and switching of energy to convert it from units of

Table 2.3
Examples of Technical Progress

Surveillance Acquisition, Tracking, and Kill Assessment
- Active discrimination concepts
- Long-life cryocooler
- Tenfold increase in long-wave infrared detector resolution

Directed Energy Weapons
- Bright chemical lasers
- Atmospheric compensation
- High-power free electron lasers

Kinetic Energy Weapons
- Endo- and exoatmospheric interceptor experiments
- Repetitive electromagnetic gun

Survivability and Lethality
- Laser shielding materials

---

hundreds of kilowatts to hundreds of *megawatts* in a fraction of a second. That power supply must also be taken into space with low cost. These issues are not the ones that get publicity, but they are critical to the feasibility of the entire SDI program.

This covers about 95 percent of the SDI budget. However, from the very beginning, we realized that as these programs proceed there will be a natural tendency, as Harold Agnew said during the Fletcher Study (1984), "for the hogs to trample the piglets on the way to the trough." This means that when one pursues a program such as SDI, there is going to be a cauldron of bubbling innovation. What do we do as the big activities start to absorb all the funds? If the central systems have a shortfall in terms of their accomplishments, there is a natural tendency to reach over and shut off innovation.

Thus, we decided to specially earmark a portion of our funds, a few percent, we hope up to 5 percent, for innovative ideas. These can come from anywhere—small business, large industry, universities. We must be able to allow innovation to play a role in the program. SDI therefore provides the seed money to get such projects off the ground, and if one turns out to be important and feasible, we transition it into the rest of the program. These innovation programs fall into many areas and we will be expanding and changing these program areas as time proceeds. There has been an enormous reaction from the academic community. We have had over 3,000 proposals—3,000 white papers offering opportunities to explore some of these uncharted regions. Although the program is only two years old, we are already seeing advances.

In our first year, the SDI has allocated almost 96 percent of our total budget of $1.4 billion. We have placed almost 1,000 contracts, we are beginning to see developments and advances in directed energy, kinetic energy, surveillance, and supporting technologies (Table 2.3). The program is building tremendous momentum. Some time in the early 1990s we may decide whether to go beyond this research phase. If successful we could build a safer and more secure world.

BIBLIOGRAPHY

Abrahamson, Lt. Gen. James. "The President's Strategic Defense Initiative." Testimony to Subcommittee on Defense Appropriations, U.S. Senate, May 15, 1984.

Adam, John A. and Mark Fischetti. "SDI: The Grand Experiment." *IEEE Spectrum*, September, 1985, 34–64.

Brzezinski, Zbigniew, Robert Jastrow, and Max Kampelman. "Search for Security: The Case for the Strategic Defense Initiative," *New York Times Magazine*, January 27, 1985.

Carter, Ashton. "Directed Energy Missile Defense." Washington, D.C.: Office of Technology Assessment, 1984.

"The Case for Star Wars." *The Economist*, August 3, 1985, 11–12.

Fletcher, James T. "The Strategic Defense Initiative." Testimony before the Subcommittee on R&D of the Committee on Armed Services, U.S. House of Representatives, March 1, 1984.

Jastrow, Robert. *How to Make Nuclear Weapons Obsolete*. Boston: Little, Brown, 1985.

Keyworth, George A. "The President's Strategic Defense Initiative." Testimony to Committee on Foreign Relations, U.S. Senate, April 25, 1984.

Long, F., D. Hafner, and J. Boutwell. "Weapons in Space." *Daedalus* 114, no. 2 (Spring, 1985) and 114, no. 3 (Summer 1985).

Office of Technology Assessment, *Ballistic Missile Defense Technologies*, U.S. Congress, Fall, 1985.

Stevens, Sayer. "The Soviet BMD Program." In A. Carter and D. Schwartz, eds., *Ballistic Missile Defense*. Washington, D.C.: The Brookings Institution, 1984, 182.

Teller, Edward, private letter to the president, July 23, 1983.

U.S. Department of Defense, *Soviet Military Power*. Washington, D.C., 1984, 34, 36.

Wallop, M. A. Letter to the U.S. Senate, July 8, 1983. Unpublished.

———. *Strategic Review*, Fall, 1979, 13–21.

Yonas, G. *Physics Today*, June, 1985, 24–32.

3

THE STRATEGIC DEFENSE INITIATIVE: WHAT, WHY, AND HOW

MAJOR GENERAL ROBERT R. RANKINE, JR., USAF

It was a little more than three and one-half years ago in a speech televised to the American people that President Reagan first set the objectives for a national research program to investigate technologies that might someday make it possible to defend against ballistic missiles. In his speech, the president discussed his continued support for strategic offensive modernization and arms control efforts, but he then challenged the scientific and engineering community to determine the feasibility of developing systems capable of destroying ballistic missiles in flight. Such defenses could provide an alternative to reliance on offensive nuclear retaliation as the sole basis for strategic deterrence, and could lead to the ultimate goal of reducing and eventually eliminating the threat of ballistic missiles.

Immediately following that speech, the president directed that two studies be instituted to investigate the policy and technology implications of an effective ballistic missile defense system (see Figure 3.1). From these two studies emerged the basis for a long-range research program the president initiated with the fiscal year 1985 budget request submitted to Congress on February 1, 1984. In October, 1984 the Congress appropriated funds for the Strategic Defense Initiative, financing a new hope for the future, first expressed by the president less than 19 months earlier. We have just successfully completed the first year of a centrally focused strategic defense research program; hence it is important to review the rationale for the program and its scope before discussion of possible commercial benefits from the SDI research program that could benefit civilian industry and commerce.

THE RATIONALE FOR SDI

In the long term, we believe that mutual defenses can enhance incentives for both the United States and the Soviet Union to agree safely

Figure 3.1
Strategic Defense Initiative Origin

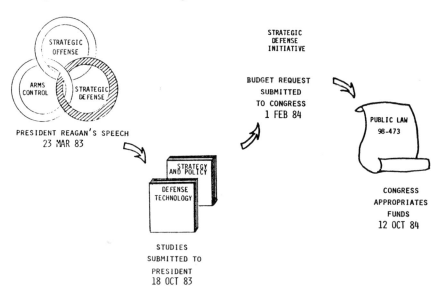

to very deep reductions and eventually even the elimination of ballistic missiles and the nuclear weapons they carry (see Table 3.1). This does not represent a shift from the basic deterrent strategy of the United States, but represents a new means for enhancing deterrence. That policy, in effect since the beginning of the nuclear era, has not changed in its fundamentals, but our ability to deter has hinged upon differing military capabilities ranging from a balanced nuclear bomber and air defense capability in the 1950s to almost total reliance on the threat of retaliation in the 1980s. The shifts in the basis for deterrence have been forced by the development of various nuclear delivery systems and not by fundamental changes in policy.

The emergence of the nuclear-tipped ballistic missiles in the late 1950s and 1960s changed the timing of nuclear warfare and thus reduced the importance of air defense in the view of many U.S. leaders. Because ballistic missiles are fast, unrecallable, and are becoming increasingly accurate, they are potentially the least stabilizing of the currently deployed systems—particularly the ICBMs, which may be targeted against each other. In order to visualize how defenses might potentially overcome that decreasing stability and contribute to increased deterrence, consider a time in the future when the United States and the Soviet Union might both have deployed defenses that were sufficiently effective

Table 3.1
Implications for Deterrence

- Initiative constitutes no change to long-standing U.S. policy of deterrence
- Effective defenses against ballistic missiles have potential for increasing deterrence and stability
  - increase in attack uncertainties
  - significant reduction in utility of preemptive attack
- To fulfill this promise, defense must be
  - effective
  - survivable
  - cost-effective

Source: All of the figures and tables in this chapter are from the U.S. Air Force, Washington, D.C.

so that a preemptive strike by either country could not accomplish any national aims. Such defenses would be designed to intercept all ballistic missiles, whether their targets are military or civilian. Under such circumstances, where the effectiveness of the defenses is sufficient to confound thoroughly the targeting strategy for each side's ballistic missiles, the incentive to initiate the first nuclear attack is essentially eliminated, since no specific objectives can be attained by a few warheads that might leak through at random locations. Under such circumstances, the nuclear-armed ballistic missile ceases to be a useful instrument for achieving national policy objectives by military means. The defensive system need not be perfect to accomplish this objective, but must meet three important criteria:

First, it must be effective against the offensive systems and countermeasures that exist or could be deployed.

Second, it must be sufficiently survivable that it would not encourage an attack on the system itself by either enemy defensive or offensive systems. If it were not survivable, then it might invite a defense suppression attack as a prelude to an offensive attack, thereby decreasing rather than increasing crisis stability.

Third, the effectiveness of defense must be able to be preserved at lower cost than any offensive proliferation or countermeasure attempts to overcome it. If that were not the case, the existence of defenses would encourage rather than discourage proliferation. Providing for cost-effective and survivable defense is the key challenge to the SDI technology program and illustrates the need for research before an informed decision to begin system development is possible.

In the late 1960s and early 1970s, the United States had done development work on an antiballistic missile system known as Safeguard. That system, which was deployed in the mid-1970s, was dismantled

Table 3.2
Hedge against Soviet Program

- Soviet Union currently
  - upgrading world's only active ballistic missile defense
  - pursuing R&D on a rapidly deployable ABM system
  - pursuing advanced defensive technologies program (e.g., lasers)
- U.S. defensive technologies program, therefore, a prudent hedge against unilateral Soviet deployment

shortly thereafter, due in part to the fact that it could not maintain effectiveness against proliferation. The United States also hoped that not deploying U.S. defenses permitted by the ABM Treaty would discourage the Soviet Union from building more ballistic missiles. However, not only did the Soviets continue to build ballistic missiles, they also relentlessly pursued technology for defending against ballistic missiles.

The Soviets have currently the world's only operational ballistic missile defense system—the one that is located around Moscow. The system is for terminal defense and similar in many ways to our former Safeguard system. The Soviets are modernizing that Moscow system and have developed a new antiballistic missile that has potential for rapid deployment as a nationwide ABM system (see Table 3.2).

Of even greater concern, however, the Soviets have been pursuing for many years extensive development of technologies that have potential for advanced ballistic missile defense applications. For example, the Soviet Union is exploring many laser technologies. They have a directed energy R&D site in the central Soviet Union that not only could provide an antisatellite capability today, but possibly a prototype for an ABM system to be deployed in the future. The Soviet's high-energy laser program, which dates from the mid-1960s, is much larger than the U.S. effort. The Soviets have built over a half-dozen major R&D facilities and test ranges, and they have more than 10,000 scientists and engineers associated with laser development. In the particle beam area, some of the advanced U.S. technology is derived from Soviet research reported in their technical literature several years ago.

The Strategic Defense Initiative program thus provides us a hedge against what might otherwise be a Soviet technical surprise. A unilateral Soviet development of such advanced defenses, in conjunction with its offensive deployments and its air and civil defense efforts, could result in a significant change in Soviet military capability and could adversely affect the security of the United States and its allies.

Critics of SDI have argued that the research and technology program

Table 3.3
Implications for Arms Control

- President's initiative consistent with current U.S. treaty obligations
  - only research on a broad range of defensive technologies
- Should a decision be made in the future to deploy an effective, advanced defense capability, such defenses would complement the U.S. goal of significant reductions in offensive nuclear armaments
  - advanced defenses have the potential for reducing the value of ballistic missiles, thus increasing the likelihood of negotiated reductions
  - offensive force reductions can further improve the effectiveness of advanced defenses

---

currently under way is inconsistent with the ABM Treaty and conflicts with arms control in general (see Table 3.3). Quite to the contrary, the initiative is totally consistent with current U.S. ABM and all other treaty obligations. The initiative includes only research on a broad range of defensive technologies to provide the basis for a decision in the future whether or not to develop systems that would provide an effective ballistic missile defense capability.

As we look toward the future, effective defenses have the potential of decreasing the value of ballistic missiles as instruments of national strategy, thereby facilitating negotiated mutual reductions in those missiles. Negotiated reductions in offensive forces, in turn, will enhance the effectiveness of the defenses; hence, we have created a defensive spiral in which both parties would be more willing to negotiate further reductions. Thus defenses couple synergistically with arms control, leading to attainment of the ultimate goal stated by the president, to eliminate the threat posed by nuclear ballistic missiles.

Defenses also facilitate arms reduction agreements by lessening the risks of undetected violations. Under the conditions that exist today, with total reliance on retaliation for deterrence, a mutual U.S.-Soviet reduction in ballistic missiles to lower levels sharply would leave each side more vulnerable to the risk of cheating. That is, the lower the agreed level of arms, the greater the danger that concealed deployments could be of a magnitude to threaten the other side's forces. But with effective defenses in place, so many illegal missiles would be required to upset the strategic balance that significant cheating could not be concealed.

An important aspect of the entire initiative is the fact that the United States is in no way decreasing its commitment to the protection of its allies but, in fact, is examining technologies for defense not only against ballistic missiles that can hit the United States, but also against shorter-range ballistic missiles that can strike our allies. As we pursue the Strategic Defense Initiative, we intend to consult closely with our allies.

The emphasis in the SDI on defending against ballistic missiles is due to their potential to decrease stability. However, while the slower moving systems, such as cruise missiles and bombers, are less threatening in this regard, there are separate efforts under way in the U.S. military services to examine the technologies required to defend against these weapon systems as well.

THE SCOPE OF SDI

It is important to understand the flight path of a ballistic missile and the various regimes in which ballistic missiles can be attacked, as illustrated in Figure 3.2. It starts in the boost phase, in which the ballistic missile, being thrust by a large chemical rocket, slowly rises from the face of the earth en route to its target. This phase can be observed as an intensely bright plume that provides a very large characteristic infrared signature. In this phase, the ballistic missile still has all its warheads attached; hence, attack in this phase provides considerable defensive leverage. In the next phase, the post-boost or bus-deployment phase, warheads and penetration aids are deployed in such a way as to attempt to confuse the defenses. This phase is followed by the longest phase, the midcourse phase. The warheads and penetration aids coast on a ballistic trajectory for several minutes on the way to their target. In the last phase—the terminal phase—the warheads and the decoys reenter the atmosphere. Discrimination is facilitated in this phase by the differing reentry dynamics and signatures of the warheads and decoys.

Developing technology that will enable us to attack ballistic missiles in any or all four of these phases will allow us to configure a layered defense system. This is a defense-in-depth approach that is not new to the military. For example, it is similar in concept to the approach used by the U.S. Navy to protect a carrier task force. We have the F-14 fighter aircraft attacking aggressors at long range using the Phoenix Missile System; at shorter ranges, using *Sparrow* and *Sidewinder* missiles; then followed up by surface-to-air missiles from the support vessels and finally by the Phalanx Gun System. Layered defenses relieve the effectiveness requirements on each individual layer and are more resistant to countermeasures.

Certain functions need to be accomplished in each of these phases for the ballistic missiles to be effectively attacked (see Figure 3.3). First, the sensor function to accomplish surveillance, acquisition, discrimination, tracking, and kill assessment; second, the weapon function to accomplish interception and destruction of the target; and third, the command and control function to integrate the allocation of the weapons and

Figure 3.2
Multiple Layered Defense

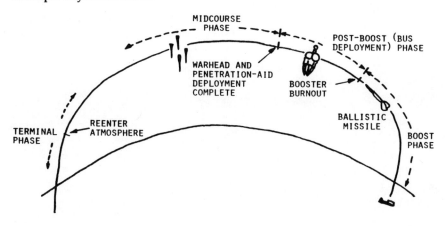

sensors and place them under human oversight to accomplish battle management. The scope of the Strategic Defense Initiative program can be discerned by identifying weapon system concepts for each function in each phase. The collection of technologies that will permit the realization of these concepts define the technical scope of the program. As an example—in the boost phase—the requirements for surveillance, acquisition, tracking, and kill assessment could be accomplished by taking advantage of the very bright signature of the booster itself. Space-based infrared sensors could detect and track the booster and pass that information to a space-based weapon that would destroy the booster. The technologies that support such a space-based sensor concept include focal plane arrays, lightweight optics, and signal processors; and programs in each of these technical areas are now being pursued under the central management of the Strategic Defense Initiative Organization. All of these key technologies were being pursued previously; hence, the SDI in one sense is not a new program, but a new focus for a collection of relevant programs.

In order to better appreciate the scope of the program, let me describe some national architectures for the sensors and weapons that might fulfill the functional requirements of a multilayered defense.

In the sensor area, five interleaved system concepts are being examined (see Figure 3.4). First, there is a space-based surveillance and tracking system that would detect launches of ballistic missiles. In the midcourse area, we perceive the need for a different kind of space-based sensor system to provide the tracking of the reentry vehicles from de-

Figure 3.3
Program Scope

BALLISTIC MISSILE FLIGHT PHASES				
FUNCTIONS	BOOST	POST-BOOST	MIDCOURSE	TERMINAL
SENSORS FOR • SURVEILLANCE • ACQUISITION • DISCRIMINATION • TRACKING • KILL ASSESSMENT	SPACE-BASED INFRARED TRACKING			AIRBORNE OPTICAL TRACKING
		SPACE-BASED LASER OR RADAR IMAGING		GROUND-BASED RADAR IMAGING
WEAPONS FOR • INTERCEPTION • DESTRUCTION	DIRECTED ENERGY			GROUND-BASED KINETIC ENERGY
	SPACE-BASED KINETIC ENERGY			
COMMAND AND CONTROL FOR • BATTLE MANAGEMENT	SECURE, SURVIVABLE COMMUNICATIONS			
	RADIATION-HARDENED SPACE-BASED COMPUTERS			

ployment to reentry. Also in the midcourse, we see the need to observe reentry vehicle and decoy deployment and thus discriminate between the two. In the terminal phase, two systems are currently envisioned, one an airborne optical system that would provide for long-range infrared tracking and discrimination of the reentry vehicles and decoys as an adjunct to the other, a ground-based imaging radar.

In the weapons area, we are considering both directed energy and kinetic energy concepts (see Figure 3.5). Ground-based and space-based kinetic energy weapons would provide for attack of ballistic missiles in all phases. In the boost phase, space-based projectiles propelled by chemical rockets or electromagnetic launcher systems would provide a capability for attacking the booster while it is still under power. These same systems would also be capable of attacking postboost vehicles and reentry vehicles during midcourse flight. In the terminal and late midcourse area, ground-based interceptors would provide a nonnuclear hit-to-kill capability to destroy reentry vehicles.

In 1984, the Homing Overlay Experiment (HOE) conclusively demonstrated that the technology for hit-to-kill intercept of reentry vehicles was viable. Some new technology breakthroughs have also occurred

Figure 3.4
Surveillance, Acquisition, Tracking, and Kill Assessment

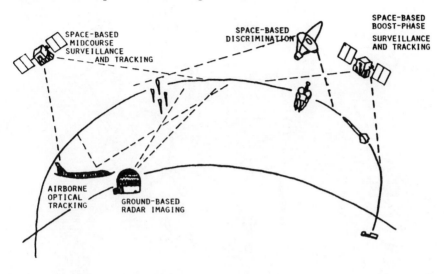

Figure 3.5
Kinetic Energy Weapons

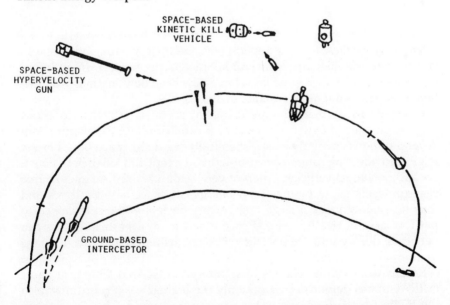

Figure 3.6
Directed Energy Weapons

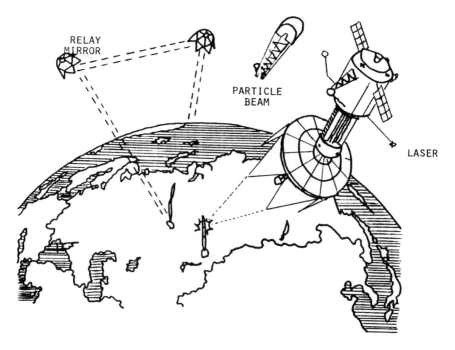

recently in the hypervelocity launcher area. We have been able to accelerate projectiles from a repetitively fired electromagnetic railgun launcher at velocities up to several kilometers per second. In addition, integrated circuits and propellants have now been demonstrated to function after sustaining accelerations of 100,000 Gs.

Directed energy weapons are being investigated primarily to attack ballistic missiles in either the boost or postboost phase (see Figure 3.6). Several options currently exist. Chemically powered space-based lasers might provide long-range, speed-of-light intercept and kill of both boosters and postboost vehicles. Alternatively, ground-based excimer or free electron lasers could bounce their energy off space-based mirrors and thus be able to attack a large number of boosters without the need to put the laser device in space. Space-based neutral particle beams can penetrate deeply into the ballistic missile, causing catastrophic damage to internal components.

Recent work on the Navy's Mid-Infrared Advanced Chemical Laser (MIRACL) has demonstrated not only the highest power, but now also the highest brightness of any laser in the free world. This laser at the White Sands Missile Range will be a workhorse for SDI, allowing us to

Figure 3.7
Possible Commercial Aspects of SDI

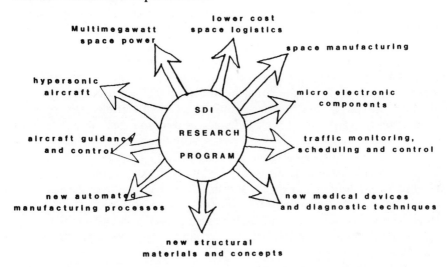

determine by actual testing the trade-offs between booster hardening and laser brightness.

POSSIBLE COMMERCIAL ASPECTS

Having described the rationale for the Strategic Defense Initiative and its scope, I will now touch on the possible commercial aspects of the program. As John McTague has already illustrated in Chapter 1, history has shown that new military technologies inevitably have an impact on industry for civilian applications. In the past, the United States made dramatic technology acceleration efforts that produced a wide range of benefits that were totally unforeseen. For example, nuclear weapons technology needs led to advances in precision machining technology, as well as in fabrication of exotic materials like Beryllium; North American Air Defense Technology efforts led to the first commercial mainframe computers and enormously accelerated progress in radars, missiles, and communications.

What commercial technology advances can we expect from the Strategic Defense Initiative program? We can only speculate, but the following may provide a beginning (see Figure 3.7).

The pointing and tracking solutions developed in response to the SDI needs may prove valuable in commercial aircraft guidance and control applications or in ground traffic monitoring, scheduling, and traffic flow.

Ultra-precise sensing and measurement technology may enable new automated process control instrumentation. Increased knowledge of interactions between high-intensity radiation and materials may produce new manufacturing processes, new instrumentation, new surface treatments, and new coatings.

The stringent requirements on mechanical structures for space applications may provide cheap and efficient devices for medical applications, as well as materials for the construction industry by providing lighter, cheaper, and stronger structures. New structural materials, design, and fabrication concepts being explored, such as fatigue-resistant metal composites and ceramic matrix composites with high fracture resistance, have widespread product potential for applications in automotive, maritime, and aerospace industries. For instance, the development of technology for cooling windows for terminal interceptor guidance may be of critical importance to the development of hypersonic commercial aircraft. The energy storage and high power densities required for space applications could have impacts on public and private transportation concepts of the future.

Lasers of various types, including gammaray, might provide new and powerful techniques for probing and modifying materials. There may be applications for microreplication and fabrication of microelectronic components where high intensity and excellent collimation will shorten the exposure time and ensure good resolution. Imaging techniques such as CAT scanners could use monochromatic radiation to permit lower doses to patients, while higher resolution would allow discrimination between molecular species, not just between density variations. Short wavelength, coherent radiation holography might permit three-dimensional observations of the structures of molecules, crystals, proteins, and genes. From the developments in particle beam generation and control and laser technology, new, safe, and efficient concepts in medical diagnostic technology and treatment may be forthcoming.

Success of nearly all elements of SDI is dependent on major advancements in space power. We estimate that potential electrically driven weapons could require power and voltage levels in excess of four orders of magnitude above current space-based systems. The technologies being pursued for these multimegawatt power sources should make power in space relatively plentiful for space manufacturing. Clearly, the potential for synergistic relationship between SDI and NASA in space power exists, particularly considering the space station. These technologies combined could make commercial space factories a reality.

In addition to all the above is affordability, the ratio between task performance and orbit weights and mass is a major support consideration for space-based power subsystems. The thrust in miniaturization of pulse power conditioning components to achieve reasonable volumes and weights for potential space-based systems should make them more affordable to place in orbit. Similarly, one of the goals in the space transportation technology area is at least a tenfold reduction in cost per pound of payload placed in orbit, based on current shuttle costs. This should translate into much more economical access to space for industry.

Potentially great increases in the numbers of space systems produced and launched due to SDI necessitate a major change in the way we reproduce and acquire space systems. Affordability is a major area of emphasis in SDI, and we must begin to address the subject even in this early stage of R&D if we are to impact the costs and producibility of potential SDI systems.

A few of the approaches SDI will take to accomplish its goal of affordable systems are consideration of commercial specifications where appropriate in place of military specifications, the requirement for producibility studies that, among other things, consider advances in manufacturing technology, affordability goals, and incentives for innovative cost-reduction ideas.

The full and enthusiastic participation of SDI contractors in these initiatives is going to be required to achieve the goal of affordable SDI systems.

The director of the SDI Organization, Lt. Gen. Abrahamson, is personally concerned, as are we all, that we not miss the splendid opportunity to capitalize on the results of the research of the Strategic Defense Initiative and apply it across all facets of our economy and society. For that reason, he created within SDI the Office of Educational and Civil Applications. Among other things, its director will be responsible for developing and encouraging the widest possible use of SDI-related technologies, consistent with security considerations, for civil use, and helping identify potential and existing technology applications and techniques that have economic benefits for the nation.

Perhaps the most significant commercial application that will come from the Strategic Defense Initiative has yet to be discovered. Perhaps one of our readers will be the one to meet that challenge.

Finally, we should consider some of the international cooperative aspects of SDI. Just a few months ago, the secretary of defense invited the participation of our allies in the Strategic Defense Initiative Research Program. We see this participation taking place in the form of cooperative research programs between government laboratories, exchanges of scientists, and by direct participation of foreign companies in U.S.-funded research either through agreements with U.S. companies or by direct competition. It has been left to each of our allies to propose the manner and extent of their participation.

CONCLUSION

I have discussed the rationale for the Strategic Defense Initiative, its scope and possible commercial aspects. Let me conclude by returning to the origin of the program.

The goal for SDI was eloquently established by President Reagan in March 1983, when he challenged the scientific community to create a means for rendering ballistic missiles impotent and obsolete.

The goal of the Strategic Defense Initiative has not changed at all since that March 1983 speech, and significant technical progress has been achieved since that time, leading us to believe that the goal is obtainable.

BIBLIOGRAPHY

SDI: A Technical Progress Report, Director, Strategic Defense Initiative Organization, June, 1985.

PART II

THE COMMERCIALIZATION OF TECHNOLOGY: PRESENT PUBLIC POLICY

4

TECHNOLOGY AND WORLD LEADERSHIP

D. BRUCE MERRIFIELD

EROSION OF U.S. LEADERSHIP

The United States emerged from World War II with a commanding lead in science and technology that translated rapidly into world preeminence in most areas of business. In recent years, that preeminence has been considerably eroded in such industries as steel, automobiles, consumer electronics, and machine tools. This erosion has occurred, even though the United States still funds about half the world's R&D and is in the forefront of scientific research in almost every area of commercial interest. In 1986, some $13 billion in basic research will be funded from all sources. This is creating a pool of fundamental knowledge that is many times greater than that being developed by any other nation. It is the resource base for many of the new products and processes that will be developed in future years.

THE PROBLEM

However, America's strong base of fundamental knowledge is not being translated as efficiently as it could be into commercial products and processes. Other nations licensing or acquiring U.S. early-stage technology make the necessary investment for its further development and then commercialize the results. Therefore, the United States has been fueling foreign competition, with a resulting slippage in its own competitive position. Of particular concern has been our inability to transfer federally funded technology into the private sector for commercial development. Currently the United States spends over $50 billion each year in federally funded technology, about $20 billion of this in government laboratories. This work has tremendous commercial potential but often has been bottled up by bureaucratic procedures in Washington. In fact, only about 4 percent of 28,000 government patents ever have been licensed. Currently some progress is being made.

The Bayh-Dole Act of 1980[1] for the first time, authorized universities and *small* businesses to retain title to inventions funded by the government but carried out in their own laboratories. In 1984, Senator Dole sponsored a follow-up bill that extended licensing rights for universities and small businesses to technology performed in government-owned, contractor-operated (GOCO) laboratories as well. For example, a university contractor operating a government laboratory now is authorized to take ownership of unclassified technology and license it to industrial organizations for further development on an *exclusive* basis. Royalties return to the university to fund additional research or faculty salaries. These bills already are stimulating a great deal of industry collaboration with universities and government laboratories.

Currently, another bill (S. 1914 in the Senate and a composite bill in the House) has been sponsored by Senator Dole. It would extend authorization for agencies to allow *large* company contractors for the first time to perform a similar function. The bill also provides that royalties from licensed technology would no longer flow to the Treasury, but could be retained by each laboratory to further enhance the mission of that laboratory. Incentive royalties to the inventors involved also are provided to encourage technology transfer.

The objective is to remove the government bureaucracy from the ownership and management of federally funded technology. Not only has the licensing function been inadequate, but technology that has commercial potential often has not been recognized and therefore has not even been patented.

As a result, unclassified work passes into the open world literature and is available to anyone. It is essential now that this advanced technology be both recognized and captured. To do this, the licensing function must (1) be decentralized to the laboratory where there is an adequate understanding of the nature of the technology, and (2) be relieved of bureaucratic red tape in the licensing process itself. U.S. competitiveness in global markets will be much enhanced if this enormous pool of technology is properly managed. But technology transfer is only one aspect of the innovation process that needs attention.

THE INNOVATION PROCESS

Innovation is not an instantaneous event. On average, it takes 7 to 10 years to produce a significant new product or process. Statistically, perhaps 1 of 20 projects that starts out in the laboratory ever results in an adequate return on investment.[2]

Innovation can be considered in a simplified model to be a three-phase process (see Figure 4.1). Phase I is the invention. Phase II involves translating that invention into a product of process that can be commercialized (about 90 percent of the R&D cost, risk, and time—Boxes 3, 4, and 5—are associated with Phase II). Phase III is successful commercialization, which also can involve considerable uncertainty.

R&D: A Form of Capital Investment

The 1981 Economic Recovery Tax Act (ERTA) has provided substantial incentives for investment in capital assets for commercial manufacturing operations (Phase III). However, the entire R&D process is a form of capital investment that must be amortized over the life of the product or process it produces. Under current law it does not qualify for incentives applied to conventional investments. In fact, it is the only form of capital investment for which no significant incentives have been available. Moreover, the cost of capital in the United States is several times higher than it is in Japan and other countries. High capital costs are a serious deterrent to investment in R&D programs that have no prior guarantee of success. As a result, many companies have not made the R&D investments necessary for them to remain competitive in global markets, especially when the innovation process has been heavily subsidized by foreign governments.

Recently, the R&D Limited Partnership (RDLP) concept has been developed to offset partially the cost of capital investments in R&D, and therefore the risk involved. Over $3 billion in private-sector funding already has been raised. RDLPs provide tax incentives for individuals to invest in R&D. These incentives reduce the cost of investing in R&D sufficiently to fund programs that have reached a preprototype or pilot plant stage (Box 4 in Phase II of Figure 4.1).

Adequate funding still is not available for the higher risk, early-stage developments (Boxes 2 and 3) that are many years away from commercial operation. If the United States is to benefit from its investments in basic research and maintain leadership in industrial technology, then it is important that the funding gap be bridged between the first technical demonstration in the laboratory (Box 2) and the preprototype stage (Box 4).

IMPORTANCE OF ADVANCED TECHNOLOGY

Those companies that have invested in advanced technology and introduced new products and processes over the past decade have done exceedingly well. In fact, over 90 percent of the high-growth industries in the United States are technology-intensive. They have grown twice

Figure 4.1
Innovation Pipeline

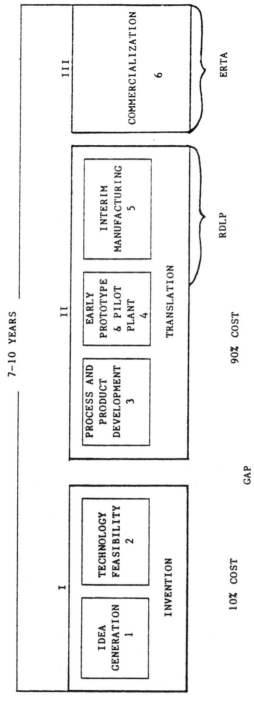

Source: U.S. Department of Commerce, Washington, D.C.

as fast as the GNP and their prices have increased at only one-third the overall rate of inflation. Their productivity growth is six times greater than that of total businesses. They have maintained themselves at the leading edge of their technology and often enjoy world leadership positions.

Moreover, it is quite feasible for even declining industries now to regain competitiveness in global markets (for example, steel, textiles, shoes, machine tools), even though they have lagged behind. In many businesses the cost/performance advantages possible with robotically operated computer integrated flexible manufacturing plants often can more than compensate for inexpensive labor and other cost advantages available in less developed countries. Introduction of advanced technology using computer-aided design and manufacturing now can restructure at least some of these industries.

In the meantime, global competition will continue to increase over the coming years, and targeting strategies by other nations can be expected to continue to capture market share in sluggish industries. Nevertheless, world leadership can be regained and maintained in most areas of enterprise if the vast array of U.S. resources can be effectively mobilized.

BARRIERS AND INCENTIVES

To mobilize U.S. resources effectively, barriers need to be removed and incentives provided. An important antitrust barrier to cooperative R&D ventures now has been removed by recently passed legislation. This legislation, the National Cooperative R&D Act of 1984, allows any group of companies or organizations to collaborate in the joint development of next-generation products or processes without fear of treble damages if they are procompetitive in world markets and meet the requirements of the law.

Other legislation also now has been introduced to strengthen patent and copyright laws and to reduce barriers to the transfer of government-funded technology to private-sector companies for commercial use. Also, legislation has been proposed both to extend and expand the 25 percent R&D incremental tax credit (which expired at the end of 1985). Under present law these credits are not allowed for start-up companies or for new cooperative ventures attempting to develop new products or processes.

Although Congress and the Executive Branch have yet to conclude their versions of these proposals, they illustrate promising new ways to reduce barriers and increase incentives for industrial innovation.

GOVERNMENT ROLE

The appropriate government role is a proactive one that removes bar-riers and provides noninterventionist incentives for innovation. More-over, nonadversarial forms of collaboration between government, industry, and academia will be critically important if U.S. industries are to regain and maintain technical and industrial leadership in a rapidly evolving and competitive global economy.

NOTES

1. The Bayh Dole Act of 1980.
2. Eugene B. Konecci and Robert Lawrence Kuhn, eds., Technology Venturing: American Innovation and Risk Taking (New York: Prayer, 1985).

5

THE DEPARTMENT OF DEFENSE POLICY ENVIRONMENT ON TECHNOLOGY TRANSFER

GERALD D. SULLIVAN

The topic of this chapter is the current Department of Defense policy environment regarding technology transfer. These views originate within the research and development community, specifically the section that is responsible for international programs. The key issue is technology diffusion—that is, commercializing of strategic defense technologies.

The first characteristic of our environment is that DOD's interest in technology is broad and perhaps the term "technology transfer" is poorly used. DOD concerns and interests cover the spectrum of basic research, technology development, engineering, and production. Clearly, each of these separate areas of technical effort involves orders of magnitude differences in funding, has different communities of participants in and outside DOD, and has quite different absorption or application possibilities for the recipients of the transfer. We do not always distinguish these differences in our review of technology transfer actions, as not all within DOD appreciate these differences. Perhaps this lack of appreciation is one important aspect of the current environment.

The second characteristic is that DOD undertakes not only large-scale programs, but also an ongoing level of technological effort that is most pervasive. Large-scale programs, such as SDI, are naturally seen as drivers of technology advancement—with high potential for commercialization. Notable examples of the past have been jet bombers, the U.S. Air Defense System (SAGE), the ICBM, atomic energy, and the man on the moon. For DOD, these have provided important products, new technologies, materials, techniques, and skills, while drawing new people into DOD interests and new technical fields. All these projects have provided important commercial spin-offs.

Although the large projects are most visible, ongoing work should not be overlooked if for no other reason than magnitude. This year's DOD R&D budget request was $39 billion, of which $15 billion is for research, exploratory development, and advance development. Moreover, alongside these directed efforts, defense firms have committed some $7 billion in 1985 to independent research and development— wherein 75 percent is authorized under overhead and 25 percent is company money. Clearly, the technology base is large and offers the potential of important developments to both DOD and the civil community.

The third characteristic applies directly to international concerns because we in DOD do not wish to see our technology become an asset for adversaries. This means we wish to prevent the direct transfer of military technology; we wish to prevent the indirect transfer of military technology through friendly and allied nations; and we wish to prevent the direct or indirect transfer of dual-use technology that has important military applications. Our attention is focused on the technology funded by DOD, on that commercialized from DOD-funded efforts, and on that which, while independently funded, results in technical data and products of significant military value. With the State and Defense Departments, we have a process of elaborate review to provide for control of this transfer. Simultaneously, we are working energetically with allied and friendly nations to have them exercise the same degree of controls. Thus the international importance of technology affects directly the domestic diffusion process.

The fourth characteristic is also international. The fact is that the United States is not able to be superior in all technologies; there are many smart people and significant investments in technology elsewhere. This results in two follow ups. First, we wish access to these technologies and our friends and allies wish in turn access to ours. Second, we have strong reasons to share technology in order to achieve our security interests, which are to field the best weapons for our collective strengths.

We indeed have compelling reasons to share. We are thus looking at allied capabilities before we start a new development; we seek to buy nondevelopmental items in order to avoid duplication of R&D; we join single consortium developments as well as initiate large numbers of emerging technology projects for near-term deployment. Overall we seek all means to minimize duplicative developments and to maximize commonality of equipment. We stress industry-industry cooperation in order that they may provide the best answers for our use as buyers.

It is important to understand the multiple agencies and mechanisms within the executive departments that focus on technology transfer within the United States and across international lines. The material that follows provides much valuable information in this regard.[1]

lata bases and
is an excellent
nent agencies,
. Of concern,
en determined
o obtain" tech-
ntages and can
lting indirectly
that until re-
standing order

1980, the Con-
ablish an office
ovide and dis-
products, proc-
state and local
quired that the
ation of Federal
rt of the NTIS.
funded bench
logy may be a
sector. A brief
he bench engi-
through chan-
ry Consortium

50 federal labo-
C coordination
ional and four
the federal lab-
eloped through
rce that is par-
r processed for
to this resource
and individual
ned to improve
nments as well
person contacts
d private-sector
in ensuring ef-

out by a dozen
the accomplish-
the Technology

HANGE

y perspective, in defense, industry,
esearch is performed in government
government by defense contractors
nd laboratories. Department of De-
earch include the Army, Navy, and
rch Office, Office of Naval Research,
rch, the Defense Advanced Research
Defense Initiative Organization.
ced technology takes place through
overnment/contractor conferences, or
mation about defense-produced tech-
h scientific journals, open meetings,
de the government. There are many
effect dissemination of information
o the American public for the express
logy quotient" and our military/eco-

nge of defense scientific and technical
y DOD directive 3200.12, "DOD Sci-
rogram" (STIP). Execution is accom-
cing DOD agency and by the Defense
ense Technical Information Center
repared by a DOD agency or defense
emination directly to other defense
demic facilities known to be partici-
pecific defense related technology.
mination of DOD Technical Informa-
dissemination of DOD technical in-
tion procedures for access to that
tiate DOD Form 1540, "Registration
tion Services," and obtain approval
acting officer's technical represent-
alified DTIC users are listed in the
shed quarterly by DTIC.
nity scientific and technical infor-
of Commerce's National Technical
S receives all DOD technical pub-
e it, "approved for public release—
. government-produced research,
rts. The NTIS has over 1 million
ign technology. Access to biblio-

graphic abstracts is obtained through on-line computer
printed biweekly and in annual indices. Obviously, thi
domestic technology transfer mechanism for all goverr
U.S. industry, universities, and the public in gener
though, is the fact that while information in NTIS has b
suitable for public release, the availability of this cheap
nology can provide our friends and allies economic adv
provide our potential adversaries an economic boost res
in enhanced military capability. It is interesting to no
cently, the Soviet embassy in Washington, D.C , had a
for two copies of every report available from NTIS.

In the Stevenson-Wydler Technology Innovation Act o
gress mandated that all federally funded laboratories es
of research and technology applications (ORTA) "to p
seminate information on federally owned or originated
esses, and services having a potential application to
government and to private industry." The act also re
Department of Commerce establish a Center for the Utili:
Technology (CUFT). CUFT was institutionalized as a p
The dissemination process is initiated by the federall:
engineer who feels that utilization of his or her techn
solution to some problem in the state, local, or privat
"Technology Application Assessment" is prepared by
neer and the laboratory ORTA officer and then provide
nels to CUFT via the secretariat of the Federal Laborat
(FLC) for technology transfer.

The FLC is an organization made up of more than :
ratories and centers from 11 federal agencies. The F
function is performed on a voluntary basis by six re
national technology transfer specialists from throughou
oratory system and their contractors. The technology de
the efforts of the federal government is a national reso
ticularly valuable in the development of new products
use by both the public and private sectors. Gaining acces
can be a complicated task because of the many agencie
laboratories involved. The FLC was conceived and desi
the accessibility of this resource for state and local gov
as domestic industries. The FLC establishes person-to
between the federal laboratories and potential public- a
users. FLC and CUFT at NTIS complement each othe:
fective execution of the Technology Innovation Act.

The domestic technology transfer arena is rounded
professional and commercial organizations that promote
ment of technology transfer. Of noteworthy mention is

Transfer Society (T²S), which held its eighth annual meeting and international symposium in June 1983 on the subject: "People Interaction— The Key to Technology Transfer."

THE FREEDOM OF INFORMATION ACT

The Freedom of Information Act (Title 5, U.S. Code, Section 552) postulates that openness in government is beneficial, and that the American public has a right to know what the government is doing.

Department of Defense Directive 5400.7, "DOD Freedom of Information Act Program," contains two policy statements relevant to technology transfer:

A. "Promote public trust by making the maximum amount of information available to the public on the operation and activities of the Department of Defense, consistent with DOD's responsibility to ensure national security"; and

B. "Release records to the public, unless those records are exempt from mandatory disclosure as outlined in Chapter III of DOD 5400.7-R."

The DOD policy obviously promotes domestic technology transfer by "maximizing" the amount of information available to the public, but, on the other hand, it has compounded the technology export "control" problem.

From a control standpoint there was previously no specific exemption that would permit the withholding of information (on unclassified technology with military application) upon request from *any* member of the public. "Member of the public" has been interpreted by the attorney general to mean U.S. citizens or foreign nationals, whether here or abroad. Once the information has been released to a requester, a public disclosure occurs, control is lost, and export may take place without the necessity of an export license. Thus, public release is tantamount to automatic export.

WITHHOLDING OF UNCLASSIFIED TECHNICAL DATA FROM PUBLIC DISCLOSURE

The Department of Defense Authorization Act of 1984, P.L. 98–94, Section 1217, has precipitated DOD Directive 5230.25, "Withholding of Unclassified Technical Data from Public Disclosure." The law and this directive provide that technical data with military or space application may be withheld from public disclosure if it is subject to license requirements of the Export Administration Act or the Arms Export Control Act. Release of the data can be made to domestic U.S. contractors with the notice that further dissemination or export may violate the law and will subject them to a fine and/or imprisonment.

TECHNOLOGY EXPORT CONTROLS

Technology export is controlled by federal laws and cabinet-level departments whose regulations define policy and procedures for "controlled" release or retention of technology (and its products) to our allies, friendly nonaligned nations, and sometimes even our "potential adversaries."

Generally speaking, classified technology is adequately protected. Unclassified technology with significant military potential, however, is sometimes not adequately protected. Many times it is excluded from consideration if it is already in the public domain, and it has in the past been exempt from export license requirements. How do international agreements and U.S. laws on technology export relate to one another? Who does what for whom?

COORDINATION COMMITTEE

In 1949 the Western allies formed the Coordination Committee (CO-COM) for multilateral export controls to implement a uniform export control system when dealing with the Warsaw Pact and the Peoples Republic of China (PRC). COCOM is now comprised of Japan and all the NATO countries except Iceland and Spain. It is a voluntary organization whose decisions can be implemented only through the national policies of its members. These national policies sometimes differ significantly. COCOM maintains three separate lists covering munitions, atomic energy, and dual-use items. The latter accounts for a majority of the trade matters considered by the group.

EXPORT ADMINISTRATION ACT

The advent of the cold war promoted passage of the Export Administration Act (EAA) of 1949. Subsequently modified in 1969, 1979, and 1985, the act provides for controls on export of goods that might enhance either the economic or military strength of a potential adversary. The responsibility to execute the EAA was placed with the Department of Commerce. The Export Administration Regulation (EAR) provides for stringent government control in licensing exports. The EAR includes a commodity control list, which identifies (1) the characteristics of the goods and processes of particular concern, (2) the country of destination, and (3) the end-use of the goods. The EAR control also encompasses "technical data". With few exceptions, all exports of technical data require a general license or a validated license. A general license is analogous to an exemption and a validated license, on the other hand, is a document authorizing a specific export. The EAR process is performed by the Office of Export Administration in the Commerce Department. Most transactions deal with government agencies other than the Defense Department, but some militarily related transactions require DOD technical input to the decision process.

ARMS EXPORT CONTROL ACT

The Arms Export Control Act (AECA) of 1976 provides for the Department of State administration of the "International Traffic in Arms Regulation" (ITAR). ITAR, first issued in 1954, sets rules for controlling the export of military systems, including the "design, production, manufacture, repair, overhaul, processing, engineering, development, operation, maintenance or reconstruction" of items on the U.S. munitions list or any technology that "advances the state-of-the-art or establishes a new art in any area of significant military applicability."

U.S. defense contractors file an application with the Office of Munitions Control in the State Department as the first step to obtain an export license. The Department of Defense is required to establish a "position" on each export license application of military significance or each munitions case.

THE MILITARILY CRITICAL TECHNOLOGIES LIST

The Bucy Report of 1976[2] set forth as its primary conclusion that the control of design and manufacturing know-how is absolutely vital to the maintenance of U.S. technical superiority. This was a shift in emphasis on export controls away from a product or "end item" fixation.

Paralleling the language of the Bucy Report, the Export Administration Act of 1979 directed the secretary of defense to prepare a list of "militarily critical technologies" (MCTL). The act defined these as technologies that, if exported, would permit a "significant advance" in a military system of any country to which U.S. exports are controlled. The act stated that this MCTL should emphasize design and manufacturing know-how, keystone manufacturing, inspection and test equipment, and goods accompanied by sophisticated operation, application, or maintenance know-how.

ENFORCEMENT OF EXPORT CONTROLS

Enforcement activities to ensure compliance or the conduct of investigations regarding the provisions of the Export Administration Act and the International Traffic in Arms Regulation are conducted by the Commerce Department Office of Export Enforcement, the Federal Bureau of Investigation, and the Treasury Department's Customs Service. Operation Exodus was initiated by the U.S. Customs Service in January 1981 to prevent the illegal exportation of strategic technology to the Warsaw Pact nations. Exodus began with a massive cargo inspection program. This represented a major policy change, as the United States previously mounted only token cargo inspection efforts. Other stages of the project focus on investigations and the active involvement of customs agents stationed overseas in violation cases.

Exporters and some members of Congress have complained that Operation Exodus is delaying legal shipments and causing customer problems. The customs service's report on Operation Exodus acknowledges these complaints, but contends that delays "should diminish substantially in the near future" with the improved training of agents and liaison with the Department of Commerce's licensing staff. Shipment inspection is obviously of limited effectiveness unless all shipments are inspected and then excessive delays would be unsatisfactory and the costs would be prohibitive. Project Exodus may not stop all illegal or "ignorant of the law" violations but it will instill consciousness and awareness to minimize violations.

The Defense Department has produced the MCTL by involving technical specialists from DOD, the military services, service laboratories, other government agencies, and industry. Approximately 80 industrial firms formally reviewed the MCTL. The MCTL is updated periodically; the latest edition was updated in 1986.

The criteria for selection of "candidate technologies" for the MCTL included:

• Technology that is not already possessed by potential adversary, nor is it readily available to them

• Technology that provides advantage to us in terms of performance, reliability, maintenance, and cost over systems currently employed by adversary

• Technology that is on the Central Intelligence Agency's projection of Soviet acquisition targets

• Technology that is related to emerging technology with high potential for having an impact for advanced military application

CONCLUSION

The National Academy of Science Panel on Scientific Communications and National Security has set forth the postulate that "security by accomplishments" is better than "security through secrecy," and that it represents a national strategy for long-term security through economic, technical scientific, and intellectual vitality.

Domestic technology transfer is absolutely necessary for the economic strength of our economy—and thus our security and growth as a nation. In the long run, the technological lead of the United States must be maintained both through effective vigorous research and development via application of developments elsewhere and through a conscious effort to prevent the "undesirable" export of critical military technologies. The collective strength of the free world depends upon the technological growth of our allies and friends and the "desirable" sharing of technical developments. This is the environment. The participation of the entire technological community is the key to effective and safe technology transfer.

NOTES

1. R. Kuhn, ed., Commercializing Defense Related Technology (New York: Praeger, 1984).
2. J. Fred Bucy (author and chairman of task force), "An Analysis of Export Control of U.S. Technology—a Department of Defense Perspective. A Report of the Defense Science Board Task Force on Export of U.S. Technology," February 4, 1976 (Washington, D.C., Office of the Director of Defense Research & Engineering).

6

PERSPECTIVES ON TECHNOLOGY TRANSFER

GEORGE GAMOTA

In the last 20 years we have seen many large-scale government programs, such as the space shuttle, very high speed integrated circuits (VHSIC), manufacturing technology, the search for a cure for cancer, and, more recently, the energy programs; but compared to SDI they were like hors d'oeuvres to the main course. It is rare to see major government programs providing new technological opportunities on the scale of SDI.

Opportunities will soon be available to research and develop a whole range of new scientific and technological capabilities to resolve not only SDI-related problems but also many that find commercial applications. This chapter seeks to provide a perspective on this potential.

ADVANCED POLYMERIC COMPOSITES

A growing array of man-made polymeric composites provides materials that are stronger and stiffer than the best structural materials. These polymeric composites are already being used in the manufacture of aircraft and sports equipment and are on the verge of being used in autos, heavy equipment, robotics, and many other commercial areas.

SUPERCOMPUTER ARCHITECTURES

Supercomputers, able to respond at about 100 million instructions per second, will soon be capable of executing 1,000 million instructions per second, rising to 20 billion in the next decade. Faster computers, accompanied by refinements in software, will dramatically expand the applications of computers to ever more complex scientific and technological problems. To illustrate, computer simulation will affect aircraft design, the development of new pharmaceuticals, the design of energy storage systems and industrial products, and the testing of the new generation integrated circuit (IC) chips. Better and real-time forecasts will be made of weather, atmospheric phenomena, wind shears, tornadoes, and earthquakes. In medicine real-time simulation of surgery will have dramatic effect in providing better health care.

SOLAR TERRESTRIAL PLASMA PHYSICS

Better understanding of the interactions of charged particles with each other and with electrical and magnetic fields will help in the effort to attain peaceful uses of fusion, improve understanding of effects of sunspots on magnetic storms and communication systems, and will provide invaluable data on breaking new ground in understanding such basic questions as origin, behavior, and location of black holes.

COOPERATIVE/CROSS-DISCIPLINARY WORK

Consideration of new funding modes, research structures, and agency organization is a major legislative issue and is driven by the growing need for multidisciplinary research. Multidisciplinary research now ranges from neuroscience—requiring the effective collaboration of biologists, anatomists, physicists, physicians, chemists, psychologists and computer scientists—to man-made structured materials—requiring condensed matter physicists, materials scientists and engineers, chemists and chemical engineers, toxicologists, and process designers and manufacturing engineers. Such work is clearly of national interest but seldom found today in a university setting or found funded by government agencies.

As Gerold Yonas discussed in Chapter 2, the technical areas of SDI break down into: systems, sensors, directed energy, kinetic energy, survivability, lethality, and key technologies. Additionally, to nurture the basic technologies needed for the above, an Innovative Science and Technology Office (ISTO) was formed. ISTO is to be to SDI as Research Offices (Army Research Office, Office of Naval Research, or Air Force Office of Scientific Research) are to the military services. ISTO is the primary interface to the universities, while the rest of SDI will presumably interface more with industry and DOE's weapons laboratories.

What are some of the potential spin-offs to the commercial world from SDI? Predicting the future, particularly the application value of technology, is dangerous territory to tread upon since even major companies have lost their shirts because of erroneous assumptions and/or predictions. Nevertheless, planning in a company is an important part of its business and R&D planning is a key part of any high tech business.

Let us look at some of the possibilities:

Systems. Possible spin-offs are the development of very large computer systems linked together to do real-time tracking of enemy missiles. To accomplish this feat we need at least two orders of magnitude improvement in our computing capability. Smaller, more densely packed, and more reliable ICs need to be developed. Virtually any progress in this field has immediate commercial spin-off and any major company working will have a jump on the competition. Japan is investing heavily in these areas so that the U.S. (SDI) effort will help protect our slipping position.

Software is one of the key ingredients that is creating much of the discussion about whether SDI is feasible. Software is also one of the major bottlenecks in wide usage of computers, ranging from small personal computers to big supercomputers. Any progress here will have obvious spinoffs.

Sensors of all sorts will provide much generic technology of wide usage, limited today by imagination alone.

Materials, again, will help the U.S. industry compete effectively with our commercial competitors. Even space materials programs can potentially find wide usage as more and more satellites and Space Shuttle/Station experiments are used for a variety of purposes. Some of those exotic materials may find applications here on earth if their cost eventually levels downward and competes with what is available. The key point here is that the R&D costs are very high and these will be borne by the U.S. government.

The same can be said with respect to communication technologies. Less certain is the degree of spin-off potential from directed energy efforts, but even here General Rankine provided us some ideas in Chapter 3. The cost of doing the R&D probably is not justified based on the commercial spin-offs alone, but, and this is a big "but," if the DOD is developing these technologies for its own defense needs, spin-offs need to be taken into account and should be exploited (since incremental costs are relatively small and potentially cost-effective).

Historically, we know that there are commercial spinoffs from DOD R&D—in fact, some compare DOD in the United States to MITI in Japan.

Direct spending by the DOD and NASA has played a major role in enhancing the competitive position of high tech industries. For example, commercial development of the integrated circuit technology was a result of programs in DOD and NASA. The Minuteman, Apollo, and other federal programs paid for most of the technology development and for the first IC production lines, and the federal government bought nearly all of the early output. In effect, not only did DOD provide the funding for the R&D but it was the only guaranteed buyer for the products.

Similarly, many if not all advances in the aircraft industry resulted from federal R&D programs or from manufacturers' independent R&D efforts to meet federal needs. Except for the rather recent Boeing 757 and 767, most commercial models had a predecessor in the form of a military plane. Much of the Boeing 747 and McDonnell Douglas DC-10 technology was developed in the course of competition for the federal jumbo cargo carrier contract, eventually won by Lockheed's C-5A.

Federal space and defense R&D programs were also responsible for the development of many plastics and other materials now commonplace in such items as the nonstick frypan.

It is generally recognized that research benefits the nation more than it does any individual company and that private firms tend to devote less resources to R&D than the public interest warrants. This is particularly true for high tech firms that perform roughly half of all commercial R&D in the United States. The defense industry gets a lion's share of this federal support for R&D. Additional support comes from the individual industrial independent R&D (IR&D), which allows a company dealing with the government (DOD or NASA) to increase its costs of selling products by the amount it spends on R&D for projects with potential government use. As were previously cited, the Space Shuttle, VHSIC, Rapid Solidification Technology, and Man Tech programs are just a few examples of where companies spend IR&D dollars to get ahead and gain some competitive edge.

I am generally bullish on future prospects, but unless proper planning is put into place, we can also run into difficulties. Let me cite just two: manpower and controls.

MANPOWER

The DOD in the 1980s, similar to NASA in the 1960s, is aggressively getting involved with higher education by creating a need for scientists and engineers in a number of SDI-related fields. The fear many of us in the academic world have is whether the support for this work is there for the long haul, or if it is going to be a repeat of the early 1970s. It is important to note that DOD, for the first time since the Mansfield Amendment days,[1] is seriously involving itself in higher education. This is happening not because it feels its mission is suddenly broader, but because of the stark realization that if it does not support graduate education in these several fields there will not be the trained manpower to carry out their critical programs. For example, in areas such as microwave tube and accelerator design, where the DOD is the only customer, there are already specialized graduate programs to fill their needs. I believe the DOD should be applauded for assuming this responsibility, but once in this role, it must also agree (with congressional backing) to carry the burden and not allow wild swings to permeate the system.

The basic question and/or concern is: Will 1971 (fallout of the Apollo program) repeat itself in 1991 (possible fallout of the SDI program)? Concurrently whose role is it to make sure that the transition, either build-up or scale-back, does not adversely affect the U.S. technical work force?

In the decade following *Sputnik*, the federal government aggressively promoted higher education. Many of us here today were in graduate school under some type of federal support program. Unfortunately, as many of us know, the push for training of technical manpower did not really bear fruit until after the peak of demand passed. Thus, the main result may have been to produce an excess labor supply for the period of aerospace and academic retrenchment that set in during the early 1970s. This created a profound disillusionment with public manpower programs whose effects have still not worn off.[2]

Today, industrial needs are putting demands on the science and engineering base as the DOD did previously. In some areas, such as large-scale computation where it is still a driving force, technical manpower resources are simply not in the position they were three decades ago.

CONTROLS

Technology concern alone might adversely impact how quickly we might see commercial spin-offs of SDI technology. There are signs, for example, that VHSIC technology is not being picked up for commercial spin-offs because companies are concerned about getting controls slapped on the products.

Obviously I have only scratched the surface with respect to the whole problem of commercialization of defense technology, and much more needs to be discussed. For example, maybe a good look needs to be taken to ensure that we have optimized the military-civilian technical transfer mechanisms. A key question is whether DOE's patent policies are going to inhibit technology transfer from its weapons laboratories, where much work is going to be done.

Additionally, how can we get the small and medium-size companies, which are the core of innovation in the United States, involved? To date, this has been one of the most obvious shortcomings, notwithstanding the SBIR (Small Business Innovation Research) program, which is starting to bear some fruit. In commercializing SDI-related technologies, how to involve small and medium-sized firms must be one of the most important issues if we really want the nation to benefit economically from our large investment.

Which of the SDI technologies have the most promising commercial spin-off possibility? And, again, whose job is it to ensure that the technology gets transitioned to the most innovative sector—namely, the small and medium industrial sector? Is government going to play a role and if so, what kind of a role? These are the crucial questions.

In 1982, three out of four dollars spent on R&D by aerospace companies were provided by the DOD. Those are big dollars and the nation can benefit tremendously if the right policies are in place and there is cooperative spirit on all sides.

NOTES

1. In the early 1970s, the Mansfield Amendment to the DOD appropriations bill stated that all DOD work must be relevant to the DOD's mission.
2. Walter McDougall, *The Heavens and the Earth: A Political History of the Space Age* (New York: Basic Books, 1985).

PART III

PRIVATE-SECTOR REQUIREMENTS FOR SUCCESSFUL COMMERCIALIZATION

7

COLLABORATIVE RESEARCH AND DEVELOPMENT

ADMIRAL BOBBY R. INMAN (Retired)

When I was first charged with putting together a joint research venture in microelectronics and computer technology, I gathered together some very competent people; we had some very good luck and a very viable venture was put together. We are proud of it and, therefore, we have given free advice to other companies that were considering similar joint ventures. More than 50 have been declared to the Department of Justice. We could have had a decent commercial line of business consulting had we pursued it, but we did not.

I do not have a commercial line of business ready on the technology transfer issue, either. Let me take a historian's view first in looking at this country's periods of great surges of creating technology and the subsequent commercializing process. Dr. George Kozmetsky has been my instructor in much of this.

If you look back at the late 1940s and early 1950s, the primary impetus for many of the technology gains was investment by Defense in R&D, largely from the Office of Naval Research and its counterparts. That effort to push the frontiers of science turned ideas into technology. Sometimes it was a vision of the kinds of weapons systems that would be created, but not always. There was often no indication at the outset of what other uses might be available. Yet that is precisely where things like computers and synthetic fibers originated.

The key to this country's great economic gain was the speed with which defense technology became available for commercial exploitation—the speed with which bright innovators, not the ones that created the technology, recognized the potential and had ideas how to exploit it.

We had a procurement cycle in Defense of four to five years. The flowthrough was pretty rapid. Now look at 1987. We began in the early

1960s trying to take a procurement system that had problems and make it "perfect." With what result? We now have a procurement system process that is 12 to 13 years. Therefore, the United States loses most of the economic commercial advantage that we once obtained from the early availability of technology created through research funded by the Department of Defense. (NASA to some degree has been a separate case.)

One of my major concerns, therefore, for this great new surge of investment for SDI, is what is going to be the length of the procurement cycles? Will they be held to all the standard DOD approaches?

I had the good fortune in my years as director of Naval Intelligence and director of the National Security Agency (NSA), to be able to set up and run a number of large black (i.e., classified) programs. They were on balance pretty successful. It wasn't that the secret covering let me hide the mistakes, it was that the black program let me avoid all the bureaucracy in the process, and my procurement cycles were reasonable. This was before we set out to improve it and to make it a "perfect" system. Rapidity is vital. The real key is what is going to be the time cycle for technology created by SDI investment to flow through for potential commercialization?

I recently had the privilege of heading a joint research venture, the largest one on this scale for in-house industrial research activity that has been undertaken in this country. In the early stages, I was quite comfortable with the definition of the research goals and with the by-laws of how the operation would be conducted, but I was very concerned about two issues: talent acquisition and technology transfer. I was persuaded then, and even more now, that these issues were much intertwined. The basic attitude I found from the original 12 sponsoring companies was one of benign neglect: They really did not worry about talent and transfer. The assumption was that all the talent I was going to need would be found in the shareholder companies, and that it was just a question of assembling it. My government experience told me to be very skeptical of that view. My skepticism tracked on through to technology transfer; the general attitude was, "Don't worry about technology transfer; the talent we send you will come home when the research is finished and they will bring the technology with them, and it will get used."

I subscribe to the certainty that human participation in technology transfer is the most important issue, but there is also a question of time. When does it become available? My previous experience, especially in my NSA years, told me that if you wait until the researchers have finished and tied a neat ribbon around their package of technology, those who are out building or procuring systems are already gone. They would have already decided on the approach that they want to use; so if you wait until the scientists are comfortable with the totality of their results, the likelihood of that technology being applied effectively, at least in a competitive marketplace, is pretty small.

As I try to look out and understand the great Japanese economic success over these past 25 to 30 years, I have a strong sense that they have not been troubled by a "not invented here" syndrome. They are devoid of that hang-up. Rather, they are constantly scanning for new technologies, new ideas to attack a problem or opportunity in front of them.

Time is often critical. For example, instead of spending a year test marketing an idea, companies should be willing to go ahead and plunge into implementation. The critical factor is understanding the potential of that evolving technology, and generating new ideas how it can be effectively used.

In my accepting employment, running the Microelectronics and Computer Technology Corporation (MCC), one condition was absolute authority over personnel matters. My determination was that a relatively lean joint research venture would work only if it was staffed by the highest quality people available. The shareholder companies agreed that MCC was not to be a turkey farm. In the early months, we accepted only about 5 percent of the candidates that were offered by the shareholders. We were fortunate that the widespread publicity triggered a great flood of resumes—not only from all over the country, but internationally as well—from people who wanted to be part of the research effort. The end result was 65 percent of the talent was directly hired and only 35 percent assigned by the companies. As reality began to take shape, we then turned back to our 21 shareholder companies to begin dealing with the problems of technology transfer. (They weren't just going to call their people home.) We spent nine months hammering out a master technology transfer plan with all the licensing arrangements. Getting a structure in place before you actually have results to argue about should be a high priority—organize an approach before somebody has an idea or an empire they feel the urge to protect.

We then spent another nine months on something that I hope most ventures will not have to worry about, i.e. building arrangements for technology transfer between unequal programs. All these 21 companies that sponsor MCC do not fund all the programs. So again, as with the government, we needed to compartmentalize programs. How do you build the contractual agreements between programs that let you share talent, expense, results?

In looking at the realities of our challenge, we ran a good prospect of producing technology with some substantial time frame advantage before our principal foreign competitors. Yet our number-one worry was, and remains, that even if we produce a three-year lead, we may still find the Japanese arriving earlier with comparable products, even though they would have accessed the technology two or three years behind us, given current commercializing approaches and the questionable availability of capital.

Thus we made a fundamental decision to put in process a continuous flow of research results to our commercial companies—the only limiting feature that can be applied by a program manager is quality control. He or she can hold up research results until he or she is reasonably satisfied that there is not a gross mistake in the research activity. From that point the data flows; we worry later about getting credit for having created it.

Our prime objective is to get the attention of those who are setting the business strategy. As early as we can interest decision makers in what we are producing, we increase the likelihood of impacting their product line some years down the way.

I have watched 21 different approaches to technology transfer from our 21 shareholder corporations. I am not uncomfortable with it. I am persuaded again that one should not try to force everyone into the same mold. But I am fascinated by how very different the approaches are. There are a few firms that, at least at this point almost three years into the effort, are receiving the written flow of reports rather passively (and the pile is growing into a huge mound of paper). These companies come quarterly to review meetings and semiannually for detailed meetings and, unfortunately, that is the extent of their visible involvement.

The other extreme are shareholders that have now rented office space and apartments in Austin, Texas (where MCC is located), and are sending their top scientists to stay two to three months at a time working in our laboratories. I am persuaded that these companies are the ones most likely to be at the cutting edge of using what we are producing.

In applying the MCC experience to SDI, I have trouble figuring out how to attract all those bright youngsters to come to one's laboratories, at least until the research can be seen on a broader scale.

How can one access defense created research? Who can be involved other than those actually working on the defense areas directly? I suspect that we will have to create some new mechanisms—some entirely different approach to the ones we have seen to date.

To achieve successful commercialization, industry's brightest thinkers need the earliest possible exposure to the nature of SDI's research—particularly where there may be some unique new approach. Let them begin to conceptualize, as soon as possible, how to perform the modern alchemy, turning technology into products.

Is our new consortium approach to technology transfer going to be better than other methods? I have hope, but no certainty. As I have gone around the country worrying aloud about technology transfer, some of my shareholder companies have told me that I ought not worry so much, or at least not in public, because there is a new dynamic at work here, one not heretofore common in industry.

Each company in the consortium knows that its competitors have equal access to the technologies we are producing. If, by way of contrast, a technology is found in their own company laboratory, and they elect not to use it because it doesn't fit the cycle, perhaps no other company will access it and they safely can wait two to three years to commercialize it. But in the case of our joint research venture, each company knows that if they don't track technology developments closely and plan to use them rapidly, the odds are high that they will have subsidized their competitors in taking new products to the marketplace. Is this a strong incentive for rapid commercialization? The jury is still out.

NOTE

This Chapter was originally given as a speech to the Large Scale Programs Institute, March 21, 1985, Austin, Texas.

8

INVESTMENT BANKING REQUIREMENTS

WAYNE G. FOX

From the perspective of an investment banker, the profitable application of technological innovation is a process that follows a consistent pattern and requires the same business inputs regardless of whether the innovation is derived from ordinary corporate R&D or from the Strategic Defense Initiative program. The commercialization of technology may be described as the arduous process by which a single invention joins the existing body of technical knowledge and by which the technology is applied to meet a market need.

The purpose of business is the creation of economic wealth both for business owners (shareholders) and for employees by providing need-fulfilling products and services to markets that are willing and able to purchase those products and services. Technology exists as society's pool of knowledge, which sets forth the limits on how much can be produced with a given amount of productive inputs. Even with these limitations, there is generally a wide range of possible methods of producing a given product or service.

The process of commercializing technology begins with research, the systematic, patient study and investigation of some field of knowledge, undertaken to establish facts or principles that may be utilized in creating new ideas or inventions. Ideas have the potential for creating wealth; however, invention has little or no economic significance until it is applied.

In a business context, invention is applied to a market need by an entrepreneur. An invention when applied for the first time is referred to an as innovation.

Entrepreneurship is the process by which a pro-active manager, whether as the owner of a small emerging growth business or as an employee in the context of a large corporate entity, organizes, operates, and assumes the risk for a business venture. The risks of technological innovation can be very high. Although research and development can provide much information about the technical characteristics and the cost of structure of an innovation, and although marketing research can provide considerable information about market demand, there are many areas of business uncertainty that can be resolved only through the actual production and marketing of a product or service.

The development of commercial applications of technology as well as the underlying research require capital funding. The funding of growing, technology-based companies takes place primarily through capital markets, which will be discussed in some detail in the following pages.

The Need for Investment in Technology

Technology is the ammunition of business competition. New ideas for products or services, new methods of producing products, new techniques of organization, marketing, and management give companies a competitive edge. The need for investment in the development of technology is clear.

America's strength lies in its technology combined with the ability to develop need-fulfilling goods and services from that technology. In the late nineteenth century, a technical revolution developed in the United States that was fostered by a rapidly developing commercial market. An emerging capital market soon followed, flourishing in the 1920s. The Great Depression of the 1930s brought the increased role of the federal government in promoting the economic welfare of the country. With the end of World War II, the country emerged as the world leader in technology, which led to rapid expansion of the industrial, commercial, and consumer markets. The 1960s brought about the technology of the Space Age as a direct result of President Kennedy's clearly defined national goal to put a man on the moon by the end of the decade and by significant developments in defense-related technology.

Clearly defined goals lead to technical innovation. The U.S. government is engaged in a number of programs to foster research and development of new technology. The Stevenson-Wydler Technology Innovation Act of 1980 set clear national goals in finding that

Technology and industrial innovation are central to the economic, environmental, and social well-being of citizens of the United States.

Technology and industrial innovation offer an improved standard of living, increased public and private sector productivity, creation of new industries and employment opportunities, improved public services and enhanced competitiveness of United States products in world markets.

Many new discoveries and advances in science occur in universities and

Federal laboratories, while the application of this new knowledge to commercial and useful public purposes depends largely upon actions by business and labor. Cooperation among academia, Federal laboratories, labor, and industry, in such forms as technology transfer, personnel exchange, joint research projects, and others, should be renewed, expanded, and strengthened.

Small businesses have performed an important role in advancing industrial and technological innovation.

Increased industrial and technological innovation would reduce trade deficits, stabilize the dollar, increase productivity gains, increase employment, and stabilize prices.

No comprehensive national policy exists to enhance technological innovation for commercial and public purposes. There is a need for such a policy, including a strong national policy supporting domestic technology transfer and utilization of the science and technology resources of the Federal Government.

The purpose of the SDI is the continued survival of the nation; however, given the magnitude of the program, a proposed R&D budget of $26 billion over the next five years, and given the interest of Congress in promoting technology, it follows that an important secondary benefit of the SDI R&D expenditures will be the commercialization of technologies that will emerge from this research effort.

As an investment banker, I approach the SDI from the viewpoint of an objective third party. It is clear that in order to accomplish SDI's objectives, significant breakthroughs in current levels of technical knowledge will have to occur, especially as they relate to large-scale computers and computer software, advanced materials, high-power lasers, electronics, communications, space technology, and other areas.

It can be argued, by analogy, that significant commercial industrial and consumer products could be derived from SDI research. For example, products in commercial use today such as radar, jet engines, nuclear power, integrated circuits, and advanced computer hardware and software are a direct result of technology developed by military-supported R&D. While few companies are financially committed to the pursuit of basic scientific research, research facilities like AT&T's Bell Laboratories have made significant breakthroughs in both basic and applied technology that have dramatically improved the quality of life for many people. While AT&T was a regulated monopoly it had the ability to spend funds on research that was not immediately actionable in their business. Now that they are in a more competitive environment, they, along with the rest of corporate America, must carefully evaluate the investment of corporate funds in basic research, concentrating more on applied research and development of commercially viable technology.

Without government support, there is little that can be done in corporate America or on Wall Street to increase significantly the pool of resources available for basic and applied research and development given current legal, competitive, and capital market environments. Corporate America is driven by profits as a relatively short-term result and by maximum efficiency in the use of capital.

THE CREATION OF SHAREHOLDER WEALTH

The objective of a profit-making enterprise is the creation of wealth for its shareholders or owners. There is a basic conflict in the corporate sector between reported earnings per share and expenditures for R&D. Current spending for R&D is an expense that reduces reported earnings and for many companies, if engaged in a major R&D project, lower reported earnings, all other things being equal, may be translated into a lower market value of equity securities and, hence, a reduction of shareholder wealth. On the other hand, the anticipation of success from an investment in R&D can enhance significantly the market value of a company's common stock and result in increased shareholder wealth if the company can adequately predict and convince investors of the future commercial gains to be received through current R&D expenditures. Much of the market value of today's high technology companies is derived from a recognition that technical knowledge leads to increased competitiveness, market dominance, and hence profitability.

For a new high technology venture, the investment of funds in R&D is extremely critical—in many cases the very survival of the new company is at stake. Corporate R&D funds may be very carefully invested. In the world of high technology ventures, capital means survival.

CAPITAL FORMATION

At the outset, I must point out that investment banking and venture capital are dependent functions. Capital formation generally does not occur until after a commercial idea is generated by matching a technology to a market need.

Wall Street is responding to increased entrepreneurial activities related to technological innovation as evidenced by:

• the growth in venture capital,
• the growth in initial public offerings of common stock (IPO's),
• the growth in R&D and venture capital funds,
• the increasing depth of the capital markets, and
• by other new financing methodologies.

Raising capital is a major preoccupation of many high technology companies. Market conditions for most forms of equity financing, the

Figure 8.1
Initial Public Offerings, in Billions of Dollars, 1970–1985

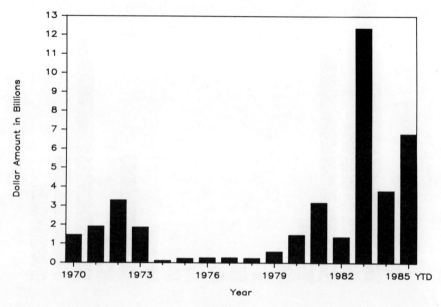

Source: All of the figures and tables in this chapter were compiled by the author, unless noted otherwise.

lifeblood of high technology growth, are very cyclical to say the least. On the following pages are presented several graphs, described below, that illustrate this point.

Initial Public Offerings 1970–1985: The IPO market is very cyclical (Figures 8.1 and 8.2). Note that during the recessions of 1974–1975 and 1982, IPO activity fell off sharply.

Quarterly Analysis of Initial Public Offering Markets: Recent resurgence of the IPO market was buoyed by lower interest rates and a strong equity market (Figure 8.3).

Venture Capital—New Funds Raised 1970–1985: The venture capital pool of funds has experienced enormous growth since 1978 (Figure 8.4).

Corporate Underwritten Offerings 1980–1985: It is interesting to note the magnitude of national R&D expenditures for 1985, approximately $110 billion, as compared to all corporate underwritten offerings for 1985 year to date, $106 billion (Figure 8.5 and Table 8.1). Government expenditures are so large that corporate financing seems relatively small in comparison. Government-sponsored R&D alone is over $50 billion per year. Government expenditures and policies regarding R&D are extremely critical to the successful development of

Figure 8.2
Initial Public Offerings, by Number of Issues, 1970–1985

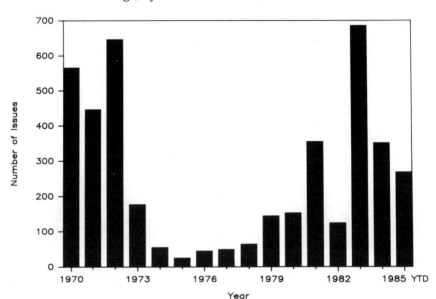

technological innovations in the United States because the federal government is the largest single investor in the pool of knowledge.

Given the business objective of increasing shareholder wealth while providing employment opportunities, we can examine the growth characteristics of high technology companies. We have found a very strong correlation between the market value of a company and its number of employees. In order to grow, a company must continually add new employees or it must increase labor productivity through technological innovation. The relationship between the market value of equity securities (shareholder wealth) and the number of employees for selected high technology and defense-related companies is presented in Figure 8.6 and Table 8.2. Given the current state of technology and its accompanying level of productivity, a theoretical limit can be derived that non-asset-valued companies cannot exceed without a technological innovation or a change in the cost structure for labor. Productivity can be measured in terms of the ratio of production outputs to inputs. The determinant of the rate of growth in labor productivity is the rate of technological change. As companies continually seek to maximize share-

Figure 8.3
Analysis of Initial Public Offering Market, 1982–Second Quarter 1985

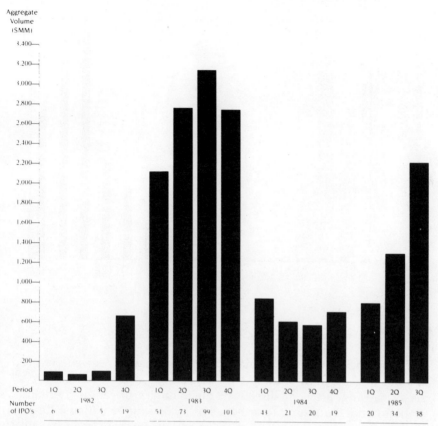

Aggregate
Volume
(SMM)

Period	1Q	2Q	3Q	4Q	1Q	2Q	3Q	4Q	1Q	2Q	3Q	4Q	1Q	2Q	3Q
		1982				1983				1984				1985	
Number of IPO's	6	3	5	19	51	73	99	101	43	21	20	19	20	34	38

holder wealth for any given amount of labor inputs, technology related to productivity becomes increasingly important.

As economic groups, both employees and shareholders share the common business dynamic of desire for increased wealth and prosperity. The employee group dynamic is derived from each individual's motivation to survive and prosper as a member of the economic group. As illustrated in Figures 8.7-8.9, this framework can prove useful in describing the relationship of capital formation to both the creation of shareholder wealth and to the prosperity of an economic group as measured by the group's ability to meet its financial commitments. Larger groups generally have a greater financial capacity to meet their group's financial commitments. Along the common business dynamic line we can array the capital formation process in its various stages as a capital formation line.

Figure 8.4
Venture Capital, New Funds Raised, 1970–1985

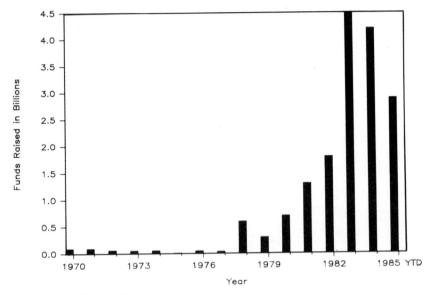

Source: Venture Economics.

The financial evolution of most companies may be viewed on a continuous line, typically starting with the earliest stage of venture capital, seed financing, provided directly by the founders, or venture capitalists, or both, and continuing (one hopes at increasing valuations) through the private markets, and then on to the various forms of financing available to public corporations. The market does *not* consist exclusively of venture capital and initial public offerings. Within the private financing arena, in addition to venture capital, there are mezzanine private placements, corporate joint-venture investments, R&D partnerships and R&D funds, accredited individual private placements, leasing, and commercial bank financing, among others. After successful completion of an initial public offering, the financing options for a company broaden further to include common stock, convertible debentures, junk bonds, investment grade debt, and ultimately commercial paper and international placements.

As you can see there are many financing alternatives available for the development of commercial applications of technology. Each of these alternatives has prescribed criteria that must be met in order to raise capital, and each alternative has a risk/return trade-off and a hurdle rate at which capital is made available. While the scope of this discussion

Figure 8.5
Corporate Underwritten Offerings, 1980–1985

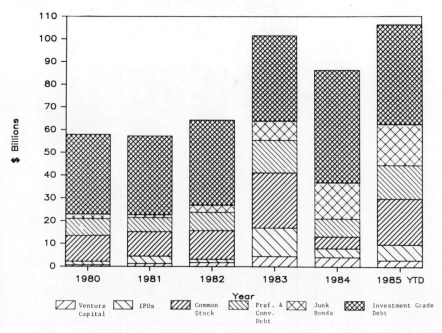

does not permit us to delve into all of these, we can briefly cover the major considerations in funding new commercial applications of technology.

MAJOR CONSIDERATIONS

There are five critical ingredients needed to develop a new high technology business venture. In the order of importance, they are: a proprietary idea or invention, a management team with business knowledge and experience, a defined market niche, technical knowledge, and capital.

The order of importance in which these ingredients are presented corresponds to the difficulty in obtaining each ingredient. Proprietary ideas or inventions are very hard to find because there is no clear path to their creation. Since approximately one-half of the nation's R&D expenditures are funded by the federal government, it logically follows that a significant number of ideas or inventions have already been created and will be created through government-sponsored R&D. These inventions may or may not be commercially viable but they are generally

Table 8.1
Corporate Underwritten Offering and Venture Capital Financing Volumes, 1980–1984

	1980	1981	1982	1983	1984	1985 YTD	Total 1980–1984
Investment Grade Debt	35,015	34,619	37,371	37,624	49,482	43,801	237,911
Junk Bonds	2,004	1,250	3,086	8,432	15,790	17,989	48,551
Convertible Debt	4,341	4,645	3,189	6,107	4,077	8,358	30,716
Preferred Stock	1,896	1,175	4,515	5,143	3,114	4,229	20,073
Convertible Preferred Stock	1,286	462	509	3,148	818	2,170	8,393
Common Stock—Non IPO	11,330	10,754	12,545	24,266	5,121	20,117	84,133
Initial Public Offering	1,458	3,180	1,351	12,385	3,798	6,802	28,974
Venture Capital	700	1,300	1,800	4,500	4,200	2,889	15,389
Total	58,030	57,385	64,366	101,604	86,399	106,356	474,140

Figure 8.6
Market Value of Equity versus Number of Employees for Selected High Technology and Defense-Related Companies

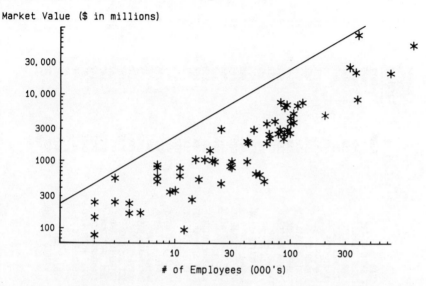

unknown outside the select group who are directly involved with the technology. One identifiable problem of government research is that it is widely disbursed throughout many different groups, which may or may not communicate owing to considerations of security or other reasons. In order for an entrepreneur to develop commercial application of technology he or she must know what is available; and the government is actively pursuing avenues of technological diffusion within the commercial sector.

Not all of the groups that find breakthroughs are qualified or capable of bringing a new product to market. Government laboratories are not in the business of developing commercial products. Large companies may believe that a market is too small to invest valuable management time in the development of a particular product. Small companies may find the task of exploiting a technology too complex or that their resources are too limited. What is needed is a mechanism that transfers technology to those who can best exploit it.

The skills required to develop a new technology are very different from those required to operate a business. There may or may not be a shortage of qualified scientists and technicians in the United States, but there is surely a shortage of qualified entrepreneurial managers and marketing executives who understand high tech markets and who have

Table 8.2
Market Value of Equity versus Number of Employees for Selected High Technology and Defense-Related Companies

Company		Market Value 10/31/85	# of Employs	Mkt Val per Empl
INTL BUS MACHS	IBM	79821	395	202
GENL ELECTRIC	GE	26236	330	80
AMER TEL & TEL	T	21946	373	59
GENL MOTORS	GM	21226	748	28
FORD MOTOR	F	8602	384	22
HEWLETT PACKARD	HWP	7744	82	94
WESTINGHOUSE ELC	WX	7641	127	60
BOEING	BA	7115	93	77
ALLIED SIGNAL	ALD	6906	115	60
DIGITAL EQUIP	DEC	6472	89	73
ROCKWELL INTL.	ROK	5234	106	49
UNITED TECH	UTX	4949	206	24
CHRYSLER CORP	C	4464	100	45
RAYTHEON	RTN	3998	73	55
RCA CORP	RCA	3857	106	36
MOTOROLA	MOT	3697	100	37
NCR CORP	NCR	3674	62	59
LOCKHEED	LK	3002	81	37
INTEL CORP	INTC	2996	25	120
TRW INC	TRW	2992	94	32
HONEYWELL INC	HON	2980	94	32
TELEDYNE	TDY	2941	48	61
GENL DYNAMICS	GD	2638	99	27
SPERRY CORP	SY	2587	78	33
MCDONNELL DOUG	MD	2551	88	29
BURROUGHS CORP	BGH	2542	65	39
LITTON INDUSTRIE	LIT	2208	66	33
TEXAS INSTRUMENT	TXN	2176	87	25
NORTHROP	NOC	1979	42	47
TEXTRON INC	TXT	1884	43	44
MARTIN MARIETTA	ML	1857	62	30
CRAY RESEARCH	CYR	1613	1	1193
GOULD INC	GLD	1439	20	72
PERKIN ELMER	PKN	1048	15	70
DATA GENERAL	DGN	1048	18	58
TEKTRONIX	TEK	1017	21	48
NATL SEMI	NSM	989	42	24
HARRIS CORP	HRS	985	31	32

Company		Market Value 10/31/85	# of Employs	Mkt Val per Empl
EG&G	EGG	979	22	45
E SYSTEMS INC	ESY	873	12	73
PRIME COMPUTER	PRM	872	7	125
LEAR SIEGLER	LSI	842	30	28
GRUMMAN CORP	GQ	807	31	26
LORAL CORP	LOR	794	7	113
M/A-COM	MAI	785	11	71
SINGER CO	SMF	652	50	13
CONTROL DATA	CDA	633	54	12
SANDERS ASSOC	SAA	598	11	54
CESSNA AIRCRAFT	CEA	592	9	66
COMSAT CORP	CQ	552	3	184
VARIAN ASSOC	VAR	533	16	33
LTV CORPORATION	LTV	505	59	9
AMDAHL CORP	AMH	496	7	71
GENL INSTRUMENT	GRL	465	25	19
CINCINNATI MILAC	CMZ	364	10	36
TRACOR	TRR	347	9	39
WESTERN UNION	WU	268	14	19
BOLT BERANEK NEW	BBN	264	2	132
ELECTROSPACE SYS	ELE	257	1	184
UNITRODE	UTR	246	3	82
WATKINS-JOHNSON	WJ	244	3	81
SCNTFIC ATLANTA	SFA	235	4	59
MATRIX CORP	MAX	230	1	230
UNGERMANN-BASS	UNGR	228	0.4	600
NORTEK	NTK	170	5	34
SCI SYSTEMS	SCIS	167	4	42
FAIRCHILD INDUST	FEN	163	14	12
GENL DATACOMM	GDC	147	2	74
STANDARD MICRO	SMSC	142	1	142
CALIF MICROWAVE	CMIC	91	1	91
VALID LOGIC	VLID	90	0.1	833
WYLE LABS	WYL	80	2	40
AYDIN CORP	AYD	79	2	40
ADVANCED SYSTEMS	ASY	70	0.5	153
TERA CORP	TRRA	31	0.2	137

Source: Merrill Lynch Equity Research.

Figure 8.7
Employee Group Dynamic and the Creation of Shareholder Wealth

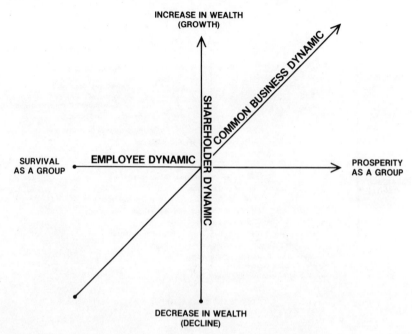

the personal productivity to take on more commercial activities. Qualification as a technician does not immediately qualify someone as an entrepreneur. Some of the skills an entrepreneur must possess are:

- an understanding of business functions
- the ability to define purpose and policy for the company
- the ability to negotiate and to convince the financial community of the viability of the venture
- the ability to motivate employees
- the ability to produce results

Good managers with the skills necessary to start a venture and make it successful are hard to find. Qualified entrepreneurs are either pursuing a venture or employed in existing businesses. The technology transfer mechanism must open communication channels with entrepreneurs; however, there is a difficulty in finding those people who can best commercialize a given invention.

The commercialization process must find entrepreneurs who can match market needs with technology. Marketing is a key factor to business success. Technology doesn't drive business; markets drive busi-

Figure 8.8
Capital Formation and the Creation of Shareholder Wealth

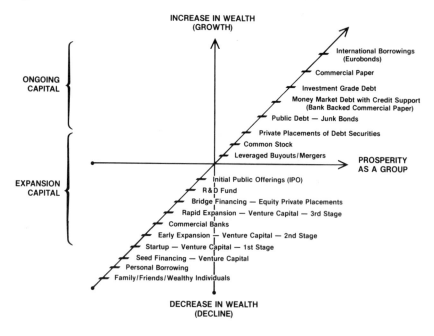

ness. The marketplace is the final arbiter of the success of a commercial venture. The entrepreneur must answer the question, "Who wants to buy the product or service?" and "Why would someone want to purchase it?" If someone is going to invest a lot of money into R&D, they have to know that there is a significant market out there to justify the development of the product at all.

There are two classes of risk in new ventures, of which commercialization of R&D is a subclass. First, will the technology be successful; that is, can the company make the technology work? Second, if the company gets the technology to work exactly as promised, (1) who is going to use the product or service? and (2) how much value does it add relative to whatever else is available in the marketplace?

Government-funded research for SDI is driven by specifications that have no bearing on private, commercial markets. This is the major risk for considering industrial spin-offs and business opportunities.

In identifying a commercial market, there are several key marketing considerations: the size of the market; the type of market: industrial, commercial, consumer; competition from other firms and products; and market growth rates and future potential. The blending of invention, entrepreneurship, markets, technology, and capital are the ingredients of business venture success. The commercialization of SDI technologies

Figure 8.9
Access to Capital

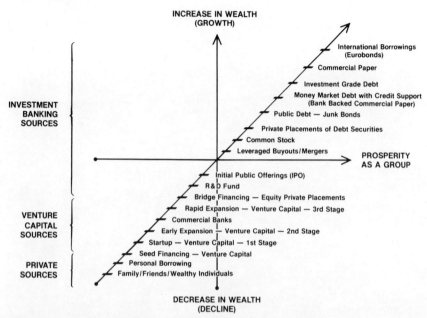

will require the full integration of many diverse segments of the economy.

In addition to the efforts that are currently being made to transfer technology and to promote the use existing of technology, there are some marketing-related ideas such as (1) developing a business/government-supported marketing research consortium to determine macroeconomic market needs and to address problems from the marketing viewpoint integrating backward to technology; (2) getting consumer products companies involved in the technology transfer process; and (3) promoting corporate marketing research involvement in the technology transfer process.

Integration is the key to success in technology transfer. The technical community must reach beyond its normal borders to communicate with managers, marketers, engineers, production people, finance professionals, investors, advisors, and others.

Wall Street is ready to raise capital for new commercial ventures. Capital should not be a constraint for viable commercial technology ventures. The capital markets will continue to seek ever-expanding growth opportunities in the creation of wealth for the prosperity of the nation.

9

INNOVATIVE FINANCING FOR EMERGING TECHNOLOGY COMPANIES

MARK LANCASTER

The financial bridge between advanced technologies and commercial markets is crucial to commercialization. Today there are several financing sources available for emerging technology ventures. Investment capital is not decreasing, it is just coming from different and more varied sources. In addition to the entrepreneur's personal resources, he or she can look to entrepreneurial investors, corporate ventures, government, foreign investors, and venture capital firms. Tapping into these sources requires an unprecedented level of energy and sophistication from entrepreneurs.

The most common source of capital for start-ups continues to be bootstrap financing: personal savings, loans, and investments from friends and family. This method, however, can severely limit the company's growth potential and its ability to capitalize quickly on market opportunities.

ENTREPRENEURIAL INVESTORS

For growing businesses, the single most important financing source is informal entrepreneurial investors. They might be wealthy individuals, retired executives, or other noninstitutional investors looking for early-stage venture opportunities. These entrepreneurial investors may complement the CEO's skills and may be identified through informal networking or private placements. These entrepreneurial investors typically add valuable experience to a start-up operation. They understand the nuances of start-up situations. They can provide the technology-oriented CEO with management or marketing expertise, and can guide a start-up venture to later-stage financing.

It takes more persistence to locate entrepreneurial investors, however.

Table 9.1
R&D Limited Partnerships

Year	Amount Raised (millions)	Number of Offerings
1983 thru April 1984	$1,200	83
1982	603	66
1981	226	17

Source: Venture Capital Journal (Stanley Pratt, publisher), 1985.

Their backgrounds and objectives are quite diverse, and there are no formal statistics available on them. Two potential ways of locating investors are informal networking of intermediaries; and formal, private placement offerings by investment bankers. Financing network contacts include attorneys, business brokers, investment bankers, local venture capitalist groups, and other entrepreneurs.

When an investor is identified, there are several financing forms. One popular form is where the investor guarantees a line of credit for the start-up company in return for a large, perhaps controlling, interest in the company. The company has access to the needed funds, and the investor's cash investment is minimal.

Another popular form for attracting entrepreneurial investors is the partnership: either an R&D limited partnership (see Table 9.1) or straight equity partnership. They offer investors some tax shelter benefits, as well as the rights to whatever technology is developed. In turn, the sponsoring company typically is compensated for project management. It also has an option to acquire the rights to the technology from the partnership through royalty, equity, or joint venture.

Several studies show a strong upward trend in the use of R&D partnerships. One study estimates the total amount of capital raised in 1983/84 at $1.2 billion, compared to $226 million in 1981. To counter some well-publicized failures of R&D partnerships, entrepreneurs and their advisors are structuring this type of deal more carefully.

CORPORATE VENTURES

Corporate venturing is one of the strongest *new* financing opportunities for emerging technology businesses. Corporate venturers can take two forms: joint ventures of emerging companies and direct investment by larger corporations. In a joint venture, two or more smaller companies combine complementary abilities for a specific project. The emerging companies achieve the critical mass necessary to carry out R&D and to market a product that competes effectively with larger companies.

Table 9.2
Direct Corporate Investments: Benefits to Emerging Company

- Management Experience
- R & D Resources
- Facilities
- Marketing Channels
- Credibility
- Potential Major Customer

Source: Author.

The second form of corporate venturing is direct investment in an early-stage venture by a larger corporation. There has been a record number of these investments. In 1984 alone, there were 200 direct corporate investment deals, totalling $500 million. Some of the larger corporations that are using this approach to acquire equity positions in technology ventures include Monsanto, General Motors, Lubrizol, A.E. Staley, Tektronics, IBM, W.R. Grace, and General Electric, just to name a few.

Direct corporate investment benefits the entrepreneur beyond the capital received (see Table 9.2). The benefits include guidance from corporate management; R&D personnel, equipment, and facilities; and marketing, advertising, and distribution channels. Association with the corporation can often enhance the start-up's credibility. The corporation itself often becomes a major user of the start-up's product.

Corporations also benefit from their direct investments. Through start-up companies, the corporations expand into new technologies, gain exposure to new markets, and tap a supply of new or related products. Moreover, the corporations enhance their image in the eyes of stockholders as a more exciting company. Also, association with an emerging fast-growth venture may liven up the larger corporation's otherwise stale culture.

The entrepreneur typically begins the search for corporate partners through investment bankers, attorneys, accountants, and corporate executives. These people can help to identify the technology or product "hook" that will get the entrepreneur in the door of a large corporation. They also have contacts in corporations that are poised for investment.

GOVERNMENT: SBIR GRANTS

The government's Small Business Innovation Research program is another financing source. The role of small businesses in federal R&D

programs expanded last year when over 1,000 SBIR funding proposals were accepted. Successful proposals received up to $50,000 for initial feasibility research. After six months, about one-third of these programs received prototype development funding of up to $500,000 dollars. By 1988, total SBIR funds will increase to an estimated $500 million.

The SBIR process is very competitive and requires a complete understanding of the grant program. Thousands of research possibilities are contained in the SBIR "Requests for Solicitations," which are available from the Small Business Administration.

FOREIGN INVESTORS

Another financing source that we see used more frequently is the foreign investor. Entrepreneurs typically tap into these sources through private placements or the formal foreign markets, such as London's Unlisted Securities Market and the Parallel Market in Amsterdam.

Foreign investments are approaching record levels and in 1985 nearly exceeded U.S. pension funds as the largest source of venture capital. To reach these investors, American entrepreneurs need assistance from professional accounting or securities firms that know these markets and already have foreign contacts.

VENTURE CAPITAL FIRMS

The final source of financing is the professionally managed venture capital firms. Although this has been a common source in recent years, a study of the 100 largest venture capital firms recently showed their total investments during 1984 to be virtually flat (see Table 9.3). The number of deals was down 15 percent. More of their investments went into mature deals rather than start-ups. With $16 billion under management now, the venture capital industry may be reaching its capacity to produce the returns that attracted the capital into the funds.

Moving toward safer investments, the percentage of funds invested in start-ups dropped to 21 percent from 29 percent in 1983—this represents 576 deals in 1984 compared to 833 in 1983. Investments in later-stage financing (second and third or mezzanine rounds) declined to 21 percent from 27 percent. But investments in follow-on deals (that is, investments in companies already in the venture capitalist's portfolio) increased to 36 percent from 30 percent. Also, leveraged buyouts, which are less risky, made up 22 percent of dollars invested, up from 14 percent in 1983. These trends have continued in 1985, and at Deloitte Haskins and Sells we've experienced these same developments with our clients.

This means that venture capital will not be the primary source of financing for many high tech, start-up ventures. The venture capitalists

Table 9.3
The Venture Capital 100

	1984	1983	Percent Change
Total invested (in billions)	$2.28	$2.33	−2
Number of deals	2,651	3,119	−15
Type of investments (percent)			
Seed/start-up	21	29	−8
Later stage	21	27	−6
Follow-on	36	30	+6
Buyouts	22	14	+8
Totals	100	100	

Source: Venture Capital Journal (Stanley Pratt, publisher), 1985.

are very selective and consider only the strongest proposals. On the positive side, however, we should note that almost 600 start-ups were funded last year. To be one of these select few, the high tech entrepreneur will need a comprehensive game plan that shows a clear opportunity to grow a company to substantial size.

BUSINESS PLAN

The single most important link to all the financing sources is a creative business plan. In reflecting on new, successful start-ups with which I've been involved, several key attributes in the business plan come to mind:

• A concise description of the product and its practical application in the marketplace
• Clear evidence that the timing of the product is right (that a window of opportunity in the marketplace exists); and a thoughtful marketing strategy to make it through the window
• Clearly defined operational milestones
• Profiles that show a strong management team; the quality of the management team is so important that some financiers would rather back a company that has a Grade A management structure with a Grade B idea

To summarize the current environment, we see several sources of financing available for emerging technology companies that have the right mix of product, management skill, and marketing savvy. The investors, however, are more sophisticated and selective. As a result, the entrepreneurial CEO must spend more time structuring a creative investment opportunity and in locating interested investors.

This is a continuous process. Emerging companies today are having to achieve three and four rounds of financing from different sources in order to continue growing, as compared to previous years when one round of investments might bring a company to the stage of going public.

FUTURE INITIATIVES

Having reviewed the current trends, let's consider some initiatives that might help emerging technology companies obtain financing in the future.

Corporate Venturing: There is increasing emphasis in large companies to act small, to encourage risk-taking and innovation. A natural extension of this trend is corporate venturing. More larger corporations will probably consider teaming with smaller technology companies on specific projects.

Government Financing Promotions: It is hoped that state and federal government officials will increase their efforts to promote seed-capital programs. Nearly half of the states have such programs, when two years ago there were only ten states that had them. At the federal level, it is encouraging that several congressmen have sponsored legislation to create the Corporation of Small Businesss Investments. COSBI, as it is called, would raise money for SBICs and minority investment companies (MESBICs) by selling securities that are backed with a limited federal guarantee. It is also encouraging that a major goal of planners for the 1986 White House Conference on Small Business is to expand and simplify the fundings from the SBIR program.

Government Tax Incentives: In an important sense, the federal income tax makes the federal government a joint venturer in all financings. By providing tax incentives for investments in emerging technology companies, the government can be a constructive partner with business in the technology transfer process. A more proactive approach could include permanent R&D tax credits, increased capital gains benefits, and other tax benefits that enhance the attractiveness of investments in R&D efforts.

Business Incubators: The final future initiative is business incubators. They have fascinating possibilities to help entrepreneurs develop their ideas while reducing the pressures associated with starting a company solely on one's own resources. These high tech hatcheries are springing up across the country. Many are affiliated with universities or supported by state governments. More study, of course, is needed to determine if the incubator, in fact, cuts down the time between idea conception and production stage, a period critical for most technologies. Nonetheless, incubators do provide a way for entrepreneurs, government, and universities to explore a unique opportunity together.

I am optimistic about current trends and future initiatives to help entrepreneurs obtain financing for emerging technology ventures—to help widen and strengthen the financial bridge between technology and commercial markets. This will generate potentially large payoffs for entrepreneurs, investors, and society as a whole.

PART IV
SDI TECHNOLOGIES AND SPIN-OFFS

10

TELECOMMUNICATIONS MARKETS

COLONEL GILBERT RYE, USAF (Retired)

This chapter will serve to place the telecommunications area in context with the overall trends in SDI technology.

A strategic defense against ballistic missile attack has to perform five functions: (1) target acquisition to search for and detect attacking objects; (2) tracking, to determine the trajectories of those objects; (3) discrimination, to differentiate missiles and warheads from decoys and chaff; (4) interception, to point and fire a weapon system and intercept an object; (5) damage assessment (often forgotten but very important), to determine what we have hit and retarget if necessary.

These five functions require a certain amount of intelligence and information and use several families of technologies: sensor technologies, to acquire and track potential targets; computer technologies, to analyze detected signals rapidly, to distinguish threatening from nonthreatening objects, and to calculate trajectories; telecommunications technologies for systems integration and battle management.

Within these broad areas, there have been major advances in recent years. Certainly the first would be in the area of microchips. In the late 1950s, the cost of a basic computing unit, or digital gate, was about $10.00. By 1963 this had been reduced to less than $1.00. The revolution of solid-state electronics and miniaturization has reduced this cost to .00002 of a dollar and this was cut in half by 1987.

In the area of computers, a $3,000 personal computer (PC) today has essentially the same capabilities as a $5 million IBM 360/40 mainframe of the mid-1960s or about $15 million in today's dollars. Also the 1960s machine required an air conditioned room, plus a marching army of operators and maintenance personnel. Today's PC requires a desk top, one briefly trained operator, and virtually no maintenance. There have been rapid advances in software, yet the increase in labor-intense programming requirements of computer systems are proving to be real bottlenecks and cost drivers. Increasing attention must be paid to cheaper ways of programming, such as firmware (hard wiring programming into the hardware), more efficient algorithms (rules for solving problems), artificial intelligence, computer processing, and data management systems.

Another relevant area to telecommunications is fiber optics, which is becoming a significant competitor to communications satellites. Fiber optics technology uses light waves for transmitting digital data by means of laser-driven signals sent through glass fibers. The cost per channel, per kilometer, is already substantially below that of terrestrial microwave transmissions. Additional attributes of fiber optics technology include: compactness of materials and resistance to electromagnetic pulse, security against tapping or eavesdropping, and suitability for digital transmission. Fiber optics are currently being used for satellite ground station systems and communications.

Satellite communications are also advancing. Trends include decreasing costs and increasing orbital lifetimes (average life in the early 1970s was three years, today it is around ten years). Other advances such as the use of higher frequency (12/14 Ghz) are showing that satellites will continue to play a viable role in the communications business, including the military.

SDI's impact on the commercial telecommunications market may be divided into two areas, general and specific. (Perhaps the general areas will be more significant than those specifically related to telecommunications.) In the general areas, the SDI office wants to concentrate on the development of lower cost space transportation that will be critical for deploying a truly cost-effective strategic defense capability. It is also critical to other elements of the U.S. space program: national security, civil, and commercial. Driving down the cost of space transport (and insurance rates, which are becoming more and more of a problem) will have a pervasive impact on satisfying a multitude of national requirements in space, including SDI. The SDI office is investing in that potential and coordinating a broader study (initiated out of the White House) conducted by NASA and DOD to assess launch-vehicle technologies that might be made available in 1995 and later years. It will be a significant study that may point the way toward new developments such as the transatmospheric vehicle, mentioned earlier in this volume. A means for developing a new transportation capability can reduce the large personnel requirements needed to sustain launch capability that we have today.

The second general area that will be impacted by SDI-related technology will be in the repair and maintenance of satellites in orbit, for which NASA is developing a capability. We will see this capability gain increased importance as SDI demands the maintaining of expensive orbital platforms in high states of readiness. This will require a sustained ability to do maintenance and repair in place, thereby keeping costs down.

A third general area will be in the development of large structures. SDI will require the ability to place certain types of capabilities in space without making large targets out of them. Economies can be realized through the development of large structures that do not necessarily represent big targets to aggressors.

Another area will be in miniaturization and development of compact systems, in order to lower the weight of a platform that must be placed in space, thereby representing a cost-effective way of placing SDI-related systems in orbit.

Increased reliability is another general area. Systems reliability will have to reach unprecedented levels: An SDI system can't fail. We will have to develop systems that are truly fail-safe in their capability to sustain themselves at increasing levels of conflict.

Finally, increased on-board processing and computer capabilities in satellites will be an important general requirement for SDI. These space-based systems must reduce this dependence on ground segments in order to enhance survivability under crisis conditions.

Many of the more specific areas related to the impact of SDI on telecommunications have been discussed. Huge masses of data will be gathered from many different sensors. High-speed signal processing and computation capability will be needed to discriminate and analyze critical information. We are gaining increased expertise in this area. Sophisticated systems internetting is a second area for two-way satellite-to-ground and satellite-to-satellite links. In spite of rapid advances in such areas as fiber optics, satellite communications will still be essential for SDI, especially with our reliance on boost-phase intercept capabilities and the need to communicate data rapidly over long distances with minimal dependence on vulnerable ground-based facilities.

Last is the development of encryption technology, which can have some applications to the commercial or private sector. There is indeed an evolving trend toward the use of private networks by corporations who need a dedicated communications capability from the United States to overseas offices. COMSAT Corporation is certainly involved, as are other companies. In order to insure the corporate user that company information will not be accessed by competitors, some encryption will be necessary.

In summary, it is important to note that battle management and C^3 (communications, command, and control) is one of the three major technology research thrusts for SDI (the other two being weapons and surveillance). It is being increasingly recognized by the Space Command in Colorado Springs that we cannot overlook the portion of the iceberg below water, the battle management and C³. These make the whole system work.

11

AUTOMATION AND EXPERT SYSTEMS

BRUCE BULLOCK

Everybody has heard about expert systems; they are discussed everywhere, from *Business Week* to *Readers Digest*. Yet many people still don't understand what expert systems really are. This chapter is intended to explain the nature of expert systems, and to show why they have industrial potential. Commercialization of this technology precedes SDI, but SDI will undoubtedly galvanize the process.

Expert systems technology, sometimes called "knowledge systems," is a subfield of computer sciences called artificial intelligence, an area that has been around for 20 years. Some of the languages used in the development of artificial intelligence go back to the time when Fortran was invented. Historically, knowledge systems have roots that go back to the beginning of computer science.

About ten years ago, an interesting thing happened in this rather academic discipline—something useful actually came out of it. The best-known successful system is called Mycin. It was built at Stanford University by someone pursuing a Ph.D. in Computer Science and an M.D. in the medical school.[1] Mycin was designed to specify antimicrobial therapy based on infectious disease information using blood data. The system was interesting because it was the first that would perform near the competence level of human experts. Mycin, in fact, remains one of the few cases that have been largely validated. (Validation studies comparing the performance of Mycin with human experts in treating infectious diseases were published in the *Journal of the American Medical Association*).

About five years ago expert systems took another step forward. A number of companies started to take this technology out of academia and move it into the commercial marketplace. Most of these smaller, innovative firms concentrated primarily on one-on-one custom system development for large corporations—the Fortune 500. For the most part the aerospace industry lagged behind in applying expert systems. It is possible that one or two individuals in a firm were aware of the technology and conducted some minor R&D effort, but for the most part they have not built large systems. Yet an increasing number of large corporations are starting to invest in the technology because of the potential for solving difficult problems heretofore unapproachable by traditional computing technology.

Table 11.1 presents an overview of major expert systems now in existence. The technology has developed from what was a relatively risky area of investment a few years ago to one that has significant potential for commercial application and exploitation.

Table 11.1
Commercial Knowledge System Sampler

Who	What	Why
ELF	Drilling advisor	Cut total drilling costs
DEC	Vax configurer	Eliminate errors ($10M)
GM	Car diagnosis	Cope with complexity
NCR	Factory order checker	Integrate company know-how
DYNAQUEST	Product recommender	Expand consulting business
X	Statistical expert	Grow/retain staff
BIG–8	Automated senior partner	Cut risks, costs
Y	Loan advisor	Standardize policies
Z	Furnace advisor	Retain expertise

Source: All of the tables and figures in this chapter were compiled by the author.

Figures 11.1 and 11.2 explain how an expert system works. A *traditional* program collects procedural knowledge, an algorithmic step-by-step sequence of actions that the computer executes. It has an instruction counter and is basically a fixed sequence that is always going to be followed. It has high-quality input, in the sense that it always has to know where input fields are. The program has to know exactly what is going to be coming in. Pieces of data can't be missing, in order for the program to give output that makes sense. At the same time the output is always fixed. One always knows exactly what is going to come out.

A knowledge system is different. It is able to use *procedural knowledge* with *judgmental knowledge*. Judgmental knowledge is a procedural mechanism that isn't necessarily a step-by-step algorithm. It may be only a few pieces of judgmental knowledge, but those few little rules could be extraordinarily powerful in building a system functionally different from an algorithmic one.

A critical difference is variable processing; the program does not have

Figure 11.1
Knowledge-Based Systems

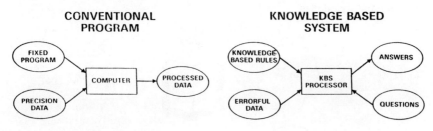

CONVENTIONAL PROGRAM

* PROCEDURAL KNOWLEDGE ONLY
* FIXED SEQUENCE
* FIXED HIGH QUALITY INPUTS
* FIXED OUTPUT MODES

KNOWLEDGE BASED SYSTEM

* JUDGMENTAL AND PROCEDURAL KNOWLEDGE
* VARIABLE (REQUIREMENT-DRIVEN) PROCESSING
* LOW-QUALITY/ERROR-PRONE DATA
* VARIABLE OUTPUT (SITUATION DRIVEN)

to sequence through a fixed series of steps. The steps can basically change, given the input data, input situation, and the user's particular need. The user can ask the knowledge system some questions, and the systems can give answers. Why would anyone want such a system? Figure 11.3 gives some summary applications of expert systems.

How is an expert system developed? The process involves taking the knowledge of an expert (if an expert exists) or some other source of knowledge, e.g., textbook or instruction manual knowledge. It can be knowledge of any form, but not algorithmic. If enough of the expertise can be captured, the average level of performance of the human work station can be improved. Studies show there is wide variation of performance for people using a work station.

Table 11.2
Added Value

- Existing value-added of computer-based systems
  - Speed
  - Accuracy
  - Consistency
  - Availability
  - Affordability
- Is extended from data processing to knowledge processing
  - Judgmental
  - Advisory
  - Diagnostic

Figure 11.2
Traditional Advantages

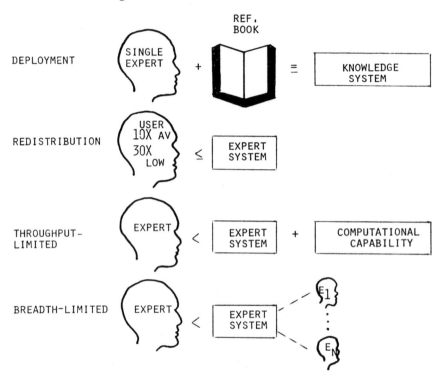

One goal of expert system application is to capture enough expertise that one can pull the average worker up by the bootstraps and make him or her perform at a higher overall level. Or, it is hoped, pull up the lower level worker. The goal isn't to surpass the expert but to approach that level of performance. Adding the traditional benefits of computer technology makes the system run faster. It doesn't take coffee breaks. It doesn't retire. It doesn't forget. Knowledge has become captured in electronics. A research issue, for the future, is trying to collect the capabilities of *multiple* experts. The goal is to produce a single system that has more capability and expertise than any single person available at that point in time. These advantages are summerized in Table 11.2.

One can consider an expert system to be a *glass box* rather than a black box. A black box is something into which you put "raw" data in and from which you get "cooked" data (based on the algorithm inside). An

Figure 11.3

M.1 and S.1 Applications: A Partial List

FINANCIAL SERVICES

CLAIM ESTIMATION
CREDIT ANALYSIS
TAX ADVISOR
FINANCIAL STATEMENT
  ANALYSIS
FINANCIAL PLANNING
  ADVISOR
RETAIL BANK SERVICES
  ADVISOR

DATA PROCESSING AND MIS

FRONT-END TO STATISTICAL
  ANALYSIS PACKAGE
FRONT-END TO A LARGE
  SOFTWARE PACKAGE
  (SEVERAL APPLICATIONS)
DATABASE MANAGEMENT
  SYSTEM SELECTION
SOFTWARE SERVICES
  CONSULTANT

**FINANCE AND
ADMINISTRATION**

LEGAL ANALYSIS OF
  CONTRACT CLAIMS
LOAN APPLICATION
  ASSISTANT FOR SCHOOL
  ADMINISTRATORS
PERFORMANCE EVALUATION
  OF DEALERSHIPS
CONFLICT OF INTEREST
  CONSULTANT
INVENTORY MANAGEMENT
  ADVISOR

MANUFACTURING

MAINTENANCE ADVISOR
  FOR MULTI-MILLION-
  DOLLAR HYDRAULIC
  SYSTEM
CONTINUOUS PROCESS
  MANUFACTURING ADVISOR
TOOLING SELECTION FOR
  MACHINING (SEVERAL
  APPLICATIONS)
DRILLING ADVISOR FOR
  COMPLEX
  MACHINING
MATERIAL SELECTION
  (CHEMICAL)
PROCEDURE ADVISOR FOR
  OIL WELL DRILLING
  OPERATIONS (SEVERAL
  APPLICATIONS)
ELECTRICAL SYSTEM FAULT
  DIAGNOSIS
GAS TURBINE ENGINE
  FAULT DIAGNOSIS
ELECTRONIC EQUIPMENT
  FAULT DIAGNOSIS
  (SEVERAL APPLICATIONS)
POWER SUPPLY FAULT
  DIAGNOSIS
MECHANICAL EQUIPMENT
  FAULT DIAGNOSIS
  (SEVERAL APPLICATIONS)
REFINERY PROCESS CONTROL
SENSOR VERIFICATION FOR
  POWER GENERATION
  EQUIPMENT

FIELD SERVICE

SOFTWARE SYSTEM
  TROUBLESHOOTER
FAULT DIAGNOSIS OF
  ELECTRONIC SYSTEMS
  FROM EVENT TRACES
  (SEVERAL APPLICATIONS)
FAULT DIAGNOSIS OF
  AUTOMOTIVE SUBSYSTEMS
  (SEVERAL APPLICATIONS)
COMPUTER NETWORK FAULT
  DIAGNOSIS

EDUCATION

PROBLEM DIAGNOSIS
  TRAINING AID
SPEECH PATHOLOGY ADVISOR
TEST RESULT INTERPRETER
WORKSHEET GENERATION
  BASED ON STUDENTS'
  PRIOR PERFORMANCE
STUDENT BEHAVIOR
  CONSULTANT
LEARNING DISABILITY
  CLASSIFICATION ADVISOR
TEXT BOOK SELECTION
  ADVISOR

SALES AND MARKETING

SELECTION OF
  COMPONENTS FROM AN
  ENGINEERING CATALOG
QUALIFICATION OF SALES
  LEADS

ENGINEERING

DESIGN OF MOTOR
  COMPONENTS (OUTPUTS
  ENGINEERING DRAWINGS)
MATERIAL SELECTION FOR
  MANUFACTURING PROCESS
  (SEVERAL APPLICATIONS)
FRONT-END FOR COMPLEX
  COMPUTER SIMULATION
  PROGRAM
FRONT-END FOR ENGINEERING
  DESIGN PACKAGE
ENGINEERING CHANGE
  ORDER MANAGER
WEIGHT ESTIMATOR FOR
  EVOLVING DESIGNS
STATISTICAL ANALYSIS
  TOOL SELECTOR
FRONT-END TO STRUCTURAL
  ANALYSIS SOFTWARE
  SYSTEM
CONSTRUCTION PROJECT
  PLANNING AND
  EVALUATION
STRUCTURAL ANALYSIS
  OF BUILDINGS
SENSOR INTERPRETATION
  FOR DRILLING
ROBOT SENSOR
  INTERPRETATION

Figure 11.4
Knowledge Systems Are Different: The Glass Box

* ACCESS TO THE PROBLEM-SOLVING PROCESS

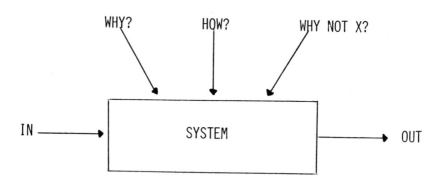

* POWERFUL KNOWLEDGE ACQUISITION FACILITY
* CREATES USER CONFIDENCE
* ENHANCED DISTRIBUTED SYSTEM "INTERCOMMUNICATION"

expert system is a glass box (as shown in Figure 11.4) in that it doesn't always have to produce a fixed answer. One can actually ask an expert system questions like: "Why did you give me that piece of information?"; or "How did you derive that result?" That performance is very different from those traditionally obtained by a program that has to go through a fixed sequence of instructions. An expert system can actually run backward and forward to a certain extent.

An expert system is constructed by knowledge acquisition. One cannot simply write a requirement specification for this system and capture all the knowledge in one swoop. It must be a progressive procedure of knowledge acquisition between someone who can facilitate the process (called a "knowledge engineer") and someone who has the content expertise. This process of drawing out such expertise is done by validating the knowledge with the expert using "Why not?" type questions at the top of the system, and then correcting knowledge within the system.

An expert system, once built, has obvious benefits: raw speed, accuracy, consistency, availability, affordability. When the element of judgmental technology is added, the system can now provide some *advisory* knowledge. Note that it just doesn't provide judgmental knowledge, but also offers *advisory* knowledge—about *why* one is getting a particular answer—and *diagnostic* knowledge—why one approached the problem in a particular way.

Table 11.3 illustrates situations in which people have found knowledge systems useful. Basically, these are embedded within organizations that require many people, trained personnel who cannot be acquired and trained fast enough. Such characteristics are often found in the military or large corporations, where highly skilled people are a valuable resource. The expert modeled (and in a sense replicated) could be one person, for example, who has special knowledge in a major industry, and that knowledge could be a very valuable, irreplaceable asset the firm can not afford to loose.

Table 11.3
Situations That Instigate Knowledge Engineering Initiatives

- The organization requires too many skilled people to recruit or retrain.
- Problems arise that require almost innumerble possibilities to be considered.
- Job excellence requires a scope of knowledge exceeding reasonable demands on human training and continuing education.
- Problem solving requires several people because no single person has the needed expertise.
- People become ineffective problem solvers because of information overload, date rate, and response times.

EXPERT SYSTEMS AND SDI

Most people in the knowledge systems industry came from government-funded areas. We understand where the technology could be used, as well as put together small prototype systems. Yet few people have assembled a whole system. In a major defense system, the bits and pieces of various subsystems would have to be combined.

Table 11.4
Smart Sensor Systems

- Reasoning-based classification and interpretation
- Multisource fusion based on judgmental knowledge
- Knowledge-based performance accommodation

Table 11.5
Key Challenge: Battle Management

Deciding what to do with the information once it is gathered:

- Keeping track of threats
- Keeping track of weapon and sensor position and status
- Allocating weapons to threats
- Maintaining data base consistency

This background suggests certain expert system components necessary for SDI: interpretation boxes, prediction boxes, diagnostics, support functions, design, and planning. All are generic to most defense applications. There are three areas in particular that are probably going to be heavily involved in SDI (see Table 11.4). The first is smart sensor systems. These will make better use of supporting knowledge in deriving results. Such systems do not just observe and classify, but apply reason to provide better interpretation of the data. The data fusion problem, interrelating diverse categories of input information is critical for SDI and ripe for expert systems.

The whole area of C^3 and battle management is another obvious area for application of expert system technology. What kind of knowledge can be applied to keep track of threats in a smarter way than just placing data in bins (see Table 11.5)? What kind of knowledge can be applied to do this at a work station?

The last potential application has to do with user interfaces—how to make better man-machine interfaces. One has the potential to provide much functionality to speed things up, to enable the operator to perform at a higher level of expertise, while at the same time ensuring his or her control. An expert system is one of the ways that this dual functionality—speed and control—can be addressed (see Figure 11.5).

Table 11.6
Smart Operator Interfaces (MMI)

- Operator-controlled system interface
  - Suggestion oriented
  - Informative capability
  - Advisory capability
- Quality control advisor

Figure 11.5
Future System Perspective

* LEVERAGE FUNCTIONALITY AND PERFORMANCE

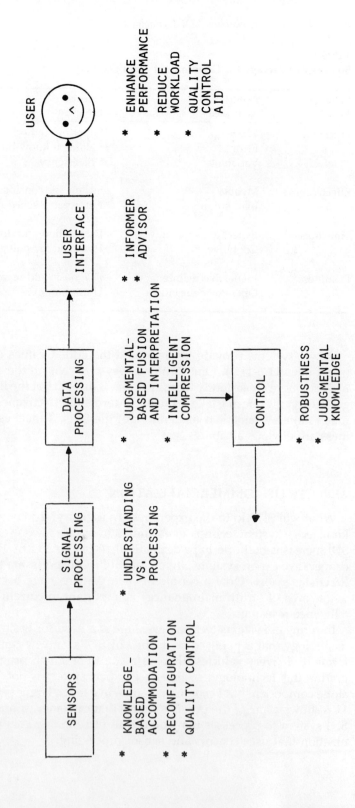

Table 11.7
Sources of Leverage for Government Applications

Value Added	Problem Addressed	Sources Exploited
Efficiency	Waste Error Variability	Superior methods Validated know-how Consistency
Effectiveness	Myopia Inattention	Systematic consideration Enforceable scheduling
Timeliness	Expert unavailability Cognitive	Duplication and distribution Heuristic reasoning
Readiness	Ineffective maintenance Operator deficiency	Diagnosis and repair expertise Utilization expertise

Expert systems provide leverage and the added values of efficiency (see Tables 11.6-11.7). One can have a system that on the average will perform more consistently than a person. It doesn't get the flu; it doesn't get hungry; it doesn't take a break. In terms of effectiveness, it makes much more systematic consideration of the facts. Timeliness and readiness are obvious attributes.

ASPECTS OF COMMERCIALIZATION

What will SDI do to the expert system industry? Today, off-the-shelf knowledge system technology is limited in terms of scope and capacity. SDI increases both, perhaps dramatically (see Table 11.8). For example, cooperative expert systems, involving multiple experts, are totally in the R&D stage now. Only a couple of such systems have been built. The whole area of "truth maintenance" is important in current artificial intelligence research.

In terms of systems technology, there is a need for basic engineering technology that is going to be pushed by SDI's large systems efforts. In terms of delivery vehicles, there is going to be much progress in integrating this technology, so that each expert system is not just a stand-alone component but becomes a module in a much larger system. Figure 11.6 shows some of the possible things that can emerge, and relates the SDI system to processes that could take place in any commercial organization that uses sensors and sensor processing.

Figure 11.6
Intelligent Defense Systems Components

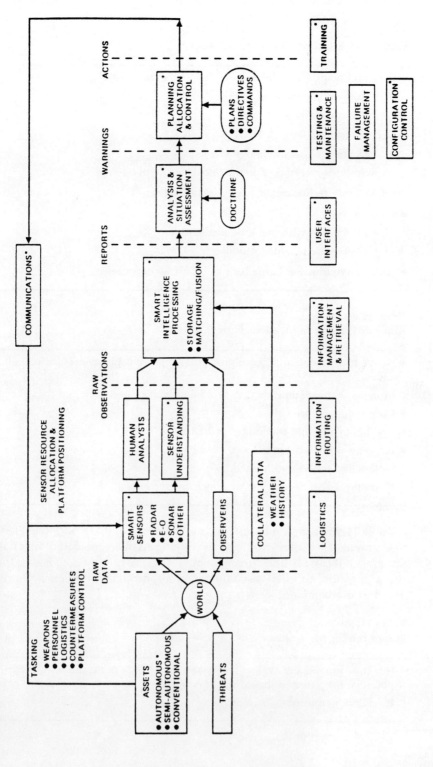

Table 11.8
First-Order Effect on Commercialization

- Basic technology: Accelerate knowledge system research
  - Cooperative systems
  - Truth maintenance
- Systems technology
  - Developing methodology
  - Systems integration methodology
- Engineering technology: Generic system modules
- Delivery vehicles
  - Integration with real-time processors
  - Low-cost embedded modules
- Technology transfer: Large base of industrial experience

Table 11.9
Kinds of Product Innovations Now Possible

- Active instruments that solve problems by producing answers instead of data
- Systems that explain how they work and how to use them
- Corporate memories
- Reasoning aids and thinking prosthetics
- Accident-proof machines
- Automated sellers and trainers
- Hypothesis and expectation management systems

Table 11.9 lists a number of kinds of products that are possible: Active instruments that solve problems producing answers instead of just data, systems that can capture corporate memories, corporate data bases, then reasoning aids, accident resistant machines, automated sellers and trainers, and management systems.

Table 11.10
Future Intelligent Systems

- Integrated intelligent system technology is the area of maximum growth potential for computer-based applications
- It will not be business as usual

Table 11.11
Management Heuristics

- Do the easy things first
- Focus on applying rather than developing the technology
- Concentrate on demonstrating success that has value and impact

Expert systems will have substantial impact on computers and computer technology automation in the industrial and commercial marketplace over the next 20 years. Tables 11.10 and 11.11 examine key issues of commercialization. First, try to do the easy things when you bring an expert system into an organization. Second, don't focus on developing the technology; rather, apply the technology. Take advantage of investments made elsewhere and apply them. Third, try to demonstrate success with high value. There are going to be more opportunities than capability, so pick applications carefully.

Table 11.12
Summary

- Knowledge systems are a young, successful technology
- Knowledge systems will play a vital role in tomorrow's complex systems
- By necessity knowledge systems will be a component of future strategic defense systems
- SDI will greatly accelerate the development and deployment of commercial knowledge system technology

Knowledge systems are a young, fragile technology. There are many holes but much potential. They will play a vital role in strategic defense systems and, recursively, SDI will advance their development dramatically (See Table 11.12).

NOTE

1. R. Dayhoff, *Computer Applications in Medical Care* (New York: Computer Society Press, 1983).

12

SPACE ROBOTICS: COMMERCIAL OPPORTUNITIES AND CHALLENGES

RONALD L. LARSEN

While the size of the human work force in space will remain small for the foreseeable future, the number of in-space activities requiring manipulative capabilities will be large and will continue to grow. These activities range from satellite servicing tasks now performed by astronauts using the Shuttle Remote Manipulator System (RMS), through assembly and repair tasks, to in-space manufacturing. These tasks are typically difficult to perform and dangerous, owing to the inherently hazardous space environment.

Space affords the opportunity to advance robotics technologies to meet national needs, expand the manipulative work force in space, and advance fundamental technologies with terrestrial spinoffs. Key results of recent Space Station studies performed by aerospace companies under NASA sponsorship confirm the significance of the opportunity (see Figure 12.1).

An architectural framework is proposed in this chapter that unifies key technological concepts for space robotics. The framework spans teleoperator systems through autonomous robots, and enables an assessment of current technology status, needs, and opportunities for the future.

AEROSPACE STUDIES OF SPACE ROBOTICS

Under the sponsorship of NASA's Space Station Program Office, a series of studies was conducted during 1984 and 1985 to investigate the potential of automation and robotics to meet Space Station requirements as well as to focus technology development on issues that have the potential to advance substantially the state of technology important to the industrial competitiveness of the United States. These studies were

Figure 12.1
Automation/Robotics Study

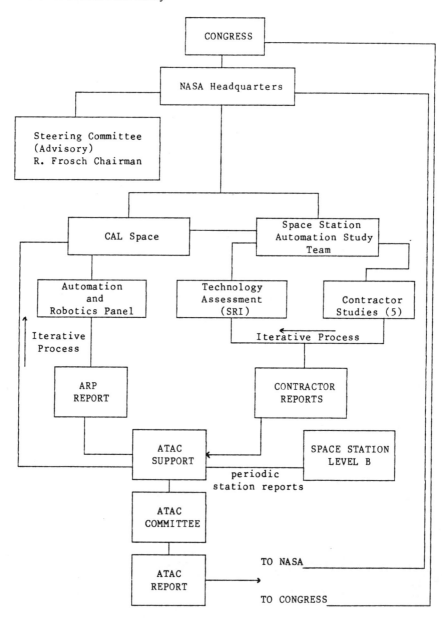

Source: The figures and tables in this chapter were compiled by the author, unless noted otherwise.

Table 12.1
Contractor Reports

- Hughes—Automated Subsystems Operations
  - Communications
  - Electrical power & thermal
  - System monitoring & control
- TRW—Satellite Servicing
- General Electric—Space Manufacturing
  - GaAs crystal production
  - GaAs microelectronics chip fabrication
- Martin Marietta—Autonomous Systems and Assembly
- Boeing—Operator/Systems Interface
- SRI—Technology Assessment

---

opportunistic in nature. Cost considerations were not a factor in exploring applications of automation and robotics technology in space. SRI International subsequently derived R&D needs implied by the applications studies (see Table 12.1).

Operator-Systems Interface

Boeing developed a concept for an extravehicular robot illustrated in Figure 12.2, and studied the means by which an operator could effectively interface with such a robot to perform in-space servicing and repair functions[1]. The commercial potential of this work includes remote manipulation in space, including the control of space robots from ground-based facilities, but extends to terrestrial applications demanding remote, highly capable robots and to applications in medicine such as interfaces to prosthetic devices and aids to the handicapped. Highly capable remote robots are required in hazardous environments such as in nuclear facilities, undersea, fire-fighting, and security applications. A key problem in developing such systems is the development of effective interfaces between the operator and the remote system. Interface technologies such as natural language and scene interpretation are vitally important, as are task planning and reasoning technologies that enable the operator to interact with the remote system at a higher level of abstraction.

Figure 12.2
Boeing Extravehicular Robot Concept

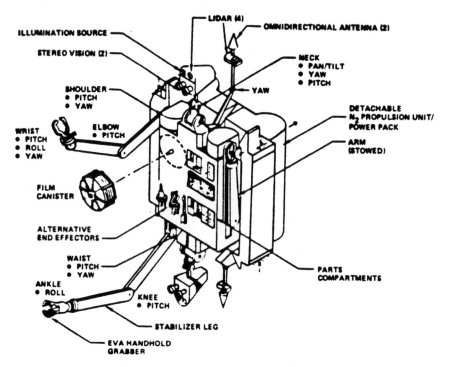

In-Space Manufacturing

General Electric developed a design for an automated in-space facility to manufacture gallium arsenide (GaAs) devices from raw materials.[2] Figures 12.3 and 12.4 illustrate the two manufacturing modules that comprise the system. One module is used to house the electroepitaxial crystal growth and wafer manufacturing equipment, while the other houses the equipment to manufacture GaAs very large-scale integration (VLSI) devices using the space-manufactured wafers. The facility is designed around the concept of manufacturing high-quality, high-yield devices automatically in space.

The successful development of such an in-space manufacturing facility requires the solution of a number of problems with terrestrial implications. Long life, continuously working mechanisms using dry lubricants will be required. The automated systems will require a self-diagnostic

Figure 12.3
GaAs Crystal Production

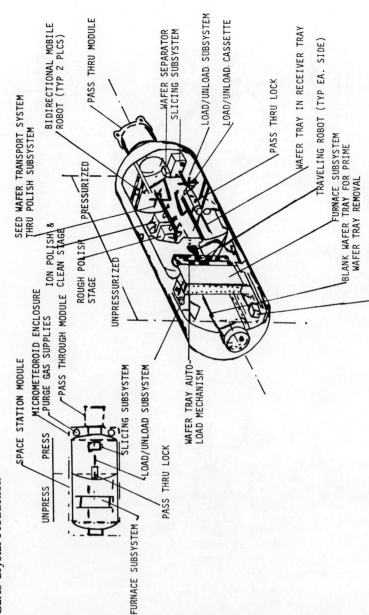

SPACE STATION MODULE
MICROMETEOROID ENCLOSURE
PURGE GAS SUPPLIES
PASS THROUGH MODULE
SLICING SUBSYSTEM
LOAD/UNLOAD SUBSYSTEM
PASS THRU LOCK
WAFER TRAY AUTO-LOAD MECHANISM
FURNACE SUBSYSTEM
UNPRESS
PRESS

SEED WAFER TRANSPORT SYSTEM
THRU POLISH SUBSYSTEM
BIDIRECTIONAL MOBILE ROBOT (TYP 2 PLCS)
PASS THRU MODULE
ION POLISH & CLEAN STAGE
ROUGH POLISH STAGE
PRESSURIZED
UNPRESSURIZED

WAFER SEPARATOR SLICING SUBSYSTEM
LOAD/UNLOAD SUBSYSTEM
LOAD/UNLOAD CASSETTE
PASS THRU LOCK
WAFER TRAY IN RECEIVER TRAY
TRAVELING ROBOT (TYP EA. SIDE)
FURNACE SUBSYSTEM
BLANK WAFER TRAY FOR PRIME WAFER TRAY REMOVAL
ENERGY RECOVERY SUBSYSTEM

Source: General Electric, "Space Station Automation Study—Automation Requirements Derived from Space Manufacturing Concepts," Contract NAS5–25182, November, 1984.

Figure 12.4
GaAs Microelectronics Chip Fabrication

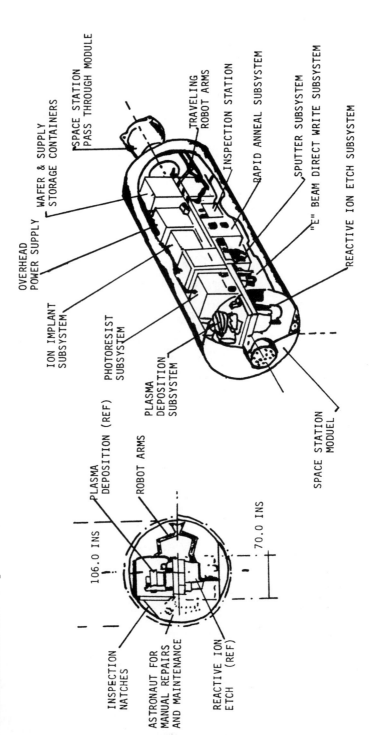

Source: General Electric, "Space Station Automation Study—Automation Requirements Derived from Space Manufacturing Concepts," Contract NAS5–25182, November, 1984.

capability and system designs will have to be fully modular with simple interfaces to facilitate maintenance and repair by robots. Handling fragile wafers in a microgravity environment will lead to innovations in dexterous end-effector design. The need for occasional human intervention will encourage the development of dual mode manipulators supporting both teleoperated and robotic operation. In addition, the successful manufacture of microelectronic devices in space will require automated techniques for performing quality assurance, a function that is currently performed largely through inspection by humans.

Autonomous Systems

Studies of in-space assembly of large structures conducted by Martin Marietta addressed an evolution of approach from pure extravehicular astronaut assembly, then introducing teleoperation of remote manipulators, adding supervisory control, and ultimately evolving to "teleautomation."[3] Technology advances in predictive displays, sensor fusion, multiple arm coordination, knowledge-based systems, automated planning and proximity, force, and touch sensing are necessary to support the proposed evolutionary approach. In addition, manufacturing advances are cited as necessary. Research into design guidelines to facilitate automated assembly is needed, and tooling, fixturing, and connecting issues must be addressed. The importance of commonality among structural elements is clearly important.

IBM researchers reported one illustration of the benefits that can accrue from designing for automated assembly.[4] A paper-feed mechanism for a copier was redesigned to facilitate assembly by robot, and the resulting mechanism contained roughly half the number of parts as the original, and was inherently a simpler, more elegant device.

Satellite Servicing

TRW examined the use of teleoperated and robotic devices to perform in-space satellite servicing.[5] Servicing functions such as refilling propellant tanks, replacing modules, and performing automated inspection tests, diagnostics, and checkout were studied. Potential time savings of typically 50 percent were reported with automated servicing aids. Figure 12.2 illustrates one servicing scenario for a Space Station attached payload. Technologies important to satellite servicing that have terrestrial spin-offs include dexterous manipulation, design-for-servicing guidelines, human-to-machine interfaces, computer vision, automated load handling and transfer, and knowledge-based systems to plan, monitor, and control robot operation. Satellite servicing differs markedly from traditional terrestrial robot applications in that the operational scenarios are typically unique. Automated satellite servicing does not benefit from the batch operations that make terrestrial robots economically effective today. Advances in the technology supporting robotic satellite servicing will enable flexible manufacturing of smaller batch sizes than are currently economically attractive.

Technology Assessment

SRI International reviewed the aerospace contractor studies and conducted an independent technology assessment,[6] identifying the major opportunities for robotics in space and the most difficult technical challenges that must be addressed to capitalize on the opportunities. Not too surprisingly, the highest priority space applications were considered to be satellite servicing, on-board monitoring and diagnosis, in-space manufacturing, and assembly of space structures. Major advances were identified as being required in design-for-automation, robotic mechanisms, sensing, automated planning, human-to-machine interface design, knowledge-based systems, and information systems architecture.

SRI recommended an evolutionary approach from teleoperation to intelligent robotics and research emphasizing visual and tactile sensing, multiagent planning, automated reasoning in a dynamic domain with subsystem interdependence, improved displays of dynamic system relationships, and system architectures that allow "rapid integration of new techniques in a way that preserves system integrity and satisfies ever-increasing performance requirements."[7] In addition, caution was advised against "premature enthusiasm" over expert systems. SRI observed that most contemporary expert systems are experimental, not generalizable beyond the original task domain, and depend on a very simple knowledge representation paradigm. They concluded that major advances in knowledge representation and reasoning are the "most important means of enabling automation of Space Station applications."

ARCHITECTURAL MODEL FOR SPACE TELEOPERATOR/ ROBOT SYSTEMS

Automation of Space Station functions and activities, particularly those involving robotic capabilities with interactive or supervisory human control, is a complex, multidisciplinary systems design problem. In this section, an abstract model is described that unifies the key concepts underlying the design of automated systems such as those studied by the aerospace contractors (see Figure 12.5).

Figure 12.5
Automation and Robotics: Technical Thrusts

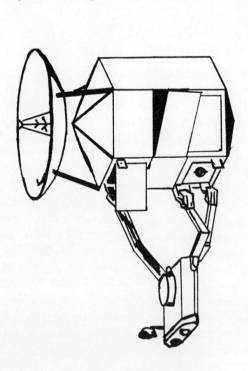

SENSING AND PERCEPTION

Sensor understanding of environment, component
identities, interrelationships, and dynamics

TASK PLANNING AND REASONING

Logical reasoning and spatial planning of alternative
task activity sequences leading to efficient task
completion

OPERATOR INTERFACE

Human factors considerations and display/control
interface requirements enabling smooth and
efficient transition of control between operator
and machine

CONTROL EXECUTION

Pattern-driven response to sensor observations,
characterized by rule-based as well as
model-based parameter adaptation

SYSTEM ARCHITECTURES AND INTEGRATION

Computing architectures enabling real-time execution
of autonomous functions. System control architectures
enabling smooth integration of these functions

Conceptual Framework

A major portion of human endeavor involves observing the state of the world and altering that state to achieve some desired outcome. Automated systems are viewed in this context as providing a transfer function between the human and the world in order to extend human capabilities. Teleoperated systems, for example, extend human reach to remote places in which it is difficult or hazardous for the human to function, and may amplify human strength and sensory abilities.

The conceptual view taken here, therefore, is that an automated system resides between a human (the operator) and the domain of concern (the external world). The system provides the operator with an ability to observe the state of the world remotely and to describe changes that are to be made to that state.

The conceptual framework consists of four major functions integrated into a unifying system architecture: (1) the operator interface, (2) task planning and reasoning, (3) sensing and perception, and (4) control execution. These functions are then organized to provide three control loops: (1) an operator control loop, (2) an executive control loop, and (3) a local control loop. The overall concept is illustrated in Figures 12.6 and 12.7.

Operator Interface

The operator interface includes displays and controls. Displays provide all of the information about system operation to the human operator, and can employ a variety of mechanisms for communicating information through the senses. Visual displays, such as graphics work stations, head-up displays, and stereo visual displays, are widely used. Force-feedback to the body, as through hand controllers or exoskeletons, can also be used, as can aural feedback and voice generation.

Controls provide the means by which the operator communicates information to the system, such as the nature or details of the task to be performed. Alphanumeric keyboards commonly provide this capability, often augmented with function keys, light pens, and similar mechanisms. Voice input, hand controllers, exoskeletons, and pedals provide additional options for the operator.

The integration of displays with controls provides the environment for human interaction with the system. It provides the means by which the human operator can communicate the description of the task to be performed to the systems, and the means by which the system can communicate the status of task execution back to the operator.

Figure 12.6
Architecture for an Automated System

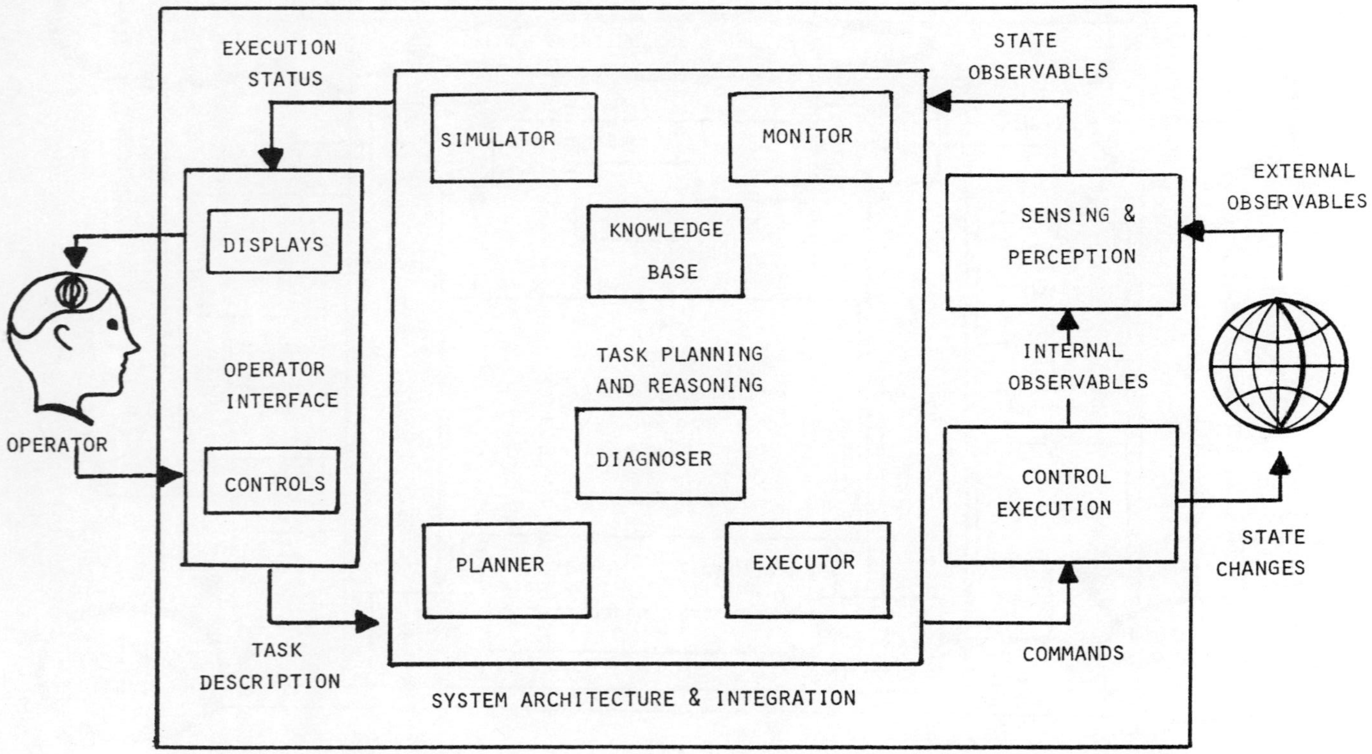

Figure 12.7
Automated System: Control Architecture

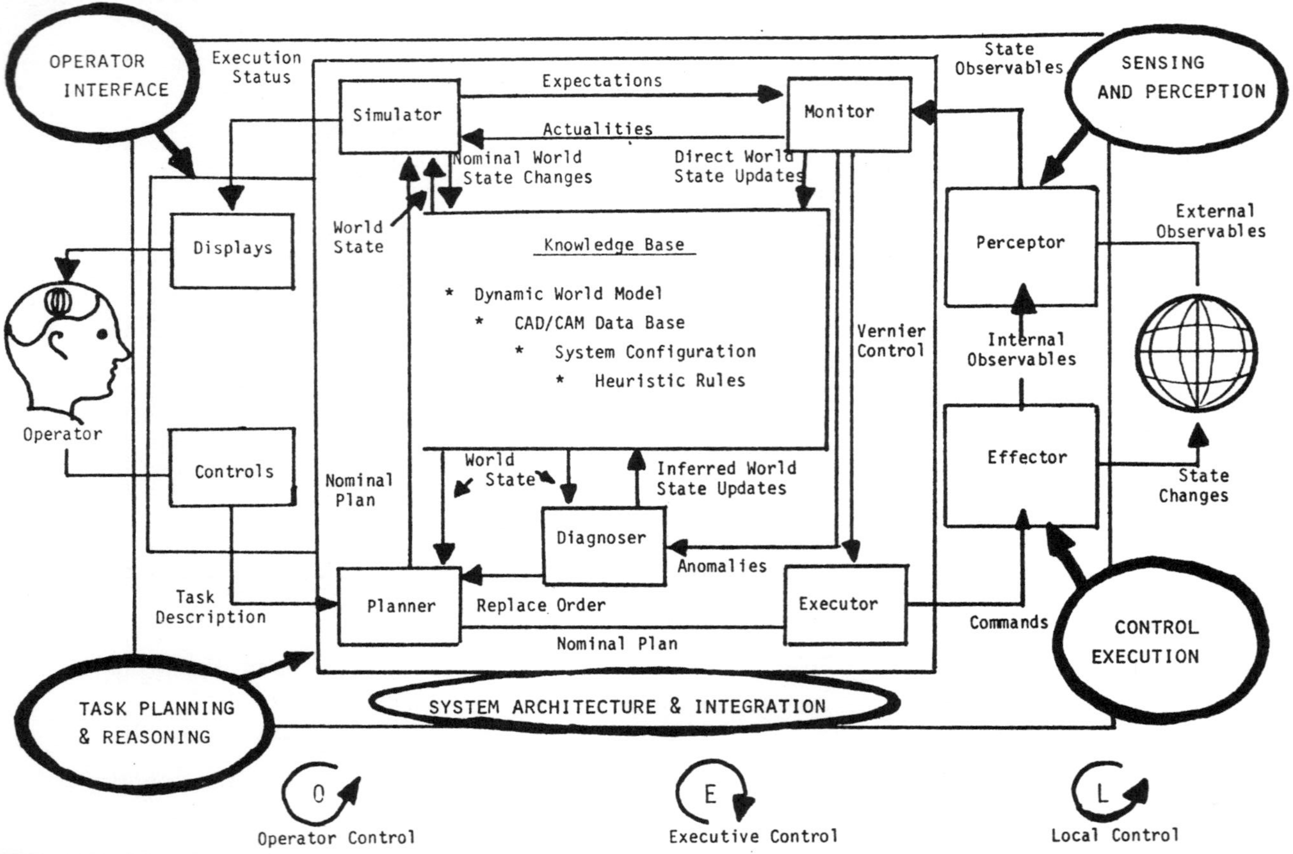

Task Planning and Reasoning

Task planning and reasoning includes most of the intelligence of the automated system. It receives the description of the task to be performed from the Controls, translates that into commands that can be remotely executed to change the state of the world, observes the changing world state, and communicates the execution status back to the operator through the Displays. Task planning and reasoning requires an extensive Knowledge Base containing all of the data required to represent and reason about the task domain. It includes a dynamic (time-dependent) world model that expresses the natural laws governing behavior of the system, a CAD/CAM-style (computed-aided design/computer-aided manufacturing) data base that provides the data required to understand the sensed world and manipulate it, system configuration data that describe the current suite of operational equipment, and the set of heuristic rules that are required to reason successfully and effectively in the task domain. The major capabilities of task planning and reasoning are provided by five functional modules: (1) the Planner, (2) the Executor, (3) the Simulator, (4) the Monitor, and (5) the Diagnoser.

The Planner receives the task description from the Controls, and the current state of the world from the Knowledge Base, including all known information relevant to the solution of the problem at hand. The Planner transforms the (typically) high-level description of the task into a nominal plan of action to accomplish the stated objective. This requires sufficient knowledge of the problem domain, the state of the system and the environment, and solution rules that lead to successful development of an acceptable plan. The plan is a time-sequenced series of primitive actions that the system is capable of performing.

The Executor accepts the nominal plan of action from the Planner and issues primitive commands in real time as dictated by the nominal plan. It also receives minor vernier adjustments that are superimposed on the command sequence to fine tune the execution of the operation in response to unanticipated discrepancies between the expected state of the world and the actual state. These adjustments are made to compensate for errors that do not threaten successful completion of the nominal plan.

The Simulator drives the operator Displays. It receives the nominal plan from the Planner, the world state from the Knowledge Base, and computes the time series of nominal world state changes, placing these into the Knowledge Base. From this nominal view of the changing state of the world, a time series of state observables is computed and sent to the Monitor. Actual world state observables are received back for display to the operator.

The Monitor uses expected values of state descriptors and receives observation data in real time from which it infers the current state of the operation and measures progress toward successful completion of the task. It updates the Knowledge Base with new world state information and detects discrepancies between the expected world state and the actual world state. New "actual" measures of the world state are returned to the Simulator, from which the expectations were received. Non-goal-threatening discrepancies are transformed into vernier adjustments, which are fed back to the Executor. Goal-threatening discrepancies (such as failure of a required device, oradetection of a broken component) require further analysis. An anomaly report is formatted and sent to the Diagnoser.

The Diagnoser receives anomaly reports from the execution Monitor. From the anomaly report and the current world state, it attempts to assess the nature of the anomaly, its cause, and potential effects. It computes an "inferred world state," i.e., the most plausible explanation and implied new system state, and places this in the knowledge base as the best estimate of the current world state. It then issues a replan order to the Planner, which informs the Planner that the nominal plan is no longer satisfactory. A new plan for the task must be derived given the new world state.

Sensing and Perception

The sensing and perception function provides a mapping from measurable internal and external parameters to an estimate of the world state. The function typically acquires its input from a multimode array of task and world sensing devices, such as cameras, force/torque sensors, proximity detectors, heat sensors, accelerometers, strain gauges, and voltage/current sensors. The objective of the sensing and perception function is to provide the Monitor with a real-time best estimate of the state of the task domain in terms that are consistent with the expected values provided by the Simulator.

Control Execution

The control execution function includes the manipulators, and effectors, and tools available at the task site that can be used to accomplish the desired task, as well as the low-level controls required to transform primitive commands issued by the Executor into state-changing actions.

Control Loops

The automated system control architecture consists of three major control loops. The Operator Control loop includes the human operator

Figure 12.8
Meshed Control Loops

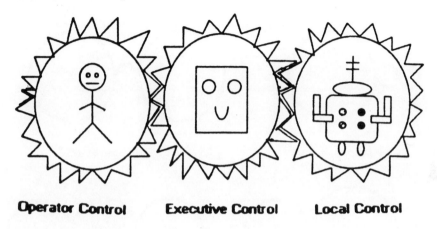

Operator Control   **Executive Control**   **Local Control**

plus the Controls, Planner, Simulator, and Displays. This loop provides the interaction between the human operator and the system. It can operate independently, providing a pure system simulation capability. This might be effective for operator training or system evaluation, for example.

The Executive Control loop includes all of the components required to operate and control a subsystem with minimal assistance from a human operator: the Planner, Simulator, Monitor, Diagnoser, and Knowledge Base. This core loop provides a generic control architecture that is equally applicable to controlling a deep-space spacecraft or an autonomous vehicle as it is to a robotic system.

The Local Control loop, consisting of the Executor, Effector, Perceptor, and Monitor, provides the low-level control for the specific manipulators used in the robot, as well as the sensor-based information extraction algorithms.

These three control loops can be visualized as a train of three gears, as illustrated in Figure 12.8. If one visually portrays the significance of the three loops for different operating modes by their relative size, one can begin to understand the robustness of the architecture. Figure 12.9a illustrates the typical factory robot, in which nearly all of the emphasis has been placed on the manipulator loop. This results in relatively dumb robots (e.g., pick and place, welding, or painting), which have simple computer controllers and minimal operator interaction except during the task programming phase. Figure 12.9b illustrates a teleoperator control

Figure 12.9
Alternative Control System Realizations

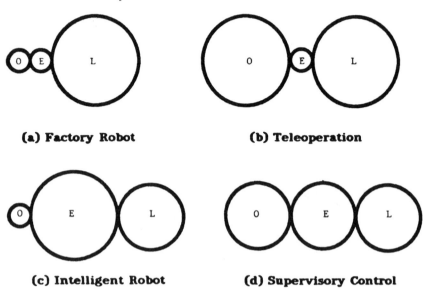

(a) Factory Robot

(b) Teleoperation

(c) Intelligent Robot

(d) Supervisory Control

concept, in which the executive control loop has been reduced to its most simple form, performing data transfer functions, but little more. The principal emphasis is on the operator loop to provide a good operator interface and on the local control loop to provide good manipulative capabilities. In Figure 12.9c, in contrast, an architecture for an intelligent robot is portrayed. Here, a massive executive control loop replaces the strong operator loop of the teleoperator. Finally, Figure 12.9d illustrates a supervisory controlled telerobot, which features a balance among the three control loops, providing the operator with the richness of a teleoperated system when the situation demands it, and providing the capability of a "semi-intelligent" autonomous robot when the situation allows it.

As the loops pictorially change in relative size, sophistication of the component subsystems changes drastically. In an attempt to maintain a consistent architecture, all subsystems are retained for all operating modes. In some cases, though, they are nonfunctional (essentially nonexistent except to provide a data interface between the other subsystems), while in other cases they might be million-line programs (see Figure 12.10).

COMMERCIAL OPPORTUNITIES

The commercial benefits deriving from space research typically defy rigorous definition or quantification, but are generally accepted to be far in excess of the cost of the original research. A recent NASA study addressing Space Station automation cites a conclusion reached by the Cleveland International Research Institute that a 38 percent growth in sales (from \$2.1 to \$2.9 billion) is feasible for assembly and inspection robots by the year 2000 as a result of an aggressive program of research on space-based robots. Other applications that could benefit from space automation and robotics research are identified in Table 12.2.[8]

Knowledge-Based Systems

The primary technology areas supporting knowledge-based systems that have particular importance to space applications include procedural planning, fault diagnosis, cooperating expert systems, and knowledge representation. Large-scale space systems such as the Space Station are complex, dynamic systems operating in a highly dynamic environment. Procedural planning addresses the automatic generation of operational plans for these types of systems. As important as generating a good plan is monitoring the execution of that plan and diagnosing the causes of faults that may occur. Diagnosis involves detection of system anomalies, identifying potential causes, establishing likely explanations of observed behavior, and possibly testing hypotheses in order to improve the confidence level of the diagnosis.

Owing to the scale and complexity of next-generation space systems, advanced automation techniques are envisioned as being required to operate many of the subsystems cost-effectively. From a systems architecture perspective, these subsystem controllers must interact cooperatively to ensure overall system integrity. Progress in cooperating expert systems technology will have potential benefit to other large-scale systems applications, as well. The organization of knowledge into effective structures for use by knowledge-based systems remains largely a research problem. Progress in fundamental knowledge-based systems technology promises to benefit many industries, including aircraft, ships, automotive, and electronics.

Figure 12.10
Evolution Toward Autonomy

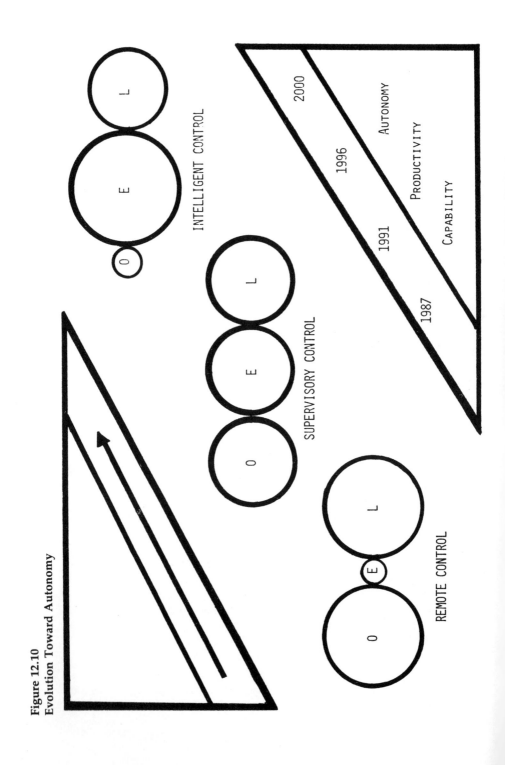

REMOTE CONTROL

SUPERVISORY CONTROL

INTELLIGENT CONTROL

1987   1991   1996   2000

CAPABILITY   PRODUCTIVITY   AUTONOMY

Table 12.1
Potential Applications of Space Automation Technology

Potential Technologies	Applications										
	Assembly	Maintenance & Repair	Product/ Process/ Structure Inspection	Plant/ Facility Security	Factory Control	Transporting & Handling Toxic Materials	Pruning, Picking & Cultivating Agricultural Crops	Medical Surgery	Computer Communications	Go-fer for Disabled	Fire Fighting
Hybrid Robot/ Teleoperator	×	×	×	×		×	×	×		×	×
Adaptive Control	×	×	×	×		×	×	×		×	×
Off-Line Robot Programming Through CAD/CAM Technology	×	×	×								
Tactile Sensors (Arrays, Force Feedback)	×	×	×	×			×	×		×	
Advanced Machine Vision (3D-Scene Analysis)	×	×	×	×			×			×	×

Table 12.1-Continued

Potential Technologies	Applications										
	Assembly	Maintenance & Repair	Product/Process/Structure Inspection	Plant/Facility Security	Factory Control	Transporting & Handling Toxic Materials	Pruning, Picking & Cultivating Agricultural Crops	Medical Surgery	Computer Communications	Go-fer for Disabled	Fire Fighting
Mobile Robot Guidance/Navigation		×		×		×	×			×	×
Advanced Planning for Robotics											
Dual Arm Robotics	×	×	×	×		×	×			×	×
Dextrous Manipulator	×	×	×			×	×	×		×	
Robot Application Modeling by Visual Simulation	×	×				×	×	×			×
Diagnostic Expert System		×	×	×	×						×
Distributed Computing		×			×				×		
Advanced Data Storage Technology		×	×	×	×				×		

132

Applications

Potential Technologies	Assembly	Maintenance & Repair	Product/Process/Structure Inspection	Plant/Facility Security	Factory Control	Transporting & Handling Toxic Materials	Pruning, Picking & Cultivating Agricultural Crops	Medical Surgery	Computer Communications	Go-fer for Disabled	Fire Fighting
Intelligent Man/Machine Interfaces	×										
Intelligent Remote Sensor Technology		×	×	×	×	×		×		×	×
Energy Management/Advanced Process Control Technology		×	×	×	×					×	×
Advanced Fault-Tolerant Disciplines					×				×		

Teleoperation and Robotics

The aerospace contractor studies established the potential of teleoperation and robotics in space. While General Electric's investigation of space-based manufacturing resulted in provocative results, the technology that would result from such an initiative could also benefit ground-based applications in automated, flexible manufacturing. Functions that might otherwise be handled manually, such as scheduling, servicing, maintenance, and repair, must be automated for an effective space-based manufacturing capability. Solutions to these problems, resulting from space-oriented research, should be transferable to terrestrial applications. Other potential technology advances that could result from space robotics research include light-weight, high-precision dexterous manipulators; multiarm coordination; sensor-based control techniques; and automated planning based on CAD/CAM data sources.

Human Interface

Human-to-machine interface technologies are of prime importance to successful space systems. Next-generation space systems will employ speech synthesis and speech recognition with natural language constructs. In addition, predictive displays and the ability to fuse multisource information into quickly discernible displays will be required to accommodate real-time interaction with processes encountering transmission delays. Without appropriate compensation, instabilities can be introduced into the operator control loop.

Owing to the anticipated complexity of future space systems, more effective system documentation techniques will be required. The paper-based approaches used to date will be totally inadequate. Advances in self-describing system design techniques are expected, resulting in relatively standard, nonthreatening user interfaces for the nonexpert. Advances made in this area should be broadly applicable to terrestrial applications. Typically, system documentation techniques have received little attention since the costs associated with poor documentation are neither well understood nor immediately apparent. Major benefits over the system life cycle are expected, though, if substantial progress can be achieved in improving the quality of documentation.

Autonomous Systems

The Department of Defense and NASA have largely pioneered the technology development for autonomous systems. Of particular interest are large-scale, highly complex systems for which robust control must be provided over extended periods using nonclassical techniques. NA-

SA's Mars Rover Project, which was canceled during cutbacks in the 1970s, provided early impetus to the development of this technology. DARPA's Autonomous Land Vehicle (ALV), being developed under the Strategic Computing Program, provides a contemporary example. The ALV is intended to be an off-road vehicle capable of successfully navigating uncharted terrain at moderate speeds using real-time sensing techniques such as computer vision.

The long-term potential of autonomous systems in commercial applications is largely unexplored, but is expected to be significant. Short-term applications in areas where operator boredom results in excessive errors may be feasible. At the other extreme, systems in which operator errors may be caused by stress and an inability to properly interpret rapidly changing system conditions may benefit. In the longer term, the integration of autonomous systems control technology with robotics is expected to yield a new generation of intelligent robots.

SUMMARY AND CONCLUSIONS

The potential of advanced automation and robotics in Space Station applications has been extensively studied by aerospace contractors, and the required technology advancements have been examined by recognized experts in artificial intelligence and robotics. These studies have confirmed the significance of the potential opportunities as well as the difficulty of the technical challenges that must be overcome.

An architectural model has been proposed in an attempt to unify key concepts underlying teleoperation, robotics, subsystem control, and autonomous systems design. This model provides a conceptual framework in which the state of technology can be assessed, technology needs determined, and progress measured.

The potential spin-offs of space automation and robotics to terrestrial commercial applications have also been considered, identifying, in particular, those technical areas in which advances in space could yield major benefits to industry. These benefits will not come easily or directly. A major fundamental research program is required to yield the space technology, and care must be taken to ensure that such a program maintains its emphasis on generic, core technology advances with the broadcast applicability.

NOTES

1. Boeing, "Space Station Automation and Robotics Study, Operator-Systems Interface," D 483–10027–1, November, 1984.
2. General Electric, "Space Station Automation Study—Automation Requirements Derived from Space Manufacturing Concepts," Contract NAS5–25182, November, 1984.

3. Martin Marietta, "Space Station Automation Study—Autonomous Systems and Assembly," Contract NAS8–35042, November, 1984.
4. J. R. Bailey, "Product Design for Robotic Assembly," 13th International Symposium on Industrial Robots, April 1983, pp. 11–44 to 11–57.
5. TRW, "Space Station Automation Study—Satellite Servicing," Contract NAS8 Space Robotics: Commercial Opportunities and Challenges, November, 1984.
6. SRI International, "NASA Space Station Automation: AI-Based Technology Review," Project 7268, 1985.
7. Ibid.
8. "Advancing Automation and Robotics Technology for the Space Station and for the U.S. Economy," Report of the Advanced Technology Advisory Committee, NASA Technical Memorandum 87566, March, 1985.

13

SUPERCOMPUTER SYSTEMS MARKETS

LLOYD M. THORNDYKE

This chapter provides one vendor's viewpoint of the present and future markets for supercomputers. Existing federal programs having impact on computer technology will be evaluated and recommendations made to address the fundamental underlying technologies. Some of the views are provocative and contrarian; nevertheless, we believe they are valid and should be aired.

EMERGING COMMERCIAL MARKETS

Supercomputers are not "an emerging commercial market." They have already emerged. The current supercomputer market is dominated by industrial customers. ETA Systems recently commissioned a market study by a well-recognized name in the market research field. The table below was developed from data contained in the study and presents the relative distribution of current installed base of supercomputers and the forecasts of this base for the years 1990 and 1995:

Market Segment Shares (percent)	1985	1990	1995
Government	38	26	23
Education	17	14	14
Industry	45	60	63

These figures are all the more remarkable when one considers that the early supercomputer market, that of the early 1960s and 1970s, was dominated by the government segment with particular emphasis on the national laboratories and other leading-edge government users. The domestic higher education market fluctuated with the fortunes of National

Science Foundation (NSF) funding, while the West European market maintained a consistent pace of a few installations annually. The only substantial, sustained industrial market during that early period was the petroleum industry, a long-time large user of high-performance computers.

It was around 1980 that the industrial segment of the market began to develop and accelerate to the point that today it outnumbers the government segment in terms of the installed base. It is also significant that this date also marks the beginning of serious competition between Control Data Corporation and Cray Research. There seems to be clear consensus within government and industry that this trend toward increasing competition and industrial usage will continue, particularly as new applications are developed and put into use.

Our need, therefore, is not a recognition that the industrial market is about to emerge, but that it is a here-and-now market that will be accelerating its growth. The challenge we face as a nation is that we must be leaders—not followers—in utilizing supercomputers to improve our economic competitiveness.

STRATEGIC DEFENSE INITIATIVE

We should examine the words "Strategic Defense Initiative" in terms of supercomputers. It is difficult to underestimate the significance of the role that high-performance computing will play in SDI scenarios—its implementation would be absolutely impossible without the availability of computing systems with supercomputer performance.

There is little question that supercomputers are "strategic" resources for the United States. Many, if not most, of the early systems were used effectively by the national laboratories in development of strategic weapons systems. Today the application of supercomputers has expanded and includes numerous uses of systems to develop and extend technology. The introduction of the supercomputer as an integral element of the design process of automobiles and increasingly denser integrated circuits are two civilian examples of this extension of supercomputer power into areas of strategic economic importance. At ETA Systems, we are using a CYBER 205 supercomputer to design our next system, the ETA-10. We will then use the ETA-10 to design its successor.[1]

If we go back a few years and examine the supercomputers of the 1960s and 1970s, we will find that they were products with 100 percent American technology content. All logic and memory components and the supporting peripheral subsystems were built in the United States. If you wanted to buy a supercomputer, you had to buy it from an American company.

Today, unfortunately, such is not the case and the situation is of more concern than is indicated by the mere fact that three Japanese companies have announced and started to deliver supercomputers, which are the direct outgrowth of coordinated thrusts by the Japanese government and industry, first into component development, then into general-purpose computers, and now into supercomputers and artificial intelligence.

There has been considerable publicity—most of it correct—about the success of the Japanese in the memory chip markets. Not only are they dominant in the "commodity-level" chips of low and moderate performance, but they are at present the sole suppliers of advanced chips that have the performance characteristics we need for supercomputers. The Japanese are also making serious inroads into the high-performance logic market, once the exclusive domain of American companies, to the point that it is not unreasonable to visualize an American supercomputer designed around Japanese logic and storage components. We must not allow this perilous scenario to become reality. We must take the necessary corrective actions to make our semiconductor vendors more competitive.

There are several ongoing federal programs designed to advance computer technologies. Unfortunately, I do not see any of them directly addressing what I consider to be the key supercomputer strategic issues. Probably the best existing government program is the establishment of supercomputer research centers at key universities and educational consortia using funds being allocated through the NSF. While the systems being purchased under this program contribute moderately to overall supercomputer sales, the more important contributions are the long-overdue investments in supercomputer software, applications research, and training of computer scientists.

The very high speed integrated circuit (VHSIC) program started by the Defense Department a number of years ago has had, at best, a trickle-down effect. Much of the effort, by necessity, was directed toward the unique requirements of the military market. I suspect that VHSIC is like all other programs of its type—there are trade-offs to be made and they will be made in the direction of the main thrust of the project: meeting military requirements.

Another new program has started up in the Washington, D.C., area, calling for the establishment of a supercomputer research center to be administered by the National Security Agency and managed by the Institute for Defense Analysis. This program could be very helpful if its mission includes assisting the American supercomputer vendors in the evaluation of technology risks. The Defense Advanced Research Projects Agency program has been under way for a short time with objectives directed toward artificial intelligence. I think time will tell as to the applicability of this effort toward furthering our standing in strategic supercomputing.

The point in identifying and commenting on these programs from an admittedly biased viewpoint is that it is not clear in my mind that this country has established an effective program to protect our present supercomputer position from erosion. We have had several examples in the past in which U.S. companies have had cooperative computer technology and marketing arrangements with Japanese counterparts. These arrangements at their inception called for the U.S. companies to be donors of technology. In every case, we have seen a reversal of the roles—the U.S. companies are now importing Japanese products.

There are lessons to be learned from the Japanese success story. Before proceeding further, I think it instructive to examine our current position. First, we have established architectures that have been proven through customer usage. Second, our domestic user base is the largest and most experienced in the world. Third, we have the experience of having developed and delivered supercomputers longer than anyone else. This list could be expanded to reach a size that would appear to be most impressive and would therefore seem to forecast that we indeed face a rosy future.

I believe that our ability to compete in the industrial supercomputer market lies, as a first step, in getting back to fundamentals and improving our technology infrastructure. The contrast in structure between the U.S. and Japanese supercomputer companies is dramatic. The Japanese supercomputers are the products of very large, vertically integrated enterprises with the capability to produce all elements of the system, including the logic and storage components. On the other hand, the U.S. supercomputer suppliers are small by any standards of measurement.

In prior years, when the United States had a monopoly on computer technology, this was not a serious concern, since one could find cooperative domestic semiconductor vendors capable of delivering high-performance components. Today we find ourselves in the semiconductor design business if we wish to buy the logic chips from domestic sources. If you want high-performance memory chips, you have no choice but to buy from Japanese sources. It has been our experience that the Japanese vendors do not make their advanced products available for use in the United States until they are in full production, assuring them of a substantial lead in the end products. This emphasizes again that the lack of domestic component sources must be of concern when we are dealing with an item of such strategic importance.

The place to initiate our line of strategic defense of supercomputer technology is at the very foundation of the business—the components. This is not an appropriate forum to debate the relative merits of one technology over another, but it is appropriate to identify some salient characteristics that most designers would agree are desirable.

We need, first and foremost, a technology that will yield fast performance at the systems level. This implies not only fast switching times, but also high logic densities. This technology must be based on proven processes and supported by design tools and packaging techniques. For this approach to be successful, we need direct participation by the users of the technology—the supercomputer designers.

A successful supercomputer system does not consist solely of fast logic circuits. It also requires a large-capacity, high-performance memory subsystem, many fast input/output channels, high transfer rate peripheral and communications subsystems, and software to facilitate exploitation of the hardware features. Some of these elements, I suppose, are being pursued in various federal programs in one way or another, but this is the very crux of the situation. We have lots of fragmented programs that will yield us lots of fragments. What we need is a unified supercomputer program.

SUMMARY

Despite current impressions to the contrary, we have already entered the stage in which the industrial segment of the supercomputer market is dominant. The world is entering an era of significant supercomputer growth. While the United States presently is in the forefront, its leadership position is threatened by the impressive technological advances made by the Japanese. We need to come up with a focused supercomputer program that addresses the development of the fundamental technologies. Otherwise we risk loss of a key strategic element in both our defense and industrial sectors.

NOTE

1. J. R. Kirkland and J. H. Poore, eds. *Supercomputers: The Key to U.S. Scientific, Technological, and Industrial Preeminence*, an IC² Book (New York: Praeger, 1987).

14

KINETIC ENERGY TECHNOLOGY

WILLIAM F. WELDON

The Strategic Defense Initiative Kinetic Energy Weapons (KEW) program incorporates two distinct technologies: missiles (near term) and electromagnetic launchers (long term). Since missiles already have an established industrial base, only the recently emerging technology of electromagnetic launchers (EMLs) will be discussed here. In so doing, the efficiency and velocity limitations imposed by theromodynamic principles are avoided. EMLs are capable of achieving much higher accelerations and velocities and in some cases higher efficiencies than their theromodynamic counterparts. The technologies required are those of generating and conditioning the extremely high levels of pulsed electrical power needed. As we will see, these new EML technologies have a variety of potential commercial applications as well.[1]

The KEW program involves accelerating projectiles to velocities far in excess of those achieved by conventional guns, for the purpose of destroying ballistic missiles by kinetic energy impact. As compared with directed energy weapons (DEW), the lethality mechanism is less controverisal, but the longer time-of-flight makes actually hitting the target more difficult. This leads to the use of so-called smart projectiles, either command guided or terminally homing. However, the topic that will be discussed here will be the launch mechanism for such weapons.

ELECTROMAGNETIC LAUNCH TECHNOLOGY

EML technology generally can be divided into two approaches: the simplest being the railgun, the more complex and potentially more efficient being the coilgun. The electromagnetic railgun (Figure 14.1) consists of two parallel, metal rails separated by a distance typically equal to their width. A projectile with a conducting armature is placed between

Figure 14.1
Electromagnetic Railgun

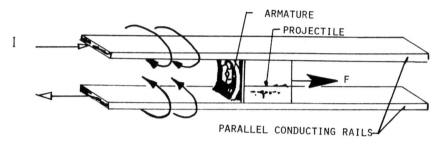

Source: All of the figures in this chapter were compiled by the author.

the rails at the breech of the railgun. If the breech of the railgun is then connected to an appropriate source of electrical current, the current will flow down one rail, across the armature and back up the other rail. The current flowing in the rails creates a magnetic field between the rails, and the current flowing in the armature interacts with this magnetic field to produce a force that accelerates the armature and projectile down the gun barrel. This accelerating force, known as the Lorentz force, reaches levels of interest only at extremely high currents ($> 10^5$ A). Unlike a thermodynamic gun in which the acceleration falls off as the hot gas expands, the acceleration in an EML can be held constant as long as constant current is maintained in the gun. Being the simplest of the EMLs, the railgun has enjoyed the most rapid development. In recent years, masses as high as 300 grams have been accelerated to velocities in excess of 4 km/s while smaller masses (1–5 g) have been accelerated to velocities of 8–10 km/s. For comparison, conventional guns are practically limited to velocities of 1.5–2 km/s.

Coilguns, while being more complicated than railguns, also offer the promise of higher efficiency and greater control over acceleration. The basic concept for a coilgun (Figure 14.2) involves a series of stationary (stator) coils and a moving (armature) coil attached to the projectile. As the armature coil passes through each stator coil, current is directed into the stator coil so that the armature coil is repelled down the gun barrel. A variety of coilgun configurations have been considered that differ in the way current is supplied to the stator and armature coils. The coilgun is attractive since it does not require contact between the armature and stator, as the railgun does, and since its higher impedance leads to higher efficiency as mentioned previously. The additional complexity of the coilgun stems from the more complicated construction of the stator and

Figure 14.2
Electromagnetic Coilgun

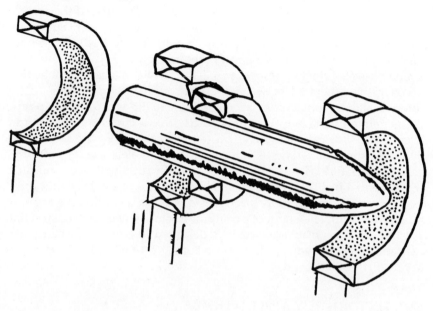

the need to synchronize the current feed to the individual stator coils
with the position of the armature.

PULSED POWER TECHNOLOGY

EMLs of interest require electrical power of hundreds of megawatts
to several gigawatts during launch. Although the basic operating principles of EMLs have been known since the early part of this century,
their enormous power needs kept then from being realizable until recent
advances in pulsed power technology (PPT). PPT uses energy storage
techniques to store energy slowly at moderate power levels and then
deliver that stored energy in a brief, intense burst of electrical power.
Energy may be stored electrostatically in capacitors, electromagnetically
in inductors, electrochemically in batteries, or in the inertia of spinning
flywheels. Recent developments at the University of Texas's Center for
Electromechanics (CEM-UT) involving the incorporation of specialized
rotating electrical generator technology with inertial energy storage have
made compact, inexpensive, portable pulsed power supplies available
for driving EMLs. Of course, the pulsed power supply must do more

than just store energy. It must deliver the desired current at the appropriate voltage level in exactly the proper time frame. Two CEM-UT developed power supplies are capable of performing this crucial task for a variety of EMLs as well as other applications. The first of these is the pulsed homopolar generator (HPG). Although the basic concept is over 150 years old, a portable HPG pulsed power supply has only recently become practical. Figure 14.3 shows the principle of HPG operation. As a monolithic conducting rotor (flywheel) spins in an axial magnetic field a voltage is generated between the shaft and outer periphery of the rotor. If sliding contacts are applied to the shaft and rotor periphery, the generated voltage can be utilized to drive a current in an external circuit. As electrical energy is extracted from the HPG, the rotor slows because its inertial energy is being converted to electrical output.

A second CEM-UT developed pulsed power supply, the compulsator, was invented in 1978. Whereas the HPG produces a single output pulse as it slows, the compulsator produces a burst or a continuous chain of pulses. The rotor and stator of a compulsator are now under construction at CEM-UT. This machine, which is designed to power an electromagnetic machine gun, will produce a burst of ten 2.5-kV, 1-MA, 2-ms pulses in one-sixth of a second.

EML TECHNOLOGY APPLICATIONS

In addition to strategic kinetic energy weapons, EMLs are being investigated for tactical weapons including artillery, antiarmor, and air defense. The technology is being developed for launching aircraft as well and has been considered for launching payloads into space. A pound of material can be fired into low earth orbit for 65 cents worth of electricity compared to a cost of $4,500 per pound for the space shuttle. EMLs have even been studied for propelling advanced space missions. For this application the EML would be used instead of a rocket engine since it can propel the exhaust material at higher velocities than a rocket and, therefore, achieve the desired propulsive force with the expenditure of less mass.

But EML technology has more down-to-earth applications as well. Metal powders fired from railguns have more than sufficient kinetic energy to melt upon impact, producing dense coatings that are tightly bonded to substrates. When coupled with the rapid-fire pulse capability of the compulsator, this metal-spraying process may some day provide an alternative to welding and casting or forging of metal parts. By varying powder composition during spraying, monolithic parts might be made with customized properties in different areas. Ceramic powders can be sprayed by this technique as well.

Since railguns easily impart to projectiles kinetic energies sufficient to

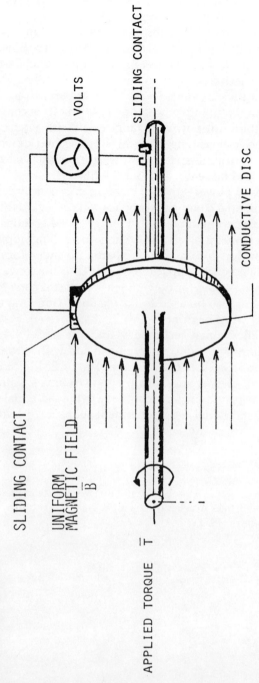

Figure 14.3
Homopolar Generator

melt or forge them (at 3 km/s the kinetic energy density in a projectile exceeds the energy density in high explosives), it is conceivable that EMLs might be used to form, forge, or draw metal ingots into desired shapes, perhaps using noncontacting magnetic dies. Since tactical EM guns will be capable of penetrating substantial thicknesses of armor plate, the same technology might be used for drilling deep holes or tunnels through the earth. As deeper wells are drilled, for example, the ability to transmit drilling power down the hole becomes a limiting factor. A compulsator-powered railgun on the surface could fire hundreds of rock-penetrating projectiles per second down a well. The limiting factor on drilling speed, in this case, might well be the rate at which debris could be removed from the hole.

CEM-UT pulsed power supplies developed primarily for EML applications have potential commercial applications as well. HPGs have been used to produce high-quality welds in large metal sections in a fraction of a second, heat metal billets for forging and rolling applications, and sinter metal powders into monolithic parts. Magnetic forming of metal parts is another potential application of HPG technology. The compulsator, originally invented for powering xenon flashlamps to drive solid-state lasers, might also be used to flash similar lamps rapidly for high-speed drying of paint or printing ink.

Electromagnetic launch technology and the closely related pulsed power technology are newly emerging fields with a wide variety of potential applications. It is the mission of the CEM-UT to develop the required technology base, perform preliminary investigations of promising applications, and transfer technology to the industrial sector, working closely with industrial and government sponsors to accomplish these goals.

NOTE

1. Richard A. Marshall, "The Acceleration of Macro Particles and a Hypervelocity Macro Particle Accelerator," Ph.D. Thesis, Australian National University, Canberra, 1972.

15

OPTICAL TECHNOLOGY

ROBERT R. SHANNON

Advancing the state of the art in optics is one of the major thrusts of technology associated with SDI. Commercial payoffs should result from work done under this initiative. In this chapter the possibilities of such commercialization will be reviewed. At this early stage, many of the suggestions contained here are speculation, but should serve as a guide to future potential.

The field of optics, an old and well-developed one, deals with the manipulation of light in all of its manifestations. The possible applications of optics can generally be divided among the four major divisions.

1. *Optical engineering* relates to the so-called classical aspects of the field, dealing with the technology required for the concentration and direction of radiant energy, either coherent or incoherent. The technology of the design and fabrication of trackers, beam directors, image stabilizers, and adaptive optical components is of interest to SDI here. The working tools of the optical engineer are a knowledge of geometrical and physical optics and an understanding of optical design. Problems to be solved are in the effective and economical fabrication of unusual optics with nonsymmetric aspheric surfaces, and the metrology of components and entire systems. The use of diffractive or holographic components for metrology or image formation is a new and growing topic. The use of dynamic optical components for precision beam steering and aberration correction of beams is central to most directed energy devices. Correction of the effect of atmospheric turbulence on beams and images is of growing importance.

2. *Quantum engineering* deals with the use of light waves as the carrier of information, either as ducted through wave guides on fibers, or in free space, and the physics of the interaction of light with matter. The various aspects of laser operation, optically controlled optical and electronic switches, and the detection and demodulation of light are considered here. This is a relatively new area of concentration in optics, and draws its strength from the use of lasers of

various types as a tool for modifying the environment. The nature of the inter-action of light with matter is most important here, and has led to new methods of molecular manipulation for industrial processes. The nonlinear properties of certain materials with respect to the intensity of the light passing through the material are central to the development of switches and optical processing devices.

3. *Computer engineering* deals with the application of optics as a medium for the computation of new information, either through analog or digital means, and is one of the most significant interests of the SDI program because of the huge potential computational bandwidth of optical computing devices. The de-velopment of data storage media, bistable computing elements, and analog signal transform systems is of interest to SDI in this part of the field. The possibility of highly parallel optical computing architectures is likely in the fu-ture. The method of data presentation and the input and output operations of computers using parallel optical transfers show promise. In some cases, optical communication within electronic computers has already been applied. The dis-tribution of massive amounts of data within a system through the use of optical storage media offers new concepts to information transfer and understanding.

4. *Image engineering* deals with the overall problem of perception and orga-nization of the state of the environment through the medium of image proc-essing, in both the pictorial and the generalized senses. The detection of specific objects among the background clutter of a scene is a typical application of image processing. The identification of a class of object within a large set is required for many SDI tasks. Not as widely noted, but possibly more significant, is the possibility of treating the state of complex systems as a generalized image that is to be searched and evaluated by complex parallel artificial intelligence pro-cedures. Smart sensors that have the capability of delivering summary state-ments about the image being observed are an eventual development in this area.

Research under SDI covers many aspects of these subjects. In what we hope will be a logical progression, the basic concepts for optical systems are being investigated prior to the development of operating devices. These component investigations should serve as the foundation for future systems to be developed. In general, the direction is toward the defensive systems required for SDI, and not toward the development of commercial products. It is hoped that some of these developments will be turned into commercial applications by aggressive entrepreneurs.

Basic optical concepts that are being investigated include many aspects of nonlinear interactions of light with materials, and the resulting switch-ing and phase conjugation processes that result. New optical component materials for substrates and coatings that may permit economical fab-rication of aspheric optics are being examined. The basics of application of artificial intelligence techniques for sorting out the essentials of images are being developed and applied to a number of possible problems. The general question of what computer architectures are suited for massive high speed parallel computations is being considered.

Lightweight optical components are being developed for eventual large-diameter segmented mirrors. These have obvious applications to astronomical purposes, but are not necessarily of wide commercial significance. Active components, along with the associated sensors and control devices, are being investigated with ever increasing numbers of actuators to drive the components.

Optical devices for sensing alignment or perturbations on the wavefront propagating through a system are under development. These may be coupled with the development of smart sensors that add some degree of intelligence to a detector array. Compact integrated sensors and image processors may emerge from these elements of the research.

Overall optical systems that are being investigated include impressive, and large, beam directors. These systems include the capability of controlling high-energy beams at high dymamic rates. The integration of beam directors with equally large trackers is a major SDI problem. There is a parallel to smaller scale problems of tracking and identifying objects amid noise or clutter.

Now, what are the areas of potential future commercial application that can be expected from SDI research fallout? The identification of products and areas is of course a subject of speculation, but the likelihood of some options is certainly greater than others. Predictions require a consideration of probable human needs in the future, as well as the opportunities that are presented by the emergence of new technologies. It is hoped that some developments of greater significance than the memorable NASA fallout of Tang can be identified and brought to the market in the future.

The hot optical topics that bear watching are manifold. They cover a wide range of possibilities, from technical applications to possible consumer products.

Complex aspheric optical components can revolutionize the industry, if they can be made economically. The need in SDI is for large components. Astronomers need large optics, but few others do. The likely commercialization here is the possible rebirth of the optical component industry in the United States using as a base some of the fabrication techniques now being developed. Optical fabrication is a traditional industry, but is amenable to some change. The largest commercial revolution already taking place is in the production of moderate to high-quality small-diameter glass components using direct molding techniques for mass production.

A more likely immediate application is some of the aspects of adaptive optics, including automatic aberration compensation and image stabilization that would improve the quality of image collection devices. Incorporating on chip image processing devices to correct for background clutter would provide a new class of imaging devices ideally equipped for use as robotic sensors.

The addition of coherent detection permits gathering or moving object signatures leading to the identification of target form. Such a powerful active image sensor would permit the automation of many processes that are hard to implement at the present time. The incorporation of artificial intelligence techniques into such a device would permit a robotic sensor to learn to distinguish the benign from threats in its local environment. Such a compact optical device would possibly make a useful local security sensor. Rather than screen incoming missiles, a sophisticated home security device could emerge from a combination of optical and electronic technologies that are being researched under the SDI label. Communication using optics and optical techniques is already big business. The extension of optical free space communications, as the tracking problems are overcome, is a likely new growth field.

Computation with an all-optical digital computer is likely many years off. SDI research should eventually lead to an investigation of computer architectures that are amenable to such processes. It is likely that the architecture and the computational bandwidth will have to be adapted to the set of human needs before a commercial market develops.

The hybridizing of optical techniques and electronics is likely to emerge as the major growth area in the near future. Optical mass memories and parallel optical data transfer to and from electronic computers have already appeared.

In conclusion, one may predict fallout from the sophistication of optical systems unable for SDI purposes. However, the reality of scale and economics must be appreciated before commercialization occurs. Since there is little tradition attached to the new areas of quantum engineering, it is likely that these will be the first areas of exploitation.

The road to commercialization in optics is a rocky one at best, and is complicated further by the requirements of an SDI program. The failure to complete SDI projects in an orderly way is an inhibition on the mature development of technologies that might otherwise make it to the commercial world. A decision process that permits consistent funding for technologies that are of general application needs to be established.

We are entering perhaps the most exciting growth periods for electro-optics. Commercialization of research results needs to be done on a timely basis in order to meet the threat of international competition. The principal initiative in optical markets left the United States some 30 years ago. The optical business in the United States has since been in the area of specialized precision optics and high technology mass-market goods, such as the disc camera. A lead on new technologies can be regained, but others are already spending significant planned effort directly upon the commercial arena. The heavy funding of technology programs by SDI appears to offer opportunity. Unfortunately the shifting sands of attention can lead to a loss of the technical momentum that is being generated.

16

ADVANCED MATERIALS FOR SDI: PROMISES AND PROSPECTS

STANLEY I. WEISS

As in other high technology ventures, the Strategic Defense Initiative depends upon technological advances in all disciplines, from the computer and data sciences through communications, satellites, sensors and electronics, and energy physics. All of these in some measure touch on critical materials, either existing or necessary to development. Some of these may eventually be revolutionary in their impact on society or at least on our engineering and scientific communities. Thus, in recent years the Apollo program nurtured a slowly developing computer and semi-conductor effort into explosive growth and utilization beyond any previous expectations. The Space Shuttle also generated some striking applications of ceramics and composites. These "generated by need" developments will inevitably have their parallels in SDI.

While it may be hard to identify all realms of new materials technology, we can certainly start the process by tracing the mission requirements for an effective strategic defense. Since most of these have been addressed previously, let me summarize by cataloging and characterizing the flowdown from mission need to material need.

In a generalized sense there are three major aspects of the strategic defense process: surveillance and identification, acquisition and tracking, and combat and weapon utilization, including self-defense and survivability. Each of these elements requires new and technologically advanced solutions for their effective implementation. All of them require interaction, together with information and data handling of massive proportions, and in the long run all of them must be achieved affordably. In speculatively assessing material requirements I would like to recatalog these missions in a slightly different fashion: (1) surveillance, tracking, and acquisition, (2) weapons systems, and (3) transportation for these systems.

SURVEILLANCE, TRACKING, AND ACQUISITION

As we look at the classes of objects and occurrences that overhead surveillance systems must successfully observe, the key material problems would appear to lie with (1) the sensor and detector systems necessary for both rapid and accurate response, and (2) the ability to translate sensing into useful data and to communicate this to the nerve centers of SDI battle management.

In addition, survivability to hostile radiation and jamming will become a large factor in their utilization. Thus, passive infrared (IR) detectors and mirrors must be capable of surviving radiation environments ranging from heat to X rays to concurrent IR frequencies. One can anticipate the expansion of use of mercury cadmium (mercad) telluride for the infrared detector devices and focal planes necessary for the passive detector systems that will be the linchpins of our satellite surveillance activity. Countermeasures to jamming and negation center on spectrally modified nongrey coatings that are derived from commercially available materials. Since these depend on the binder components, resistive to high temperature, their development can clearly expand their existing commercial applications for the same.

Another aspect of the surveillance systems is their need to carry much more substantial payloads than current programs; thus weight criticality is an increasingly important factor. Relative to this area of concern, and also associated with survivability, is the use of composites, which together with applications being exploited in aircraft and other weapons systems designs will lead to improved and more economic processes. In addition amalgams with other elements will yield proliferated use of metal matrix materials and a lowered cost for other applications. Some metal matrixes, especially alumina fiber-reinforced aluminum alloys, are just starting to see application in wear-resistance applications—as silicon carbide whisker-reinforced aluminum composites are finding initial usage where high rigidity and moderately high-temperature lightweight structures are required.

While not exclusively a province of satellite payloads, antiradiation vulnerability aspects likewise will expand and even hasten the practical development and affordability of gallium arsenide microelectronics. These crystals, which have been laboratory items for the past ten years, are starting to receive the investment emphasis that will take them to practical availability and widespread uses in design for survivability as well as for the densely packaged electronics necessary for these powerful satellite systems. Other elements of survivability will also occasion the use of optical fibers for internal circuitry, particularly those connecting command and control networks that, along with the GaAs technology, will be necessary to support the speed of processing required for these detection and targeting systems.

We are also becoming increasingly aware that lasers in various frequency domains can be effectively used to negate our satellites and even our antiballistic missile weaponry. Here the need for resistant optical coatings and for materials with supertoughness to sustain radiation damage represent critical development needs. For the former, use of silicon carbide mirrors and high-purity silica for stiffness and high-thermal figure of merit represent a potential for new materials, while perfectly pure beryllium and defect-free molybdenum mirror development are leading to techniques for processing these hitherto unworkable metals. By learning to work with these materials that have not been exploited because of processing difficulties, there should be many applications.

Availability breeds attempt. Here I might note that the "LI900" virtually pure silica thermal protection material used for the Shuttle tiles is just finding its initial application to antennas requiring survivability under laser attack; this may lead to other special uses that this relatively high-cost material can satisfy.

I should not depart from the surveillance topic without dealing with the ground-based systems necessary to process and transfer data derived from the sensor intelligence device uses. These are associated with command and control elements that are intrinsic to the overall networks tying surveillance, acquisition, and targeting and the battle management control of weapons together. Achieving survivability in space-borne elements is insufficient if the communications and ground-based processing and management systems are themselves vulnerable. Thus fiber optics become a major contribution to ground-based links as do materials that counter electromagnetic pulse and high-radiation nuclear burst environments, the same considerations for which the electronics involved were cited in space systems.

WEAPONS SYSTEMS

On the weapons side there are many potential ground- and space-based systems that provide incentives if not demands for unique material developments. While I cannot cite all of them, a number of intriguing possibilities should be noted. The first of these could be associated with hypervelocity weapons driven by small nuclear bursts and/or strong current pulses within a confined barrel, i.e., the equivalent of a super cannon. Here those high temperature shocks and loads induced by the high heat and pressure pulses suggest requirements for high ductility and high fracture toughness materials that maintain these properties under high heat loads. One can conceive of special ceramic linings for high-purity metals or special alloys used for the barrels. One can also visualize surrounding this cannon in a cryogenic gas coolant.

High-velocity kinetic vehicles launched through the atmosphere as terminal or midcourse weapons will also require high-friction heat resistance with relatively light weight as a critical factor. The alluminum alloy research toward a 900° metal and the very-high-temperature titanium base materials programs initiated by the Air Force Materials Laboratory augur unique potential for these needs. Perhaps even more important for this type of weapon will be the survivability of the homing and terminal sensors in the 2,000° temperatures induced by these 7 km/sec projectiles—unique materials, especially if devised for mass production, will indeed tax our laboratories' skills.

TRANSPORTATION

Of course, another realm of SDI requirements lies in the transportation of all its elements, whether satellites to orbit or weapons to critical deployment locations and altitudes. Certainly conventional aircraft, rockets, and space boosters will play major roles, but one new program to be supported by the SDI initiative may bring as many new material developments as all others combined: This is the Hypersonic Vehicle leading to an aircraft flight in the early 1990s. This Mach 4–14 reconnaissance weapons carrier, single stage to orbit craft, initiated by DARPA and NASA, is already cited as dependent upon critical materials developments. Mission characteristics can lead to actively cooled structures, ultra-lightweight tank concepts, and advanced hydrogen-fueled propulsion. Materials for high-temperature operations and extremely high strength/weight ratios lead not only to carbon-composites, but silica-based ceramics noted earlier and rapid solidification metals. Among these is niobium, a low-density refractory metal, promising because of its excellent ductility and resistance to thermal shock, with a high melting point of 2,470°C. The use of rapid solidification techniques and containerless processing are proposed to permit creating new niobium-silica alloys for strength ductility and toughness and, importantly, superior oxidation resistance. One can of course envision applications to commercial ultra-high-speed aircraft as well as uses similar to those found for titanium and particularly for rocket motors and hot gas management systems.

COMMERCIALIZATION

How do we relate the materials developed for, or associated with, the development of the Strategic Defense Initiative to potential applications for commercial purposes? Let's take some of the SDI-required materials noted above and address a few of the possible applications.

With respect to sensor and electronic materials, one could envision the use of mercad telluride in earth sensing systems, particularly for broadband coverage—that is to say 4 to 12 microns. One can even contemplate their application for infrared "radar" systems for obstacle avoidance for cars and other vehicles, robotic or driven, or even as locater and homing devices. The high-fracture, high-toughness materials clearly have applications for naval ships and icebreakers and are likely to be highly beneficial in oil drilling facilities, including submersible systems, both manned and unmanned. Applications for commercial rocket motors and for very advanced gas turbine and cryogenically fueled engines should also be expected. Applications of this sort should lead to others not easily defined by one whose background is largely in the aerospace business. For example, titanium is now being used increasingly in chemical plants—something that would not have occurred technically or economically but for expanding uses in aircraft and missiles. Some of the needed ceramics can well find another role in ultra-high-speed turbine blades and the coatings for sensors for application to high-temperature processes. Here, control systems involving cameras and robots in high-temperature environments become obvious candidates.

In this brief chapter it has been possible to provide only a few speculations. It is hoped that scientists in the laboratories that support this vital program will be stimulated to invent and imagine many others in their paths to meeting SDI needs in practical, affordable fashion. We should remember that most new commercial technologies were not predictable from their original inception elsewhere, but came about by unique contributions of creative individuals filling perceived needs. And history will repeat.

17

BIOTECHNOLOGY, BIOPROCESSING RESEARCH, AND SPACE: INGREDIENTS FOR NEW HEALTH CARE PRODUCTS

BALDWIN H. TOM

The new health care and pharmaceutical products for the twenty-first century will result from today's developments in the biotechnologies. We will be fed, maintain health, control disease, clean and control our environment utilizing genetic engineering technology. Indeed, super-intelligent, high-speed computers run on biochips may serve to orchestrate the new world of genetically engineered cells and organisms.[1] In this chapter I will discuss biotechnology's role in the future and space bioprocessing as a new frontier for biological discoveries.

Biotechnology will be the dominant driver in developing new health care products in the twenty-first century. In support of the biotechnology efforts, however, new developments in large-scale cultivation of mammalian cells in bioreactors will be necessary. In addition, production-scale purification techniques will be important in isolating the desired products from dilute solutions. The latter areas are both domains of bioprocessing research. The availablity of the space environment through the Space Shuttle, and subsequently the Space Station, will provide another tool and unique resources to support bioprocessing technologies. If space bioprocessing succeeds in supporting biotechnologies, the United States can expect to maintain its preeminent position in developing new biomedical technologies.

BIOTECHNOLOGY

What is this biotechnology? Biotechnology is the study of the engineering of a product from a living cell. Genetic engineering (e.g., gene cloning, recombinant DNA processing) and hybridomamonoclonal antibody production are examples of biotechnologies. It has been estimated that 40 percent of our consumer products are from organic synthesis.

By the twenty-first century, this percentage should rise considerably. These advances will require the close collaboration of engineers and biologists.

What is the value of these technologies? In 1985 the monoclonal antibody diagnostics market was $207 million. It is projected to exceed $1.7 billion by 1990, an eightfold increase.[2] Cancer therapeutics and diagnostics sales are projected to be $2 billion by 1995. This is impressive from an industry less than ten years old. The first genetically engineered product, insulin (from Genentech and marketed by Eli Lilly), is on the market and produced $25-30 million in 1984.[3] While our focus is on health care products, the applications of these biotechnologies in agriculture and animal husbandry could yield even greater monetary returns.

BIOPROCESSING

Since cells must be grown in nutrient broth, the materials produced by genetically engineered cells and microorganisms are invariably mixed with other cell products, along with an abundance of fluid. Consequently, the key to success in producing desired products includes not only the ability to grow large amounts of cells, but also the means to isolate and concentrate the high-value product from the aqueous mixture. The large-scale *production* of cells and the *purification* of products underlie bioprocessing research (Table 17.1). The Bioprocessing Research Center at Houston, along with the Center for Separation Science in Tucson and the Bioprocessing and Pharmaceutical Research Center in Philadelphia, were all developed in 1985 to begin focusing on these problems.

SPACE: BIOLOGY'S NEW FRONTIER

Overview

The decision by the United States to develop a Space Station to ensure America's continuous presence in space brings with it new potentials and scientific challenges. Space is a new frontier for biology. Space, as a potential research and production laboratory for biological sciences, has accomplished two things: (1) generated a new sense of teamwork in the research community, and (2) provided the United States a new resource in the highly competitive biotechnology field.

Without considering commercial ramifications, or new technological developments, one major response to the access of space from the research community is the fostering of new collaborative relationships between scientists of diverse backgrounds and of different institutions

Table 17.1
Space Resources and Biotechnology Needs

		Resources
● Shuttle	Space Station	• Microgravity
		• Vacuum
		• Temperature extremes
		• Radiation
		Requirements
● Biotechnologies	Bioprocessing	• Large-scale growth
		• Purification

Source: Compiled by the author.

focused on exploiting the resources of this new frontier. Space is serving as a *catalyst*, rekindling the pioneer spirit that was once in all of us. There is a new sense of mission, a new community spirit among research scientists to brainstorm, to discuss, and to investigate this new challenge. The team we have assembled includes scientists from four Houston-area universities, NASA, the Johnson Space Center (JSC), and McDonnell Douglas. The benefits from the team efforts generated by space research opportunities, such as in the bioengineering and biomedical fields, will include the efficient use of resources, funds, and manpower. When minds of different persuasion interact in this atmosphere, one should anticipate new bursts of ideas and creativity. The scientific frontiers that are being explored are so fascinating that financial reward may be incidental.

Current Status

Space serves as another tool for scientists. It provides unlimited resources of microgravity, high vacuum, extremes of heat and cold, and full-spectrum radiation (see table 17.1). A key element in the development of genetically engineered pharmaceuticals is the ability to grow large numbers of cells and subsequently to be able to separate the desired pharmaceutical product from waste products released by the same cells. This purification is greatly affected by gravity-driven influences, such as sedimentation and heat convective mixing. Space, with the gravity complication eliminated, has now been proven to have great potential for the purification of clinically valuable pharmaceuticals. Based on early studies by Dr. Grant Barlow on the Apollo-Soyuz flight, McDonnell Douglas developed an electrophoresis system capable of purifying production quantities of human hormones and cells. Recent space shuttle

Table 17.2
Candidate Products for Space Bioprocessing

Typical Products	Medical Use	Estimated Number of Annual Patients (U.S.)
Immunoglobulins	Emphysema	100,000
Antihemophilic factors VIII and IX	Hemophilia	20,000
Beta cells	Diabetes	600,000
Epidermal growth factors	Burns	150,000
Erythropoietin	Anemia	1,600,000
Immune serum	Viral infections	185,000
Interferon	Viral infections	10,000,000
Granulocyte stimulating factor	Wounds	2,000,000
Lymphocytes	Antibody production	600,000
Pituitary cells	Dwarfism	850,000
Transfer factor	Leprosy/multiple sclerosis	550,000
Urokinase	Blood clots	1,000,000

Source: Adapted from D. R. Morrison, "Bioprocessing in Space: An Overview," The World Biotech Report 1984, Vol. 2 (Middlesex, U.K.: Online Publications, 1984).

experiments with the Continuous Flow Electrophoresis System (CFES) demonstrated that over 700 times more protein per unit time can be purified than on earth by the same method. This has been described as equivalent to one year's work in an afternoon.[4] This project is the farthest along in yielding a pharmaceutical product for commercialization. Sometime in 1990 McDonnell Douglas will fly their 2.5 ton production unit (equivalent to 24 basic CFES units) in the shuttle's cargo bay. Some candidate pharmaceutical products for processing in space are listed in Table 17.2.[5]

Future Growth in Space Bioprocessing

In part, continued growth in space bioprocessing will depend on the successful development of McDonnell Douglas's pharmaceutical product. NASA/JSC has already made a commitment to design a space bioreactor to complement the CFES. This should support future production of other cellular products and enhance the attractiveness of space as a usable cell culture laboratory. Cultivation of cells in space may have distinct advantages for some cell populations, especially if the cells are fragile (Table 17.3). Also, there has been a suggestion that some cells may secrete more product in space than on earth.

The first made-in-space product is the latex microspheres presently

Table 17.3
Space Bioprocessing: Advantages in Microgravity Processing

● Large-scale growth
  • Reduced cell damage
  • No sedimentation
  • Enhanced product secretion
	● Purification
	  • No heat convective mixing
	  • No particle sedimentation
	  • No zone sedimentation

Source: Compiled by the author.

Table 17.4
Products, Services, and Technologies for Space Bioprocessing and Commercialization

● New technology
  • Bioreactor
  • Monitoring
  • Miniaturization
  • Purification
	● Inexpensive drugs
	● New Drugs
	  • Protein crystals
	  • Synthetic drugs
	● New cell biology
	● New membrane production

Source: Compiled by the author.

being sold by the National Bureau of Standards at $434,000 per ounce, or $384 for a five milliliter vial of 30 million spheres.[6] Although these uniform spheres are being used as calibration particles for instruments, other types of "tailored" spheres could be produced for uniform packing of chromatography columns for protein purifications. Some enterprising group might develop this into a new space service. Another area of promise is the production of protein crystals in space. In the absence of heat convection and sedimentation, large and uniform crystals have been formed.[7] The significance in producing such protein crystals is in their use for characterizing molecular structure with X ray crystallography. Structural information on a molecule is essential for "redesigning" new molecules, such as for cancer therapy. Hence, a potential exists for developing a service to provide high-purity crystals. As more space-related research is carried out on earth with an eye toward exploiting space resources (See Tables 17.2 and 17.3), it is anticipated that other products, services, and technologies will develop. A list of potential candidate areas is in Table 17.4.

At present it is not possible to assign a meaningful market value to space commercialization. Early estimates were provided by the Center for Space Policy, Inc., which ranged from $16 to $50 billion by the year 2000.[8] A comprehensive study on space bioprocessing's commercial opportunities and market projections is being prepared.[9]

SUMMARY

In this chapter, we have suggested the coupling of biotechnologies with space bioprocessing as a means to develop new commercial markets in the health care field. Although there are several potential products, it is still too early to predict whether this space biotechnology industry will become a commercial success. On the other hand, those of us involved in this research are acutely aware of the challenge of the Japanese for our present preeminent position in the biotechnology world. Although the biotechnology industry is still developing, its promises and potential for producing new technology and new goods are awesome.

In 1983, the United States provided $520 million for biotechnology research, with 98 percent in basic studies; 2 percent ($10.4 million) was used in applied (commercialization) research. During the same period, the Japanese spent $60 million on research, with over 50 percent, or $30 million, in applied research.[10] There is little doubt that Japan believes that biotechnology efforts will provide a handsome return. The Japanese Bio-Industry Development Center predicts $60.7 billion in biotechnology-derived sales by the year 2000.

The National Commission on Space recently held hearings in Houston to solicit ideas on the civilian use of space.[11] The comments touched on the various components and conditions needed to fully utilize space and its resources:

1. NASA must maintain and, indeed, reduce the cost for shuttle flights in order to attract greater use from entrepreneurs. NASA should develop a second-generation shuttle for commercial use in contrast to the transportation focus of the present shuttles.

2. Government needs to provide tax benefits, subsidies, and insurance assistance to minimize the high risk of space ventures and to attract more investors.

3. Universities need to provide adequate education to produce future practitioners of space science, technology, and commercialization.

4. Financial (investment) institutions need to educate their members to the potential and strategic significance of space commerce, and to support these ventures.

The United States still maintains a preeminent position in space sciences and in biotechnologies. These positions can be retained only through national initiatives, and these will be costly. However, it is critically important that adequate amounts of funds and opportunities are provided so our best minds can explore and develop these resources. How we respond to the above needs will determine the future success of space biotechnologies and the new health care products of the twenty-first century.

NOTES

1. J. B. Tucker, "Biochips: Can Molecules Compute?" *High Technology*, February, 1984, pp. 36–47.
2. D. Stipp, "Biotechnology Becomes Business in Transition," *Wall Street Journal*, September 3, 1985, p. 6.
3. A. Klausner, "And Then There Were Two." *Bio/Technology* 3, no. 7: 605–612, 1985.
4. P. Todd, "Space Bioprocessing." *Bio/Technology* 3:786–780 (September, 1985).
5. D. R. Morrison, "Bioprocessing in Space—An Overview." *The World Biotech Report 1984*, Vol. 2, Middlesex, U.K.: Online Publications, 1984.
6. D. Dooling, "Orbital Processing." *Commercial Space*, Summer 1985, pp. 14–20.
7. Todd.
8. G. Miglicco, "Shuttle Launches of Satellites Are Making Space a Bottomline Business." *Commercial Space*, Summer 1985, pp. 36–39.
9. *Space R & D Alert Newsletter*, September 2, 1985 (350 Cabrini Blvd., New York, NY 10040).
10. M. D. Dibner, "Biotechnology in Pharmaceuticals: The Japanese Challenge." *Science* 229:1230–1235, 1985.
11. C. Byars, "Space Panel Listens to Ideas on Goals from Houston Public." *Houston Chronicle*, October 16, 1985.

PART V
PERSPECTIVES ON COMMERCIALIZATION

18

VIEWS ON SDI COMMERCIAL POTENTIAL

WILLIAM GREGORY

The commercial potential of SDI is much on the minds of the aerospace industry in the United States. It is also much on the minds of European aerospace and defense companies. Part of this interest relates to the amount of R&D resources destined for this program as they directly affect future sales. An equally substantial part of this interest bears directly on the question of this volume: the potential commercial fallout from the Strategic Defense Initiative.

Critics of the so-called Star Wars Program (a name that causes the program director, Lt. Gen. James Abrahamson, to groan with dismay) argue that the technical challenge is so immense that the goals of the research are not achievable. There are many in industry who share the concern over the difficulties that lie ahead for a workable missile defense. Where the two camps divide is over the question of whether the game is worth the candle. Industry skeptics consider the potential strategic advantages as worth the risks themselves. Furthermore, they believe the technological stimulation will be immense—the biggest of its kind since the Apollo Program. It is this fallout that convinces the middle of the roaders that the game is indeed worth the candle.

From my perspective, technology transfer is analogous to the person extolling the wonders of a new golf ball to his partner: "It has day-glo paint to make it easy to see in the dusk. It has a beeper to find it in the rough. It emits a stream of bubbles to mark its lie in the water." His partner cried, "fantastic. Where can I buy one?" to which the owner replied, "I don't know. I found it."

Where technology transfers come from is about as obscure as the source of that golf ball. Industry generally accepts the notion that technology from defense or NASA space programs does transfer to the commercial sector, but the trail from defense item A to commercial product B is often a tortuous one. Defense hardware is usually too expensive and overdesigned to move directly into the civilian world. It may also be too temperamental or require too much skilled maintenance for direct adaptation.

The transistor is a veteran example of transfer, yet the transistor was not invented in a military-funded program. It came out of private development at Bell Laboratories. Considerable military allocations went into its development, but so did considerable private money. Military development of miniaturized electronics clearly led to the development of consumer products like the Sony Walkman or the pocket calculator, but I will wager that the circuitry and components are hybridized rather than out-and-out adoption of military hardware.

In recent years, commercial development of components has gone its own way, and the military found its requirements were getting short shrift in the world of much larger commercial markets. So the military has had to fund its own development program for very high speed integrated circuit development. Eventually, I am sure, VHSIC technology will transfer to the commercial marketplace even though the commercial marketplace has not stimulated the research effort the Air Force felt it needed.

Technology transfer is a two-way street, an example being the jet engine. Its development in World War II was purely a military project, but it was not long into the 1950s when the British put the jet engine into a commercial transport, the Comet. Many skeptics argued that the jet engine accelerated too slowly, burned too much fuel, and would cost too much to maintain or operate in the commercial world. (The turboprop engine was thought to be the hybrid that would solve these problems.) Most of that, of course, was wrong.

Accidents ruined the advent of the early Comet, but had nothing to do directly with the jet engine. They related to structural fatigue with high fuselage pressurization and frequent cycles. The Air Force J57 military engine modified for commercial service powered the first Boeing 707 and DC-8 transports and instantly displayed reliability, with immense passenger appeal in speed and smoothness that left the turboprop confined to smaller aircraft fields. Acceleration and fuel consumption were indeed problems and the commercial marketplace stimulated the development of the turbofan engine that alleviated these shortcomings. The fan was fed into the military market. An Air Force large cargo transport, the Lockheed C-5, sponsored development of the high bypass fan engine, but Pratt & Whitney in this country and Rolls-Royce in England developed higher thrust requirements in their C-5 engine, and also developed bigger powerplants for civil aircraft. In the most recent turn of the wheel, commercially developed turbofan engines are due to power the Air Force C-17 cargo transport. As I started out to say, technology transfer is a two-way street, with lots of bends in the road.

Recognizing a bright idea is also an impediment. During the war, the U.S. military had a vehicle called "The Duck" for traversing swampy ground, or water, or whatever. It had a rudimentary system for adjusting tire pressures from a central location during operation. The U.S. forgot about the idea after the war, but not the Soviets. They had U.S. ducks via lend-lease and set about improving the system. We found out about the improvements and now LTV's Hummer has a much more sophisticated central system for changing tire pressures for operation in soft sand. Goodyear has a similar system on its candidate vehicle for a small mobile intercontinental ballistic missile system. It seems like a natural system for commercialization in off-the-road vehicles, or even for passenger cars, but Goodyear indicates nothing is in the works.

There is a parallel in antiskid braking systems. Military aircraft had them back in the 1950s and commercial aircraft adopted them quickly. Now antiskid systems are available for cars and trucks, but the transfer process was a long one, for reasons that included availability of alternate approaches to the skid problem, like tires with improved traction.

Another reason why technology transfer is not an obvious process is that hardware—products—may not be involved at all. When the Rockwell Company acquired North American Aviation 15 years ago, technology transfer was a principal objective. As the Rockwell people told me at the time, however, they were as much interested in processes as in product. Manufacturing processes do not have the pizazz of hardware and get relatively little attention. That is deliberate, for processes are at the heart of know-how, as in good old American know-how. Processes are basic to industrial leadership, but their transfer into and out of government programs is difficult to trace because of confidentiality and the small number of people involved in any one of them.

All this is saying that industry visualizes the same sort of technical fallout from the Strategic Defense Initiative that it did from the jet engine or that it expects from the VHSIC program. There are lists of the specific kinds of technologies that will benefit from the research program. They include advanced high-speed computing capability, laser technology, sensors, and precision pointing. My opinion, though, is that the eventual fallout technologies are still over the horizon, but will emerge from the basic university/industry research that the program is sponsoring.

My guess is that these lists are valid as far as they go, but that in the end the technology that falls out is only dimly perceived now and probably has not even been invented yet.

Something is analogous to the Strategic Defense Initiative in the gestation of commercial space. Numerous forecasts have been made about the commercialization of space, e.g. pharmaceuticals. One manufacturing development program has already flown a couple of times on the space shuttle and several pharmaceutical companies teamed with universities are planning small, getaway, special-type experiments in orbit. The John Deere Metallurgical and General Motors' Crystal Growing work have been covered in the press, for they are rare examples of nonaerospace companies putting their own money into space research.

These research efforts are aimed at better understanding crystalization for improved materials. But production is intended for earth. A significant part of the commercialization of space is expected to be just this kind of work: basic research in a gravity-free enviroment for a better understanding of how things happen in nature. Manfacturing in space may not result at all from these experiments.

Another facet of technology transfer in commercial space is Max Faget's new company, Space Industries, Inc. of Houston. Max had a long career at the Johnson Space Center, and played a major role in most U.S. Manned Space Flight Programs. After retirement from NASA, he started a company to build a free-flying module that the Space Shuttle would drop off in space and revisit for service and replenishment. It is aimed at commercial users like 3M or John Deere. Interestingly enough, Space Industries is not going exclusively to aerospace companies to build this platform, though one may be selected as an integrating contractor. High prices may be one factor, but Max is also interested in the experience of a contractor like Brown and Root in ocean-based oil drilling platforms and the dynamics of their industry. It could be a typical case of mixed technology transfer: some from aerospace, some from the commercial world and, in the end, a difficult trail to follow.

Space Industries's platform is not directly connected with the Space Station. It will come first, and NASA is hoping for reverse technology transfer from the commercial platform to utilize in Space Station design and development. There will be technology from the Space Station that ought to be ripe for commercialization. One example is the work at NASA Langley on quick-connect, quick-disconnect couplings for truss members to be used on the Space Station power tower structure. Langley has an astronaut's space suit glove for demonstration, and, on earth at least, it is perfectly feasible to work with these couplings while wearing a cumbersome outfit.

European industry is as vitally concerned with the commercial possibilities from the space station as it is with the Strategic Defense Initiative. In the Space Station case, European industry is eager for participation. The governments are worried about costs and benefits, and about who get what piece of the program.

With the military strategic defense program, the attitude is much more guarded. There is significant political complexity regarding European participation in SDI. Part of the reason is security. The assasination of a German jet engine company head in his home by terrorists left European industry with a bad case of the jitters about cooperation with the United States in a military program, particularly one as politically charged as SDI.

At the same time, European industry is just as aware as U.S. industry of the potential technology bonanza from SDI. Despite concern over costs, European industry fears it will be left behind if it does not join the party. Furthermore, it is worried over a new brain drain to the United States if U.S. companies are working on such state-of-the-art technologies and European companies are not.

Reaction is the same on a broad spectrum of technology transfer questions. Industry is concerned about cost and risk in commercialization of space. Critics of the Strategic Defense Initiative warn of cost and risk in this program. European governments and industry worry about cost and risk in the space station and in the strategic initiative. The bottom line seems to come out the same, nevertheless. In today's technological competition, no player can afford not to participate.

Perceptions are critical to technology transfer. It's like the fellow who bought a water bed, surrounded it with mirrors and soft stereo music, and told a friend he was going to name it the tides of passion. His wife sidled up to the friend later and whispered: "he ought to call it the dead sea." Technology transfer in the view of some engineers has been something of a dead sea. Engineers know that there is technology sitting in the bank that could have commercial uses. Getting the word around about its existence is a difficult challenge. Making the transfer successfully is even more complex. It helps to have a dedicated effort to develop technology transfer the way the Strategic Defense Initiative is doing. There will be results, but they will take patience.

19

LEGAL PERSPECTIVES OF COMMERCIALIZATION

RICHARD A. GIVENS

THE CHALLENGE

A strong technological base and the dedication of our people are essential twin pillars forming the foundation of long-term national security.

The development of our technological base is powerfully assisted by defense purposes themselves, as most spectacularly illustrated by the efforts required by World War II and the "Arsenal of Democracy" on our productive capacity. At the same time, civilian technology furnishes the broader foundation upon which advances crucial to national defense—and the basic strength of the national economy—must rest.

Thus it is obvious that multiple-purpose technologies, with both defense and civilian applications, occupy a special position, with multiple benefits for defense, both direct and indirect. For this reason, affirmative actions to stimulate such cross-fertilization are of strategic importance.

To achieve the greatest results, these efforts must include means to insure that the legal system functions as a support mechanism for such development, rather than primarily as an obstacle.[1]

Some of the questions that need to be confronted to realize this objective include the following:

1. Identification of civilian technologies that may have critical defense applications, and hence defense benefits if accelerated—such as alternatives or sources for scarce strategic materials, or materials subject to political or other hostile interruption.[2]

2. Development of means to insure that existing agencies use current authority to promote national goals to the greatest extent possible.[3]

3. Development of means to accelerate approvals, permits, and favorable interpretations of existing law where possible, especially where multiple agencies

at multiple levels of government may become involved in permitting or impeding developments important to the national interest.[4]

4. Securing public support where necessary without disclosing critical information to totalitarian adversaries.[5]

5. Preventing the handing over of key information to totalitarian adversaries, while at the same time permitting (or where possible encouraging) use of technologies for civilian purposes, where the benefits of widening the base for their development offset the risks of doing so.[6]

6. Promoting the commitment of private capital to technological developments vital to the national interest where financial risks, the expense of longer time horizons, are balanced by appropriate financial rewards. (We must in this context appreciate the "escape" of benefits to society at large; when commercial returns are not fully capturable by the inventor or investor, suboptimal investment are the result.[7]

POSSIBLE APPROACHES

Numerous possible approaches to these challenges can be developed, many of which have multiple applications to more than one of the problems. While none can be fully canvased here, the following represent possible options that may justify further consideration:

1. *Education of the public concerning the importance of technology to the nation's future.* The primary reasons why we are materially better off today than in prior centuries are, in addition to advanced technology, our relatively feisty, open economy that permits correction of some of its mistakes more than do heavily bureaucratized systems.[8] Today, concerns about the abuses of technology have led to a "technology assessment" movement, focusing on review of proposed technological activities with a view to stopping those that may be harmful. This is too narrow a perspective. By affirmatively identifying and encouraging needed technologies—and substitutes for troublesome ones—the national interest may be served more effectively, creating new options for the future. Efforts to explain this wider perspective to the public—and means of implementing it—are critical.

2. *Focus on long-term commitments.* Our society has the tremendous advantages of its relatively open marketplace and freedom of expression permitting correction of both economic and political errors more readily than is the case in obsolete bureaucratic systems. At the same time we lack mechanisms for making long-term commitments crucial to development of strategically vital technologies on a sustained basis.[9] The causes? In the public sector, annual budget uncertainty and focus on the next election; and in the private sector, concentration on the quarterly bottom line and fear of hostile takeovers if the price of the stock falls.

Both mechanisms sometimes obscure longer-term goals.[10] With the additional advantage of enhanced focus on longer-term goals, open societies might possess an overwhelmingly decisive advantage.[11] The mere promulgation of the Strategic Defense Initiative itself, of course, represents a step in this direction.

3. *Enhancing the scope of national goals.* It may well be that over the long pull, totalitarian dictatorships are inherently incompatible with the internal restraints on rash or unwise action necessary in the nuclear age. If so, the national goal of the peaceful victory of freedom suggested by President Harry S. Truman in his valedictory State of the Union Address of 1953[12] and taken up by both Richard M. Nixon and John F. Kennedy in different ways in 1960,[13] may again become worthy of articulation in today's new circumstances. Such a peaceful victory might occur if future leaders in totalitarian nations were forced to recognize that their systems had become decisively obsolete. A goal of this scope could well generate efforts on a corresponding scale—by means that would necessarily include those under discussion here.

4. *Explicit definition of technological objectives.* By executive action or through a mechanism created by legislation, national scientific and technological goals requiring additional encouragement in the national interest could be articulated.[14] This would help lead existing agencies to use their vast discretionary power to promote those goals. Space industrialization and colonization, for example, would furnish the base from which immense strategic advantages would flow; the society— open or closed—that leads in the development of the resources of the solar system will obviously decide the course of events on this planet. The economies of scope and scale created by both defense-related and economic developments will mutually accelerate each other.

5. *One-stop approvals.* If legislation were enacted pursuant to which goals were defined, the "Supremacy Clause" could be utilized to permit one agency to handle all approvals relevant at all levels of government.[15] Otherwise, executive action might accomplish this at the federal level alone.[16]

6. *Use of long-term funding.* Where direct defense objectives are involved, multiyear funding is more cost-effective as well as goal-effective—and releases time of congressional overseers to look at systemic issues rather than details.[17] Where private efforts have synergistic benefits to national security, and thus deserve encouragement beyond what would be provided by the commercial market *alone* (as recognized by the business roundtable[18]), public investment through such means as loans or loan guarantees may be justified. Such support, however, must be limited to research and development only and not extend to actual ongoing economic activity that would compete with other private-sector

activity and require bailouts if unsuccessful[19] (recall the synfuel subsidies). Where commercialization is possible, the advantages of this approach over straight contract or grants are:

- potential payback to the program, creating a strategic R&D revolving fund (or to the Treasury);
- involvement of private capital and private entrepreneurial energy to limit costs and bureaucratic delays, and to promote follow-through of successful research.[20]

Existing avenues for such support for private research vital to defense objectives but with commercial benefits as well include:

- the Defense Production Act (50 U.S.C. App. §§ 2091, 2092), currently subject to tight monetary limits (§ 2161), which may not reflect the current importance of such research, and
- potentially of even greater importance, the broad discretionary authority of the Federal Reserve System, which includes both persuasive power and the technical powers to rediscount paper from actual commercial transactions (12 U.S.C. § 343) and for member banks that may extend credit for such purposes (12 U.S.C. § 345).

The mere existence of this authority may be enough to permit steps to insure the critical ingredient of *attention* by financial institutions to the potential profitability of defense-related investments with commercial applications—and, of course, evaluation of profitability is relevant to the worthwhileness of investments of this type under our free market system. Such authority was used to prevent consequences of collapse of the silver market and to promote bailout of the Continental Illinois Bank and other troubled institutions.

7. *The proper combination of secrecy where necessary with the necessary availability of data for commercialization where appropriate.* This combination can be achieved under the indispensable secrecy regulations discussed in L. Storch's "Issues in Government Contracting and Secrecy Controls,"[21] with the necessary sensitive approach that takes into account the gains to the national interest from both confidentiality and availability, each where appropriate. To achieve this, consideration might be given to:

- Moving toward consolidation of all approvals in a single agency (Defense is the irreducible agency that must be involved), with other agencies having the opportunity to participate as advocates where they wish.
- Developing articulated goals, taking both aspects of the national interest into account, including the extent of risk from disclosure, the likelihood or unlikelihood of adversaries developing the information quickly or readily from

other sources, and the benefit to the industrial base from availability of the information to the extent proposed.

• The possibility of limiting the location where research is carried on, so that the United States or members of an allied consortium will have the jump on others even if they steal information, because we will have moved a stage beyond by that time. This is even more important in industry than patents or trade secrets in many cases according to Richard C. Levin of Yale University.[22] Such consortia might also help to cement relationships originally developed during World War II and postwar periods.[23]

8. *Developing the strongest possible cadre of sophisticated technological experts with long-term tenure and knowledge of both defense and civilian aspects of critical advances.* At present, military officers assigned on a medium- or long-term basis to procurement projects are often at a disadvantage because of mandatory retirement ages that would not apply to similar technological experts elsewhere, lack of promotion opportunities, and "up or out" requirements that may force them out of the service in spite of outstanding performance. This may cause high turnover or even cause some of the best officers to try to avoid such duty in order to have the best chance to continue to serve the nation. All of this is ripe for reexamination.

If an adequate corps of technological experts were developed with the duty to promote both defense and commercial applications, they would also be in a position to take the lead role in determining whether secrecy or commercial expansion should predominate with regard to particular applications of mixed-use technologies.

Numerous other measures to remove obstacles to industrial innovation are possible,[24] but even more important than specific measures is the general recognition of the critical nature of technological advance for national survival, and of the need for attention to the legal structure for promoting it.

NOTES

1. See, generally, David, "Science Futures: The Industrial Connection" 203 *Science* 837 (1979); Starr and Rudman, "The Parameters of Technological Growth" 1982 *Science* 358 (1973).
2. See Cohen, Heine, and Phillips, "The Quantum Mechanics of Materials," 246 *Scientific American* 82 (1982) (the ability to create materials "to order" from parameters of material desired).
3. For a more detailed exposition of the author's views on this point, see R. Givens, *Legal Strategies for Industrial Innovation*, Chapter 12 (Colorado Springs, Colo: Shepard's/McGraw-Hill, 1985 supplement).
4. See Richardson, "Cutting Regulatory Tape" *New York Times*, December 13, 1984, p. A31.

5. The Task Force on Simplification of the New York State Bar Association is considering recommendations to reduce public disclosure of details of procurement plans through overly specific published appropriation law or committee report provisions, and through public announcements of the issuance, identity of awardees, and locations of implementation of critical defense contracts.

6. See L. Storch, "Issues in Government Contracting and Secrecy Controls," American Bar Association National Institute on Legal Problems of Innovation, Chapter 11 (1983).

7. See Business Roundtable, "Strategy for a Vital U.S. Economy" 31 (May, 1984); "Cover Story," *Business Week*, July 4, 1983, p. 62.

8. For a long-term perspective, see G. Childe, *What Happened in History* (1946).

9. Compare Davis, "New Projects: Beware of False Economies," 85 *Harvard Business Review* 2 (March 1985), p. 95.

10. See Yorke, "What Killed Long-Term U.S. Business Planning," *New York Times*, January 1, 1982, p. A30; "Companies Feel Underrated by the Street," *Business Week*, February 20, 1984 (60 percent of executives believe company undervalued); Sansweet, "Carter Hawley's Trials Show Risk in Adopting Long-Range Strategy: Moves Hurt It in the Short Run and Led to Takeover Bid that was Costly to Fight," *Wall Street Journal*, July 19, 1984, p. 1. " . . . money managers, bankers, accountants, stockholders, and business leaders should be challenged to deemphasize simple short-term financial measures, utilizing instead measures more consistent with long-range competitiveness and profitability." President's Commission on Industrial Competitiveness, Summary of Recommendations 52 (1985).

11. Compare Pipes, "Can the Soviet Union Reform?" 63 *Foreign Affairs* 47 (Fall 1984) with A. Sakharov, *Progress, Coexistence and Intellectual Freedom* (1968); W. Heisenberg, *Physics and Beyond* (1971); B. Klein, *Germany's Economic Preparations for War* (1959).

12. Eighth Annual Message, January 7, 1953, in 3 *State of the Union Messages of the Presidents* 3008–09 (Chelsea House 1966).

13. See references cited in 52 ABAJ 1046 (1966).

14. See New York County Lawyers Association, Report F-1 (1985).

15. See references on preemption authority cited in Handler and Zifchak, "Collective Bargaining and the Antitrust Laws" 81 *Columbia Law Review* 459 (1981).

16. See, generally, Richardson, "Cutting Regulatory Tape," *New York Times*, December 13, 1984, p. A31.

17. See Art, "Congress and the Defense Budget: Enhancing Policy Oversight," 100 *Political Science Quarterly* 227 (Summer 1985).

18. See Business Roundtable, "Strategy for a Vital U.S. Economy," 31 (May 1984); compare "Cover Story," *Business Week*, p. 62.

19. See Givens, Chapter 15, pp. 307–08; Schultze, "Industrial Policy: A Dissent," *Brookings Review* 3 (Fall 1983); Passell, "Banker of Last Resort: But Could an RFC Be Insulated Against Patronage?" *New York Times*, June 4, 1982, p. A30; Pasztor, 'Synfuels Plant Sees $700 Million in Losses by 1995," *Wall Street Journal*, April 11, 1983, p. 3.

20. See Nelson and Langlois, "Industrial Innovation Policy: Lessons from American History" 219 *Science* 814 (February 18, 1983).

21. Storch.
22. R. C. Levin, "Interindustry Differences in R&D Appropriability and Technological Opportunity," Table 2, Preliminary Report, 1984. See also K. Mendelssohn, *The Search for Absolute Zero* (1966) (importance of location of low-temperature laboratories); Norris, "Halting the Flow of High-Tech Bargains," *New York Times*, February 26, 1984, p. F3 (international consortiums, which would obviously function on the basis of contributions and reliability, not one-nation-one-vote or one-nation-one-veto).
23. Compare Anders, "Europeans Offer Reasons for Research Lag," *Wall Street Journal*, February 1, 1984, p. 28; Dickson, "New Push for European Science Cooperation" 220 *Science* 1134 (June 10, 1983).
24. For the author's views, see R. Givens, *Legal Strategies*.

20

COLLABORATIVE ASPECTS OF COMMERCIALIZATION

EUGENE E. STARK, JR.

International attention indicates growing interest in potential commercial spin-offs from the Strategic Defense Initiatives program. This attention reflects demanding technology requirements, including fast, reliable computation and control; high-performance optics and other materials; rugged precision systems; and the underlying manufacturing and quality-control technologies. Thus, the promise is great for a variety of technical breakthroughs to become valuable in the commercial as well as the defense sector.

The commercial potential of these technologies becomes an important issue in the economic strength and international competitiveness of the United States and its partners in SDI. Because economic strength affects national strength and the ability to contribute to a stronger world economy, the net result is a basis for peace through increasing world prosperity.

This important potential impact of the SDI program can be realized only if deliberate, early efforts are made to identify and exploit new technologies. This chapter will cover the important characteristics of the SDI program that impact on commercialization; a general perspective on technology transfer; an analysis of some important issues; and a specific proposed approach to technology transfer in this program.

THE SDI PROGRAM AND COMMERCIALIZATION

SDI has a single, overriding mission: to strengthen the stability of East-West relationships with important defensive technology. The potential for commercial value can be only a secondary aspect of this mission. Because of these clear priorities, a technology commercialization program must complement the SDI program, indeed even contribute to its primary mission.

Understanding the institutional character of SDI is an element in developing a commercialization program. This institutional character comprises an extensive set of organizations of different types, with both cooperation and competition contributing to program success. Participating organizations include: federal laboratories, both government-operated and contractor-operated; large, medium, and small businesses; universities; private research institutions; and various consortia or teams of these participants. Each is different in size, location, institutional culture, and breadth of its role in SDI.

Competition is an aspect of this program, providing the best ideas, innovations, approaches, and costs for the national program. Simultaneously, cooperation is also an element. System R&D requires the complementary expertise of a team of participants; and a system concept it progresses from research to development to prototype construction and eventual deployment; results and expertise may be handed off from some team members to others.

This same diversity is characteristic of efforts to commercialize the resulting technologies. In some areas, cooperation will be needed to recognize, package, develop, and market opportune technologies. In other cases, participants may compete in R&D and in the marketplace with similar technologies.

The match between the SDI program structure and technology commercialization efforts should be developed carefully. Mission-driven cooperation must take absolute precedence over any potential competition for commercial technologies. Commercialization efforts should contribute wherever possible to the SDI prime mission, e.g., by improvements the marketplace can make in cost and performance of technologies needed in SDI systems, and by providing additional channels of cooperation and technical strength among SDI participants. Further, these efforts will place some additional emphasis on innovation and cooperation on a broader scale than just specific SDI system teams.

TECHNOLOGY COMMERCIALIZATION: PERSPECTIVES AND METHODS

Innovation and cooperation are underpinnings of both mission programs and their spin-offs. Much of the perspective described in this section is applicable to both aims, thus reemphasizing the synergistic value to SDI of an effective associated technology commercialization program.

One of the strongest lessons learned in federal laboratory technology transfer is that there is not one magic approach or process; rather, success requires a variety of working methodologies exercised by results-oriented professionals. The heart of these processes is the involvement of individuals networking to recognize and exploit innovation opportunities. Those involved include individual scientists and engineers engaged in research and development, those who serve as technical mentors or opinion-leaders, those with a particular interest in new ideas and their applications, those who are inclined to network extensively with their colleagues in other organizations (gatekeepers), and those who will "champion" a new technology.

A similarly diverse set of methods can move new technologies from one organization to another. These include methods involving individual institutions as well as major cooperative initiatives:

Individual Initiatives

- *Informal personal collaboration*: Sharing of results and plans by individuals not necessarily linked by a formal program structure.
- *Formal collaboration*: This would be between groups or individuals whose parent organizations are programmatically linked.
- *Staff exchange*: Assignment of technical staff from one organization to another, directly exchanging the know-how of the two organizations.
- *Entrepreneurship*: Building a new business enterprise around a specific innovation (or family of innovations) is often the most effective method of exploiting the innovation, because of the entrepreneurial zeal of the key individuals. The entrepreneur may be an inventor, a member of the innovation team, or sometimes an outsider working in cooperation with the innovators.
- *Intrapreneurship*: Entrepreneurship within an existing corporation.
- *Use of Special Facilities*: Facilities constructed for mission purposes may have time available for other uses. These can include either mission-related experiments or R&D efforts aimed at commercial applications.
- *Intellectual Property Licensing*: If inventors or authors of copyrighted material (e.g., software), or their employers, choose not to exploit their technology, it can be transferred under a licensing agreement to another organization.
- *Technical Assistance*: Innovation can be driven by existing needs rather than by technology seeking an application. Cooperation with numerous public and private-sector entities can elicit problems and needs that can be addressed by SDI technology and expertise. The networking of the Federal Laboratory Consortium for Technology Transfer can provide efficient matching of need and source.
- *Professional Communications*: Some technologies can be communicated through the technical literature or at professional meetings in sufficient detail for their use by others.
- *Special Workshops*: Workshops or short courses are effective when many indi-

viduals or organizations can use a new technology, and a tutorial format is needed to transfer the know-how.

Major Cooperative Initiatives

- *Research Cooperatives*: The Microelectronics and Computer Technology Corporation (Austin, Texas), associating 21 high tech companies, is a prominent example of a research cooperative. A specific technology or commercial goal may be too risky or too expensive for one company to develop alone; it may form a research cooperative with other companies to share both the results and the costs of the development. The federal government has facilitated this approach by permitting prior review for compliance with antitrust regulations.
- *R&D Limited Partnerships*: Government policy, through the tax laws, encourages individuals' investment in R&D programs. This approach provides short-term write-offs of R&D expenditures and capital-gains treatment of future returns. This is another approach to pooled risk-taking, but by individuals rather than by corporations.
- *Coordinated University-Industry-Government Efforts*: Several initiatives have been taken to develop project cooperation among these dissimilar entities for commercial projects. There is a biotechnology center at the University of Maryland, involving also the National Bureau of Standards and Montgomery County, Maryland. Riotech is a recent initiative of Senator Domenici to focus industry cooperation and support on joint programs of New Mexico's universities and federal laboratories. Similarly, the Federal Laboratory Consortium is organizing "common interest groups" of universities, large companies, and small businesses to facilitate their cooperation with the federal laboratories.
- *Major Entrepreneurial Initiatives*: Major investments in new technology opportunities have been made by several types of organizations: one or more venture capital companies; "incubator" facilities; and existing large and small companies.

SOME IMPORTANT ISSUES IN COMMERCIALIZATION

There are five major issues in commercialization of the Strategic Defense Initiative:

1. *Program Culture*: Although it was argued earlier that the SDI program can have only one overriding mission, it is important that its culture (and that of the participating organizations) respect and reward innovations—both mission-related and those with strictly a commercial value. This seemingly ephemeral aspect can be very important. The institutional respect for entrepreneurship at MIT and Stanford, for example, has been cited as a major reason for the development of the Route 128 and Silicon Valley foci of technology-based businesses, in contrast to the dearth of such developments at other technically excellent universities.

2. *Rapid Initiatives*: The policies and methods of technology commercialization must permit rapid commitment and action. In today's competitive environment, a new technology's advantage may be lost if it is not introduced rapidly into the marketplace. The general trend of federal policy in the last ten years has significantly speeded up and simplified the hurdles to commercialization. To maintain this momentum, both policies and the interest of program leaders should be pragmatically encouraging.

3. *Classification*: This process must safeguard against the improper use of classified or export-sensitive technology. The commercialization efforts can be structured to assist actively in the identification and control of these sensitive technologies. The same motivation and analysis that uncovers the commercial potential of a new technology can also be directed toward uncovering any negative impacts of its dissemination. For example, several Navy laboratories have combined in one office the responsibilities for domestic technology transfer and technology export control efforts.

4. *Proprietary Information*: An important challenge is to pursue commercialization efforts without compromising the proprietary positions of companies that are participating in the SDI program. At a minimum, the individuals involved in the commercialization effort should be able to accept and protect the companies' proprietary information. It is presumed that, under PL96–517, that small businesses, universities, and some contractor-operated federal laboratories will receive title to inventions made under SDI program support. To the extent that these inventions can stand alone in the marketplace, the responsibility for their commercialization can be left to these organizations. If these institutions are not interested in promoting commercialization of their discoveries, or if the discoveries of several institutions must be "packaged" to yield a commercially attractive opportunity, an outside enterprise or venture may be required.

5. *Technology Management*: A businesslike approach should be taken whenever possible with new discoveries. For example, good cooperation between the mission technical staff and the commercialization program can ensure protection of foreign patent rights without delaying application of the discovery to mission needs.

A TECHNOLOGY COMMERCIALIZATION PROGRAM PROPOSAL

This section presents the skeleton of a commercialization program consistent with the issues, concerns, and needs outlined earlier. It is assumed that the SDI program's institutional culture will support the smaller spin-offs—via professional communications, technical assistance, etc. This proposal also would not interfere with the legal rights of SDI program participants to commercialize technologies they discover, should they choose to exercise those rights.

- The core of this effort would be a cadre of individuals whose full-time assignment is to assure optimal exploitation of SDI technologies. Most would be current experts in major SDI technology areas, supported by people with technology-based business skills (marketing, patents, etc.).
- This cadre would be responsible for identifying, evaluating, and exploiting technology opportunities developed in the SDI program. They would, for example, maintain an extensive network of contacts in all SDI program organizations, and particularly with the technology leaders ("gatekeepers") in those organizations.
- They would have the authority to suggest technical opportunities to individual companies or venture groups for exploitation; or to encourage the formation of industry consortia to pursue large-scale opportunities. If requested, they would assist the source and user organizations to design a transfer program. They could accept and protect any organization's proprietary information—and suggest to organizations with complementary interests that they cooperate.
- Because of their networking and technology-seeking functions, they will have a strong understanding of SDI technology, both in detail and on a broad scale. Thus, they will be in the best position to: (a) assure rapid information transfer for mission needs (outside preexisting channels of cooperation), (b) advise the SDI office on the classification and export-control issues in the various technology areas.
- By direct contacts, or through cooperation with the Federal Laboratory Consortium, they can become aware of technology needs of U.S. industry as well.
- This commercialization organization should be in the private sector, to permit flexibility and incentive in this activity. It might be supported initially by the SDI office, based on competitive proposals, and would always receive some government support for its mission-supporting efforts. It could also receive fees or equity from groups that exploit SDI technologies as a result of its efforts. As examples, it could receive (in fees or equity) finders' fees from venture capital groups, from general partners in R&D limited partnerships, from new businesses, and from new research cooperatives.

The following are anecdotal examples that indicate the efficacy of this approach:

- The Materials Science and Technology Division at Los Alamos conducted an inventory of available technology from its 700-member organization. The vast majority of the technologies reported were the result of one person's effort, through a network of contacts throughout this diverse organization.
- The Hot Rock Geothermal Energy Program at Los Alamos required the use of

many advanced technologies in drilling, logging, and fracturing, because the underground conditions are very different from those encountered in the oil field industry and even the hydrothermal, geothermal energy industry. The networking of one individual with all sectors of the oil industry identified the needed technologies and tools and arranged for their use in the Los Alamos program. The results of his efforts also made these technologies available for special applications worldwide in the oilfields and standard geothermal energy areas.

• The basic innovations on fluidics applications for logic and instrumentation were made at the Army's Harry Diamond Laboratory (HDL). There resulted numerous R&D efforts in all three services and in industry. Two of the HDL innovators formed a Government Fluidics Coordinating Committee to provide a strong network among those working in this area, including both government and industry. These individuals' initiative led both to valuable R&D program cooperation and to applications of this technology in the aerospace and biomedical industries.

A decade from now, I'd expect similar stories from SDI.

21

CASE EXAMPLES OF COMMERCIALIZATION

ROBERT P. STROMBERG

In review of prospects for commercializing technologies resulting from the Strategic Defense Initiative, examination of past similar programs may prove useful. These previous programs indicate there will undoubtedly be a tremendous outpouring of technology as a result of this new initiative.

This chapter reviews information compiled by the Technology Transfer Officer for Sandia National Laboratories in Albuquerque, New Mexico, and Livermore, California. It is an engineering laboratory where the primary assignment is the design, development, and maintenance in stockpile of the nonnuclear parts of our nuclear weapons arsenal. For the past few years documentation has been made of commercialization of technologies developed in that program as well as in our nonweapons programs. It occurred to me that these results may be quite useful in predicting what will most likely happen as the Strategic Defense Initiative proceeds. A few numbers and examples from Sandia illustrate how this process results from the weapons program.

The current record at Sandia for fiscal years 1981-1984 lists over 600 companies making commercial use of some 171 technologies. Even though it is not the purpose of weapons work to produce commercial technologies, a significant number of examples arise where work directed at weapons applications finds commercial use. Approximately 18 percent of lab activities are directed toward energy programs where the ultimate purpose is to transfer the technology, so the record is proportionately better in these areas than in the weapons programs; yet the weapons programs results are quite impressive. Quoting from Sandia's Annual Report for FY 1984, the following table describes the program source of technologies:

Weapon R&D	54	Combustion research	11
Solar energy	23	Fission energy	8
Geothermal energy	21	Nuclear Waste management	3
Fossil energy	16	Fusion energy	3
Safeguards	12		

In this table, 66 of the total are defense-related examples. This record indicates that a significant amount of spin-off has occurred. A similar release of commercially useful technology might be expected from SDI activities.

EXAMPLES

Batteries: Some years ago a weapons need arose for a long-life battery, similar in size to the common flashlight battery, to be used in the systems that allow our weapons to protect themselves against unauthorized use. Sandia's materials scientists found the problem causing existing battery failures to be in the insulator around one of the terminals of commercial batteries. After analysis, it was determined that a glass with a lower silicon content would resist attack by the lithium in the battery. We formulated a new glass, applied it to our batteries, and now find many commercial organizations using this glass for their batteries. This will result in longer life for medical uses such as pacemakers, add reliability to performance, and extend the interval between surgical replacements.

Pulse Reactor Studies: An experimental annular core research reactor at Sandia Laboratories has been used for pulse radiation studies on weapon components. In an effort to extend its capabilities, a heat transfer study has been under way jointly supported by Sandia, G. A. Technologies, Inc., and the University of New Mexico. This study is related to the low-velocity, low-pressure natural convection heat transfer of annular core reactors such as the one at Sandia. This joint project is contributing to basic knowledge of heat transfer in the transition zone between laminar and turbulent flow. The results would indicate that heat transfer is greater than was anticipated. These results will allow us to increase safely the pulse level of our reactor. They also have encouraged our commercial partners to consider the possibilities of safer reactors. Design for post-accident reflood cooling in power reactors may produce much lower hazard and even point toward lower risk designs in the case of total cooling pump failure.

Radiation Hard Microcircuits: Miniaturization of weapon systems requires the use of microcircuit technology, but their susceptibility to ionizing radiation imposes limits on the survivability of the weapon when subjected to radiation from other nuclear weapon detonations. Subsequently, an extensive program in basic science and application has resulted in a process at Sandia for producing microcircuits that operate after being subjected to more than 1 million Rads of ionizing radiation. This technology is also desirable for use in commercial satellite devices intended to survive long periods in space where radiation is one of the mechanisms known to degrade performance. The process has been transferred for commercial use and microcircuits using the technology are commercially available.

Low-Density Foam: One of the materials resulting from the Sandia program to protect nuclear weapons from seizure by unauthorized persons is a special low-density foam that can totally fill a room, making it impossible for people to seize a weapon or even find their way through the interior of a building. The foam is currently licensed to people interested in its use as a means for more efficiently applying fertilizers and insecticides to crops.

METHODS

Methods of technology transfer vary widely. The one common factor seems to be a personal exchange between people who understand the technology. As a closing example, I would like to describe an anecdote that resulted in transferring a component used in nuclear weapons for medical applications.

A Sandia supervisor had a daughter with diabetes. In the course of arranging for a summer camp for his daughter, he met with a group of volunteers at an Albuquerque home. A nationally recognized endocrinologist had volunteered to help arrange for the summer camp. Our engineer had been convinced that glucose measurements were absolutely necessary and that controlling insulin input alone would not be medically satisfactory. He had an idea for using a rotary solenoid that arms and safes weapons as a little parastoltic pump, but "knew" the idea would not be acceptable without a glucose monitor. After all the arrangements were made for the summer camp, the doctor doing research in this very area tried to convince our engineer such a device would be extremely useful. The two were asked to take their arguments outside as the evening became very late. The endocrinologist told me that on the front lawn of the host, he finally convinced the engineer that the device would be extremely useful. The rest of the story is relatively straightforward—with National Institute of Health grants, experimental implants, and now commercial development of an implantable insulin pump for some types of diabetics. The process goes on in many ways.

SUMMARY

Work on the Strategic Defense Initiative will involve systems and activities such as batteries, fuel cells and flywheels, pulse forming, fast switches, power conversion, and glass to metal seals, to name a few subspecialties. Continued work on radiation-hardened microcircuits will also be done for SDI purposes. There is absolutely no doubt that this work will produce records of spin-off for commercial use, significantly strengthening our economy.

BIBLIOGRAPHY

Stromberg, R. P. "Annual Report Technology Transfer, Sandia National Laboratories Fiscal Year 1984." SAND85–1085, August, 1985.

22

INTERNATIONAL TECHNOLOGY TRANSFER ISSUES:THE SDI AND EUREKA

RODNEY W. JONES

Little public attention has been given to the international technology transfer issues of the Strategic Defense Initiative or those raised by Eureka,[1] the French proposal for European research collaboration on similar technologies. Yet those issues are presently under active government-to-government negotiation, at least between the United States and certain West European countries. This chapter is a preliminary, conceptual effort to outline the terrain of these technology transfer issues.

The chapter focuses on the policy context and policy implications of the transfer of high technology from a strategic standpoint rather than on the details of SDI or like technology. It is concerned primarily with international technology transfer policy issues. Facilitating the transfer of technology generated through public-sector research and development to the private sector—i.e., the commercialization of technology—is an important related issue area,[2] but a separate subject, and treated in this chapter only indirectly. The strategic issues of international technology transfer are not only military, however; they are also political and economic, and would be, even if the genesis of Eureka with a civilian thrust had not made that clear.

The terrain of international technology transfer raises fundamental issues of purpose: Why transfer technology? Why control its transfer? Much has been done in the postwar world to give special answers to these questions. The SDI technology program reopens these questions in a different light. There are also institutional arrangements, export-control legislation, and treaty obligations that bear on these questions, one of the most obvious being the Anti-Ballistic Missile (ABM) Treaty provision that prohibits certain transfers. This chapter examines these issues as they could intersect with SDI and Eureka at a general level.

TECHNOLOGY TRANSFER AND CONTROL: STRATEGIC PURPOSE

High technology can be strategically significant quite apart from its specific military applications. It is an indispensable ingredient, if not the driving factor, in modern economic progress. Effective application of high technology sustains national economic health and resilience. Being at the leading edge with high technology is the basis for what has come to mean "leadership" in world affairs. It guarantees trade competitiveness. It creates for its possessor the ability to confer assistance and thus to exert power or influence. It conveys prestige. Thus, it is much sought after. The role of high technology in conferring strategic military power is even more direct and compelling as well as better understood.

The postwar advantages of the United States in science and technology became a matter of high policy concern once the Cold War emerged. An embargo was placed on export of military hardware and technology to the Communist bloc. Dual-use technology was scrutinized for its strategic and military implications. The mechanism of COCOM (or the Coordinating Council) was brought into being. It provided a framework for sensitive export policy cooperation among most Western nations and the criteria for restricting nuclear and other strategically sensitive technology flows to the Soviet bloc.[3] By concentrating on what should be excluded from trade with the Communist countries, COCOM also functioned to support the confident expansion of trade and related technology transfer among the nations of the West.

Selective denial of technology has a strategic purpose.[4] It is a means of affecting relative weights in a future balance of power. But purposefully withholding capability from adversaries is only one side of the equation. The other side, and the source of many dilemmas for exercise of control over technology flows, is that technology has to be supplied to allies and friends for the common defense and for the maintenance of the balance of power. Supply and denial both are important.

A series of issues regarding the best policy methods and techniques for purposively controlling or denying technology, and related issues of technology definition, should be mentioned, though this is not the place to resolve them. While it is not unusual to think of technology in terms of manufactured products (devices or components, or, in the computer era, also software), technology more precisely is the "know-how" underlying products. It is not only the knowledge of scientific and engineering principles that are applied in a product, but also knowledge of the manufacturing process and quality control. Trade controls are easier to impose, at least in principle, on manufacturing processes than on the diffusion of scientific knowledge or movement of products. It has been persuasively argued that export controls on technology are most likely to be effective if they concentrate on restricting knowledge of manufacturing processes rather than on denying products.[5]

Because of the diffusion of scientific knowledge (not to speak of espionage), using trade controls on particular products and embodied technologies to withhold them from an opponent tends to be effective only temporarily. Such controls are most useful in a context of steadily advancing technology in which the emphasis in control policies is on the most advanced technologies, for which those policies must constantly be updated. In one perspective, technology transfer denial is less important than maintaining a technological lead, and denial may even work at cross-purposes with the expansion of economic capacity and productivity, which are important to maintaining that lead.

IMPACT OF ADVANCED TECHNOLOGY MOBILIZATION

In large part, SDI is a goal-directed program for the accelerated investigation and development of highly advanced technologies. The goal is strategic defense against nuclear attack, a gargantuan objective that places extraordinary demands on orthodox conceptions of technological potential.[6] Subsumed under this goal are the development of new physical principles for target observation and destruction by operations in space, and computational capacities for ultra-high-speed signal and information processing that presuppose artificial intelligence. Most of the technology principles being explored by SDI have dual or multiple potential uses. The same is generally true of the technology categories specified by Eureka, despite the nonmilitary character of the program (see Table 22.1).

SDI is a strategic military program.[7] The technologies that would underwrite strategic defense capability could also enhance certain strategic offensive capabilities, including antisatellite capabilities, and also the survivability of strategic offensive command and control systems. SDI research may also generate numerous spin-offs for conventional military purposes, offensive and defensive. The military technology transfer implications are not just those denoted by ballistic missile defense (BMD) or other forms of active defense. They also embrace foreseeable conventional military capabilities of direct interest to our alliance partners and to overall NATO military planning.

Although SDI is military in purpose, the stimulus it gives to the development of dual-use and civilian spin-off technologies at the high end of the technology spectrum is profound. There are two aspects to this. One is the stimulus to space exploration and commercial exploitation; while the commercial benefits from space could be substantial, the immediate payoffs have more to do with prestige and strategic military balance perceptions. Leadership in outer space activities has become one

Table 22.1
Eureka Projects

A. Focal Technology Areas, Initial Conception, April, 1985

    Electro-optics and sensors
    New materials
    Microelectronics
    Supercomputers
    Artificial intelligence
    Lasers and particle beams (directed energy concepts)

B. Programmed Research Fields, Eureka White Book, July, 1985
    Euromatique: micro- and macrocomputer components
    Eurobot: robotics and lasers
    Eurocom: advanced telecommunications
    Eurobio: modern biotechnology
    Euromat: advanced industrial turbines

C. Industrial Participants and Agreed Projects: Examples

    Matra S.A. and Norsk Data A/S: high-powered scientific computers
    Matra S.A. and STS (Italy): integrated circuits
    Cie des Machines Bull and Siemens A.G.: supercomputers (i.e., the
      "Eurocomputer")
    Messerschmitt (MBB) and Aerospatiale: avionics and aeronautics
    N.V. Phillips, General Electric (U.K.), Siemens A.G., and Thomson-CSF:
      microprocessors for high-speed communication
    MBB, Messer Griesheim, and Robert Bosch: industrial lasers
    De Danske Sukkerfabrikker A/S and Lyonnaise des Eaux & de l'Eclairage
      S.A.: artificial membranes, filtration

Source: Compiled by the author.

of the key factors, if not the dominant one, in worldwide perceptions of the relative capability and status of the superpowers, and space program leadership is increasingly important in differentiating the newcomer spacefaring nations as well.

The other aspect is the collateral stimulus in SDI to civilian high technology R&D, particularly in the areas of high-power computers, artificial intelligence, microelectronics, robotics, and advanced energy sources.[8] Here the goal-directed or accelerative feature of SDI is pivotal. Those countries that value a high level of technological self-reliance and fear they are lagging behind in technological innovation (common features today in Western Europe), recognize that a goal-directed, heavily funded high technology program in the United States could leave them even further behind.[9]

As a consequence, the West Europeans, whether allies or neutrals, find it virtually imperative either to participate in SDI or in some analogous technological effort. Japan seems to have adopted much the same perspective. To the extent that one or another of these nations chooses to abstain as a matter of policy from involvement in the SDI, it is almost bound in view of limited resources to seek to collaborate on high technology development with others that refrain from SDI. France's deliberate decision to stay out of SDI was the genesis of Eureka,[10] an appeal to other West European countries to form an alternative technology development consortium aimed at civilian rather than military purposes.[11]

TECHNOLOGY TRANSFER: CONTROL AND COLLABORATION

The defense military objectives of the SDI program probably do not depend technically on European (or Japanese) collaboration; the technical success of the program is more likely to depend on U.S. resources and ingenuity. The European contribution, however, could enhance the rate of technical progress, at least marginally.[12]

The primary reasons for soliciting European collaboration are three. The first reason arises from NATO defense requirements and their connections with strategic stability; a program to deploy active strategic defenses would be imprudent without NATO membership support, as has been recognized by U.S. policy statements regarding future SDI decisions. NATO membership support for eventual deployments could not be counted on, moreover, unless the coverage of the defenses would include Western Europe. Such support is much more likely to be forthcoming if there is European participation in the research stage of the SDI program, where it would be possible to judge firsthand whether the technical basis for defenses is attractive, than if there is not.

The second reason is that domestic public support for SDI may not be sustainable if strident opposition to SDI prevails for a long period of time in the European membership of NATO. This in turn would under cut the domestic support in the United States for strategic modernization as well as the U.S. bargaining position in strategic arms control negotiations with the Soviet Union, where the U.S. SDI potential seems to be a potent asset in pressing for offensive arms reductions. Thus for purposes of a strong defense as well as effective East-West negotiations, it may be necessary that the United States be able to count on strong NATO support for its overall strategic policy posture.

The third reason concerns the future strength of the West as a whole in technological and economic capacity. The stimulus of a goal-directed emphasis on antinuclear defenses could be highly beneficial to the economies of Europe and Japan as well as of the United States. The overall benefit for Western security of strong allies is self-evident. Thus it is logical for the United States in a major effort such as SDI to invite research participation and look with favor on the resulting technology transfer to its allies as commonly beneficial.

The Reagan administration has voiced on more than one occasion the notion that SDI results might be shared with the Soviet Union to facilitate a cooperative and presumably stabilizing approach to deployment of active defenses. The U.S. view of the persuasiveness of nonnuclear technology-based defense concepts indeed is being shared through the arms control talks at Geneva. It is unrealistic, however, to suppose that the United States would deliberately transfer (or sell) strategic military technology to its primary adversary. Therefore, East-West controls on exports to restrict the flow to the Soviet bloc countries of advanced technologies that arise from the SDI program are bound to be a focal concern.

This suggests the need in turn to have a clear understanding of how SDI-related technology transfer policy is to be conducted with respect to the NATO allies and other Western nations. It raises an issue whether the treatment in technology transfer terms of nations that do and do not participate in the SDI program can be the same. At first glance, this issue raises discriminatory overtones, which could be cause for serious political difficulty in West-West relations. Thus it is important to take a closer look.

CONSTRAINTS IN THE ABM TREATY

The problem can be simplified somewhat by distinguishing the military and nonmilitary elements of SDI research and by recognizing the ABM technology transfer constraints that presently exist in the ABM Treaty.[13] The Reagan administration has confirmed that the United States plans to adhere to the ABM Treaty in shaping the SDI program during his second term.[14]

Virtually all of the advanced technology research of SDI is dual-use rather than necessarily military in nature, a fact highlighted by the Eureka selection of essentially the same technology categories for what are declared to be civilian purposes (see Table 22.1).

The military features of the SDI program that are well-defined reside primarily in the realm of traditional ABM systems and components, which are essentially terrestrial and fixed-site rather than mobile or space-based.[15] The military features of the advanced, and especially space-based, technologies are unlikely to be well-defined until a postlaboratory stage has been reached where systems and components must be built and tested in forms that are recognizable as operational military prototypes. Moreover, there is ample room for research compartmentalization of projects on advanced technologies so that the findings of individual projects could not be viewed as dedicated to or directly applicable to military purposes.

The ABM Treaty constraints on technology transfer by the superpowers to other nations are significant, but are not necessarily major impediments to research cooperation on nonmilitary elements of high technology nor even on military significant research that is not specifically on ABM systems or components. The relevant treaty provisions are two and read respectively as follows:

Article IX: To assure the viability and effectiveness of this Treaty, each Party undertakes not to transfer to other States, and not to deploy outside its national territory, ABM systems or their components limited by this Treaty.

Agreed Statement G: The Parties understand that Article IX of the Treaty includes the obligation of the U.S. and U.S.S.R. not to provide to other States *technical descriptions* or *blueprints specially worked out for the construction of ABM systems and their components limited by the Treaty* [italics added].

In essence, as long as the treaty is unamended and faithfully observed, these provisions mean that ABM systems or components—including ABM interceptor missiles, launchers, and radars, and ABM-capable components substitutable for the named components—may not be transferred by the United States to other countries, even in the form of technical descriptions or blueprints from which construction could be undertaken. This would seem to apply, however, to developed systems or components that would be fit for deployment. It would not seem to apply to fundamental research on physical principles or applied research on the functions of engineered technology in earlier stages, such as in laboratories.

It is also the case that the prohibitions and restrictions of the ABM Treaty apply strictly to ABM systems and components—those that are capable of intercepting "strategic" missiles. While the concept of "strategic" has not been fully defined by agreements between the United States and the Soviet Union, it is understood to exclude "theater" or "tactical" and short-range ballistic missiles. Defenses against tactical missiles (antitactical ballistic missile systems, i.e., ATBM or ATM systems) are not restricted by the ABM Treaty. Development, testing, and deployment of ATBM systems is permissible.

There is considerable difference as a practical matter in the capability required for ABM systems and in that required for ATBM systems, but the operational nature of both types of systems in other respects can be quite similar. Some regard this as a loophole in the treaty, since it not only is conceivable that ATBM development and deployment could be used to mask ABM development activities or patterns of deployment prohibited by the treaty but also there is evidence that the Soviet Union has engaged in this practice. The point here, however, is that international technology cooperation in or technology transfer of ATBM systems is not legally restricted by the ABM Treaty. But this does not end the matter because the distinction between ABM and ATBM systems is not rigorously defined.

A major concern arises in this connection among those European states, such as Britain and West Germany, that seem inclined to participate in the SDI research program provided they can be satisfied with the terms. It is that the United States may share ATBM-related projects and research but withhold similar ABM-related projects and research on the grounds that a conservative interpretation of the treaty so requires. The effect of such an approach, or so it is feared, would be to share more at the low end of the military technology spectrum and relatively little at the high end. From a military defense standpoint, this also implies that European states may benefit mainly from ATBM types of defense, which are presumed (correctly) to be essentially terrestrial in nature, while the coverage of space ABM types of defenses could be confined essentially to the continental United States.

A second major concern of these countries is that while much of the SDI research may consist of technologies applicable to civilian purposes, the United States would be in the position as a practical matter to determine what is and is not militarily strategic and therefore to cordon off areas of inquiry at its own discretion as highly classified on grounds of national security or on grounds that it would be inconsistent with the ABM Treaty provisions to leave such areas open to participation by other states.

Under these circumstances, one feared effect for participating states is that they may get incomplete knowledge of overall SDI research program results and be ill-equipped to express their views about the merits of defense deployments, or to judge the appropriateness of possible modifications in, or of U.S. withdrawal from, the ABM Treaty, in the event these issues arise at a later stage. The other feared effect for participating states is that they would lose access to high technology applicable to civilian and commercial sectors, with the lion's share of advantage in this respect kept by the United States or by U.S. companies.

COMPETITIVE BIDDING FOR PROGRAMMED RESEARCH

European high tech companies have been more eager than national governments to become engaged in SDI research by bidding for SDI contract funding. The British, West German, and Italian governments have been interested in defining the basis for participation in some fashion that guarantees that their own industrial firms will be able to compete successfully in commercial terms and be able to retain and build on their technical talents rather than losing them to U.S. industry or R&D establishments. The British government took the lead in negotiating a government-to-government memorandum of understanding, or a framework agreement, that guarantees a certain level of technology access, financial return, and rational sectoral participation of leading British companies precisely in their areas of known technical expertise. Underlying this British effort was the interest in reducing impediments from U.S. regulations and, to some degree, of establishing in advance an agreed share in the allotment of future SDIO contract allocations. The British agreements, of course, set precedents that West Germany, Italy, and others can seek to apply in similar negotiations, though there may be variations in the agreements concluded with each country.[16]

The British interest in carving up the contract activities in advance encountered obstacles from congressionally mandated rules for U.S. defense contracting, especially those that require competitive bidding. Competitive bidding among foreign (and domestic) firms would give the SDI office managers an opportunity to choose among companies and contract proposals, irrespective of national origin, the best technical fit between research objectives and what a firm can bring to bear at a given cost. By their nature, competitive bidding regulations stand in the way of a priori judgments about the qualifications of particular companies or preagreed shares of contract allocation among countries from a particular nation.

Finding ways through this thicket probably will require a combination of informal understandings and commitments about commercial matters and formal definition of levels of access in areas of sensitivity. Achieving such results, moreover, may be an iterative process that gains in clarity for both sides as experience is generated with earlier stages of participation and further talks occur to refine understandings.

It seems likely that the iterative process of generating experience and refining understandings through foreign government-monitored, foreign company participation in SDI will also address COCOM concerns as a matter of course, given a degree of bureaucratic coordination within each government concerned. It is worth noting historically that the COCOM process itself has depended heavily on consideration of cases in light of experience, and in that respect is analogous.

COMPETITION FROM EUREKA

There may be a temptation to exaggerate the competitive implications of Eureka and overlook the positive and synergistic features of parallel technology programs that serve West European national and multinational interests and identity. It remains to be seen whether Eureka will achieve coherent program definition or a sufficient level of funding to produce significant technical innovation and the hoped-for commercial returns. But it is not only reasonable that European efforts to harness resources and retain technical talent be pursued; it contributes to the maintenance of plural centers of strength and commitment from which the alliance has benefited in the past and which may be needed more in the future. It is significant, moreover, that this French idea is so explicitly dedicated to European international cooperation, even if its potential benefits from a French national point of view are also obvious.

Three points about Eureka deserve reflection. First, it has won, at least in political terms, widespread, if not universal, West European support and claims serious inquiries even from Japan. While few governments have been willing to endorse SDI, they have had no political inhibition about endorsing Eureka. The European "neutral" countries are officially enthusiastic about Eureka. Second, the few governments that have gone on record in support of SDI research are also inclined to be involved in Eureka, even though there are some differences of view on the likely value (the British being more skeptical, for instance, than the West Germans at this stage). Third, in the universe of West European high technology companies, the biggest and most technologically well-endowed are likely to participate in both projects, in SDI as well as Eureka, even in those cases where the parent governments have been unwilling to endorse SDI.

The fact that most big high technology European companies will play a part in both programs is probably the most salient point for thinking about the international technology transfer problem. It is the primary intersection between Eureka and SDI, whatever their other differences. Although big companies may compartmentalize their efforts voluntarily or under contract restrictions, there could be, in many cases is likely to be, a good deal of technology cross-fertilization and synergy across national lines as a result of private-sector participation in both of the umbrella projects. In fact, one might describe Eureka partly as a European framework designed to assure that trans-Atlantic technology transfer from SDI to Europe, at least in the civilian but perhaps also in the commercial military domain, is organized and made to occur, even if many European governments are unwilling or politically unable to participate in SDI.

While undoubtedly competitive in part, one should be aware of the implicit support that Eureka gives to the prospects of SDI. It is a mechanism to make sure European states do not lose out on a high technology push defined by SDI; the other side of the coin, however, is that Eureka is a mechanism for indirect European participation in much of the technology potential of SDI. With participation comes technical if not political support, and perhaps eventually political support.

CONCLUSIONS

There may be a variety of impediments to a free flow of SDI-stimulated technology from the United States to Europe and vice versa, including some not considered here, such as in the domain of antitrust laws and proprietary and patent rights. ABM Treaty and COCOM issues certainly will be part of this picture. But the promotion of Eureka or of other high technology consortia under European auspices are much less likely to serve as impediments than as facilitators of international technology transfer, despite the first impression one has of competitive implications. The key factor is the intersection of private corporate sectors in both large-scale programs.

It is much more likely that technology transfer across national lines will take place as a matter of course, whatever the legislative or treaty-related regulatory impediments that exist, than that there will be highly efficient commercialization of that technology in the civilian or conventional military marketplace. In the international transfer of technology arising naturally from SDI and possibly from Eureka, there is bound to be considerable scope for European opportunities to recover a significant degree of high technology momentum, probably more scope than the governments and corporations involved will successfully exploit.

There is a good deal here, then, for governments to do, but even more that will fall on the private sector to do, both to make the promised programs flourish technically, and to harness the benefits for technology commercialization and economic expansion. That there is a broad European response on these matters of opportunity is more important than the fact that there are competitive connotations for SDI in that response. The salient point about competition in this context is how likely it is to be traded in for reciprocal support.

NOTES

I wish to thank my colleague, John Yochelson, Director, International Business and Economics Programs at Georgetown University's Center for Strategic and International Studies for reviewing this chapter; Steven A. Hildreth, now of the Congressional Research Service, for support while still on my staff; and Joseph Lovece and Hans Hermann for research assistance.

1. Eureka stands for European Research Coordination Agency, a concept proposed by President Mitterrand in Paris in April, 1985 as a basis for a civilian high technology consortium in Europe. The Eureka proposal was a reaction

to U.S. Secretary of Defense Caspar Weinberger's March, 1985 overtures to European governments and firms to commit to participation in the SDI research program. The French government feared that U.S. financial inducements from SDI to European industrial firms would drain Europe's best technical talent unless an alternative, high-profile European program was launched with its own aims and funding in order to keep native technical talent in place. For additional background on Eureka, see Samuel F. Wells, Jr., "The United States and European Defence Co-operation," *Survival* 27 (July/August 1985), pp. 163-168; and Steven A. Hildreth, "EUREKA: The Political and Technical Challenge to the United States," *CSIS Alert* (September, 1985), pp. 5-6; "Europe's High-Technology Eureka Project," *Wall Street Journal*, November 5, 1985, p. 34.

2. See George Kozmetsky, "Summing Up: Commercialization of Strategic Defense Technologies," IC² Institute, The University of Texas at Austin, October, 1985.

3. For background on COCOM and postwar export control, see *Technology and East-West Trade*, Congress of the United States, Office of Technology Assessment (Washington, D.C.: U.S. Government Printing Office), 1979, particularly chapters VII-IX.

4. See William E. Odom, "Soviet Force Posture: Dilemmas and Directions," *Problems of Communism*, July-August, 1985, pp. 1-14, especially pp. 12ff.

5. See the well-known "Bucy Report," more formally referenced as Defense Science Board Task Force on Export of U.S. Technology, *An Analysis of Export Control of U.S. Technology: A DOD Perspective*, Department of Defense, Office of Director of Defense Research and Engineering, 1976.

6. SDI emphasizes ballistic missile defense or active defense against long-range offensive ballistic missiles, but the program also takes into account the means of defense against "air-breathing" strategic offensive delivery systems such as bombers and cruise missiles. For basic policy statements, see "The President's Strategic Defense Initiative," The White House (Washington, D.C.: U.S. Government Printing Office), January, 1985; "The Strategic Defense Initiative," Speical Report No. 129, U.S. Department of State, June, 1985; U.S. Department of Defense, "Statement on the President's Strategic Defense Initiative," by Richard DeLauer, Undersecretary for Research and Engineering, before the Committee on Armed Services, U.S. Senate, 97th Congress, 2nd sess., March 8, 1984; Gen. James A. Abrahamson, "Statement on the Strategic Defense Initiative," before the Armed Services Committee, U.S. Senate, 98th Congress, 1st sess., February 21, 1985.

7. For a study of possible SDI requirements and strategic policy implications, see Rodney W. Jones, with Steven A. Hildreth and Paolo Stoppa-Liebl, *Strategy, Arms Control, and Strategic Defense Requirements* (Washington, D.C.: Georgetown University, Center for Strategic and International Studies), July, 1985.

8. For the most thorough public description of the technology sectors and research tasks involved in SDI that is currently available, see *Report to the Congress on the Strategic Defense Initiative*, U.S. Department of Defense (Washington, D.C.), 1985.

9. See "Eureka?" *The Economist* (London), November 2, 1985, p. 18.

10. The French government's decision not to participate in SDI did not, however, involve a government ban on French companies, including companies partially held in the public sector, from bidding for SDI contract funds privately; indeed, the French disposition seems to be quite open, informally, to French private-sector participation in U.S.-sponsored defense contracts.
11. See Wells, p. 163.
12. It is unclear what amount of resources will be committed to Eureka. The largest figures talked about for pooled government funding for Eureka, essentially guesswork, amount to the equivalent of about $6 billion over several years. So far, however, France is the only government to specify a financial commitment to Eureka, and that is only $125 million. In contrast, the Reagan administration proposed to use $26 billion for SDI research over six years; the proposed annual installments on this figure so far have been trimmed somewhat by congressional budget cuts, but the total could easily be $20 billion for the period. Industrial contributions to the cost of R&D are expected in both programs. U.S. companies could easily double the public allocation by private, i.e., industrial or IR&D, funding for SDI research. Whether European companies could make a proportionately similar contribution to Eureka remains to be seen. In all likelihood, however, SDI is likely to dwarf Eureka in resources committed.
13. For broader reviews of the meaning of the restrictions in the ABM Treaty as they affect military R&D on capabilities for outer space, see Rodney W. Jones, "Space Arms Control and Constraints on the Military Uses of Space," CSIS Nuclear Policy Studies, Project on the Military Uses of Space, 1984, (mimeo); Alan M. Jones, Jr., "Implications of Arms Control Agreements and Negotiations for Space-Based BMD Lasers," in Keith B. Payne, ed., *Laser Weapons in Space: Policy and Doctrine* (Boulder, Colo.: Westview Press), 1983, pp. 36-105; and George Schneiter, "The ABM Treaty Today," in Ashton B. Carter and David N. Schwartz, eds., *Ballistic Missile Defense* (Washington, D.C.: The Brookings Institution, 1984), pp. 221-250. For contemporary discussion of the issues of ABM Treaty constraints on planned technology experiments and demonstrations of the SDI program, see Thomas K. Longstreth, John E. Pike, and John Rhinelander, *The Impact of the U.S. and Soviet Ballistic Missile Defense Programs and the ABM Treaty* (Washington, D.C.: A Report, March, 1985).
14. In October, 1985, a controversy surfaced from within the U.S. government over interpretation of the ABM Treaty's restrictions on SDI downstream program activities. Until this point, the prevailing interpretation was that the ABM Treaty prohibits "development" and "testing" of ABM systems and components based on "new physical principles" (such as lasers and particle beams) in any ABM configuration or with any ABM capability, possibly excepting those associated exclusively with ABM systems in fixed-site, land-based modes. Robert McFarlane, the president's special assistant for national security, declared on October 6 what amounted to a change in policy view by indicating that the only certain limit in the treaty regarding such ABM systems or components was the prohibition on "deployment" without first conducting negotiations on the matter with the Soviet Union. This broadened interpretation turns on the treaty's Agreed Statement D,

which implies that joint negotiations to define limits on such systems or components would be needed in the event they are created (i.e., developed). While this broadened interpretation, if adhered to, would expand the scope of permitted testing activities in the SDI program, it would have no effect by itself on the treaty's technology transfer restrictions as discussed below.

15. The ABM Treaty is quite explicit about ABM systems and components, referring to ABM launchers, ABM interceptor missiles, and ABM radars, the last being defined also with quantitative measures of capability. Transfer of these kinds of hardware dedicated to ABM purposes, or the design information for their construction, is prohibited by the treaty.

16. According to a recent report, Italy is on the verge of completing an industrial security annex to the General Security Military Information Agreement with the United States as a prerequisite to Italian participation in SDI. The annex is to provide safeguards "for a variety of sensitive U.S. defense technologies, including those related to SDI." A draft of a separate SDI agreement covering areas of research and compensation for Italian companies also is close to completion. See *Aerospace Daily*, November 4, 1985, p. 10. This layered structure of agreements for one nonnuclear weapons NATO state may be a model for what would be negotiated with West Germany.

The inclination of West Germany's government under Chancellor Helmut Kohl to establish a similar basis for participation in SDI has been singled out for Soviet pressure in the form of intimidating letters and statements declaring that West Germany's participation would be a violation of the ABM Treaty. Such pressure helps to explain the ambivalence in Kohl's government—different views of the Defense and Foreign Affairs ministries—and its desire that other NATO allies go on record first as participants in SDI. See William Drozdiak, "Moscow Warns Bonn on SDI," *Washington Post*, November 14, 1985, pp. A33 and A36.

23

COMPREHENSIVE NATIONAL SECURITY: THE POWER OF AMERICAN SCIENCE

ROBERT LAWRENCE KUHN

The commercial benefits of the Strategic Defense Initiative can be explored only within a context of the economic impact of American (U.S.) science. Science and economics are no longer independent entities, and to understand the latter we must appreciate the former.

Science separates present from past. It is the critical difference between savages living like animals and humans living like people. Science is more than subjects in school; it is the foundation of our world, the progenitor of present-day society, the source of contemporary civilization. Science, in short, is axial to our way of life.

Science is both process and content, the mechanism of discovery as well as the object discovered. The scientific method is the core paradigm of modern man; it is the shortest and surest distance to factual truth, the line of thinking most logical and reproducible. The scientific method is perhaps mankind's greatest conceptual tool: unbiased data collection, creative hypothesis generation (induction), rigorous analytical reasoning (deduction), comprehensive hypothesis testing, and independent repetition and confirmation—all are necessary wherever and whenever truth is desired, irrespective of content area, whether "science" in the traditional sense or any other facet of human awareness.

Science is not a field of knowledge; it *is* knowledge. The advancement of science is the enrichment of mankind. What we call "human progress" is quite literally the historical sum of innumerable scientific steps. Derived from the Latin *scientia* meaning knowledge, science, in its broadest sense, conceives most concepts and sculpts most objects. Science, today, is wonderous, and scientists, in a sense, are worshipped.

There is one area, however, where science is controversial, where inquiry is questioned and advancement criticized. Science in the service of national defense triggers hot debate. Some would say that scientists have the moral right to control the potential use of their personal creativity, and the moral imperative to prevent their innovative output from producing weapons of war. This lofty position bespeaks high tone and laudable ideals, yet is flawed fatally by inconsistency and illogic.

The simple syllogism, framed for the United States, is thus: (1) such lofty positions can be espoused only in a free society; (2) a free society will remain free only by military strength; (3) military strength will be guaranteed only by state-of-the-art science. This is the real world. (Examples of free societies flourishing devoid of military strength? They only prove the point: All rely, at last resort, on the United States.)

National defense demands technological superiority. Parity in military science, for a nation without aggressive intent or expansionist designs, is not good enough. Equality just will not do—it's too close, a slight error and you're behind. And being behind is no place to be, not in this game, not with all the chips in the pot. In an electronic fairyland of blinking black boxes, where battlefield microprocessors command, control, and communicate in real time, "leapfrogging" is the ever-present danger. A nation dedicated to peace cannot allow itself to be jumped over. Not ever.

In past wars we could survive a slower tank or shallower sub, but in future encounters missing a scientific breakthrough in missile defense or sub-location technology could be disastrous. Our country is committed upfront: We will not be the aggressor. When the other side picks time and place, we had better field superior weapons and surer systems. When we concede quantity and number, we had better stress quality and expertise. The issue, of course, is more deterrence than triumph. We must *prevent* the next war, not win it.

Yet the world moves on. Subtle shifts redefine the nature of power. Today, nearing the final tenth of the twentieth century, security in the United States stakes out broader boundaries than ever before. More is encompassed within our vital needs as a nation. The economic thrust of Japan, for example, is a threat every bit as real as the military menace of the Soviets. Not the same, of course, but every bit as real. Computers and communications are also extending security boundaries. The profusion of information amplified by the ease of transmission lowers entry barriers for those with disruptive intent.

The battles of the future will be fought on vastly more complex grounds, contested more with ideas and products than with armies and navies. Confrontation among nations—attacks, provocations, insults—will assume new forms and novel shapes. Troop movement across Europe is virtually an anachronism—superpower nuclear stand off has seen to that. We must secure the stand off with military strength through technological supremacy, but that is not enough. An irrefutable defense capability, in the words of the logician, is "necessary but not sufficient" for national security.

This, then, is the *new* vision of national security, a broad concept embedding economic, social, educational, cultural, and intellectual components as well as military ones—a concept increasingly being called *"comprehensive* national security."

Scientific superiority must maintain U.S. comprehensive national security just as it must assure the subset of preeminent military might. The first nation, for example, to mass-produce future generations of integrated circuits—1024K and beyond—will capture high ground and strong position. The country that pioneers genetically enhanced food production will wield commanding influence in world politics, well in excess of Arab oil's peak power.

Comprehensive national security must become our redeployed concept of self-protection. Mechanisms of competition, not machines of warfare, will become increasingly critical. We must construct a *comprehensive* secure country, in both economics and defense, and American science is our primary building block for both.

Following is the domain of comprehensive national security, with each area evincing the central role of science:

Military: Maintaining technical superiority in weapons and delivery systems is the *sine qua non* of national security. Until a fully enforceable, policeable transnational inspection system is in place, or until the hearts of men are miraculously changed, the United States will remain compelled to define the state of the art in military technology. Responsiveness, reliability, and redundancy are cardinal characteristics. American science should be proud to participate in sustaining freedom.

Economic: Strengthening the industrial base of the United States is a quintessential component of comprehensive national security. In past centuries countries could make up with military aggressiveness what they lacked in economic resourcefulness. This is no longer possible. Countries will survive and prosper or suffer and fall in direct relation to their productive capacity and commercial acumen. The premier growth industries of the next decade—telecommunications, personal computing, biotechnology, and health care—are all science-based. Scientists are not only involved in creating novel high tech ventures but also in developing fresh approaches to traditional businesses. Both are prescribed for American economic health.

Social/Political: Structuring society for the benefit of all people is our contemporary mega-problem, labyrinthian in complexity, long-term in solution. We must be able to meet our soft-stated goals of equality, opportunity, care, and concern for citizens of every age, sex, race, creed, religious belief, etc. A populace well-pleased is an intrinsic part of comprehensive national security. Though human systems are fiendishly more intricate than material systems, social scientists are as clever and inventive as their physical science counterparts. The use of sophisticated techniques in sociology, political science, and the like provides a core of hard data, certainly superior to the self-serving rhetoric of political palaver.

Educational: The minds of the young are the blueprints of the future. What we teach, and how they learn, will plot the course of the United States—with the trajectory now being set in our schools. Science, here, contributes more than tools, though the personal computer will revolutionize both teaching and thinking. (Free enterprise has given the United States a jump of at least half a generation over the Soviet Union in acclimating children on personal computers.) Science teaches logic, how to use it, when to overrule it. It catalyzes enthusiasm for investigation and analysis; it teaches respect for proper rationale and confirmed proof; it offers the thrill of exploring unchartered areas, of using insight, of making discovery, of finding truth. Science replaces rote by rigor and memorization by reasoning. Science is no longer the exclusive domain of the elite; it is the language of all.

Cultural: The identity of a nation affects its cohesiveness; self-image determines self-confidence. Building U.S. culture buttresses U.S. security. Science, the complement of culture, supports its promulgation and propagation. Culture thrives on wide accessibility, and science provides the nutrients of transmission: television, radio, cable, satellite, video dics/cassettes, motion pictures, computer networks, interactive video. Science has fashioned marvelous techniques for enhancing effect, making culture more pleasurable and more veritable, conveying emotion and making impact.

Intellectual: In the twenty-first century information will be the new medium of exchange. (Money, that archaic commodity, will be bytes in computer memories and numbers on computer screens.) International leadership will be framed in terms of cerebral skill not military prowess. A nation's prestige will be built by its intellectual endowment, not the number and size of its bombs and rockets. Scientists from all disciplines will contribute, from philosophy and astronomy to mathematics and music; new information will be prized, even from fields without direct economic benefit—human values will have changed and human worth redefined.

This is the context within which the Strategic Defense Initiative emerges to impact U.S. security. For whereas the military vulnerability of its systems may be open to debate, the economic endowment of its technology is not. The curious contribution of SDI to U.S. society is its amplification of American science, with a resultant massive commercial spin-off in all directions. This is a real benefit to the United States (and a potential threat to our adversaries). SDI will catalyze great jumps in computing power, directed energy, electronics, electro-optics, robotics and automation, artificial intelligence and knowledge systems, advanced materials, and telecommunications, many of which will inevitably circle back to build the civilian sector of society. Thus, by the natural force of the market, SDI will enhance each of the above-discussed facets of the

United States: The economy, society/politics, education, culture, and intellectual development will all be strengthened by an intense commitment to SDI.

A word here for *pure* science. Basic research is the foundation of science, the platform for progress, the precursor of revolution. One cannot know in advance where seminal breakthroughs will come and what application technologies may have. Instinct and intuition, not program and project, are the requisite sources of energy. Basic research is a stimulant for creativity; it is, in all fields, an absolute necessity.

Sensitivity to scientists as well as appreciation of science is vital for optimizing national output. Scientists, by personality, are not easily coerced, not easily directed. Indeed, such is their strength. Scientists must be free to wander and explore, to confront blind alleys, to shatter tradition. Society must establish incentive systems to encourage scientists, giving them maximum motivation to imagine and construct. We must nurture and develop America's premier natural resource.

SUMMING UP:

INITIATIVES FOR COMMERCIALIZING SDI TECHNOLOGIES

GEORGE KOZMETSKY

This volume is not traditional. It is a poineering effort. *Commercializing SDI Technologies* has not simply concentrated on the current science and technology defense research markets nor prematurely speculated on markets for subsequent development and deployment of defense systems. This volume addresses, perhaps for the first time, the Strategic Defense Initiative from the perspective of what can well become one of the most exciting national research and technology programs in history. In many ways, the ongoing SDI program signals a significant transformation in American society. The program breaks with the past and represents a true initiative.

SDI carries with it its own unique requirements for successful accomplishment of its own goals as well as provides a catalytic driver for timely commercialization of the resultant technologies and know-how. The emphasis is on the phrase "timely commercialization."

The motivations for any large-scale national program, according to Dr. Michael I. Yarymovych of North American Rockwell,[1] consist of three elements: security, profit, and pride. We have identified, discussed, and examined all three motives. Moreover, these motives were viewed from the perspectives of the public at large, the Office of the President of the United States, individual scientists, the Department of Defense and other federal agencies, our nation's allies, universities and colleges, private-sector defense and nondefense institutions, and the financial communities.

Needless to say, no overwhelming and generally acceptable consensus emerged with respect to the SDI research effort. Nor was there any attempt to do so. On the other hand, there is a deep underlying consensus with regard to the role and scope of the SDI program. Most would agree that *pride* in doing it the American way is an important

motive. The fact that SDI can be openly and publicly debated and challenged is important to doing it the American way. The linking of the
security and profit motives was perhaps best expressed by D. Bruce
Merrifield who said, "Technology leverage is the theme—on the battlefield or in the economic arena.[2]

In many respects, this volume focused on identifying requirements
for successful accomplishment of the SDI program in terms of the comprehensive security of the United States. A number of authors stressed
in their own way that our nation's security and global economic position
as well as our private sector's economic well-being depend on our individual institutions' abilities to support and diffuse the newer technologies. In simple terms, these requirements for successful
accomplishment of SDI will depend on (1) a continuity of public and
political support; (2) sufficient supply of competent, skilled, and properly
committed and dedicated personnel; (3) newer institutional developments that transfer and diffuse the SDI technologies to provide for American economic leadership; and (4) timely legislation that provides
incentives for and removes barriers from the innovation process.

Perhaps three of the more important discernible underlying trends
that we perceived during the course of this examination are as follows:

1. Meeting critical strategic defense needs calls for new technologies that are
   more complex and interdisciplinary than required heretofore. Moreover,
   many of the key technologies are not as yet "in place." Nor is there yet in
   place the required infrastructure for development, manufacture, and training
   for the SDI Program. On the other hand, the infrastructure is key for meeting
   SDI's main criteria for assuring that it is more cost-effective to embark on
   defensive strategic weapons than to continue offensive weapons buildup,
   thereby leading to ballistic missile reduction and control.

2. There was acceptance that national research and development programs
   such as SDI bring with them an implied commitment to both solve the near-
   term defense program mission requirement and maximize longterm comprehensive economic benefits.

3. Public support for both the program and for building the required infra-
   structures for technology leveraging requires visible accountability and unprecedented openness in operations and assessment of key milestone results.

This volume focuses on the requirements for successful commercialization and overcoming the traditional innovation gaps of technology
transfer and diffusion. We are striving to redefine commercialization of
defense R&D in light of the new challenges posed by SDI.

Commercialization is the process by which research and development
results are transformed into the marketplace as products and services.
It requires the necessary constituencies to interchange ideas and opinions that are technological in nature. When technologies are utilized in

both defense and nondefense markets, the commercialization process may benefit through increased scale of production, higher quality, and lower prices. The SDI program can profoundly change the relationship between defense and commercial markets. This effort has unequivocably established that one market is not isolated from the other.

During the 1950–1970 period, the technology diffusion of defense market to commercial market was perhaps too imperceptibly accomplished. It was easy to built the 707 once we had the B-52. It was feasible to reduce the production costs of both when the same corporation designed, manufactured, and marketed both. The first supercomputer development for the Livermore and Los Alamos National Laboratories was just as easy to build for the commercial market. There was, however, a larger and more profitable commercial market for electronic data processing using more limited systems. So the outcome was that the supercomputer market stayed limited to the government market until recently.

The SDI program is one of the most complex systems undertaken for research and technological feasibility by any nation in history. The matching of commercialization of defense with nondefense markets is also of unprecedented historic importance. For some time now, we are not as a natural matter of course in defense procurement policy matching commercialization with defense needs—and this is a primary point for the successful accomplishment of SDI program goals.

Where applicable, sharing technology between the defense and nondefense markets can result in less displacement in labor markets as a result of disarmament, renewed detente, or the loss of markets in declining industries. Such commercialization also helps to define the educational and training requirements for present and emerging marketplaces. Comprehensive commercialization can thus be a major driving force that invigorates newer industries and rejuvenates mature industries by utilizing technology as a resource. National security concerns must, of course, be taken into consideration to ensure the protection of those technologies exclusively required for defense.

For much of the period from the 1950s to the 1980s, the United States generally assumed that scientific research would, in one way or another, transfer naturally into developments or technologies and subsequently be commercialized. For most of this period, not enough attention was paid to how science was transformed into technology that was subsequently transferred for specific commercialization purposes and then diffused throughout all industries, nationally as well as among our allies. The traditional paradigm has been that basic research innovations would be utilized for applied research and development and that their commercialization would automatically follow. Diffusion to other uses would occur when R&D results were both economical and better understood. The utilization of technology as a resource was perceived as an individual institution's responsibility. It was expected that all regions of the United States would in time enjoy the benefits of this paradigm in which new innovations from research were followed naturally by timely developments, commercialization, and diffusion.

There is evidence of an emerging, new paradigm for the commercialization of national R&D programs. This paradigm involves newer institutional developments that complement and extend more traditional institutional relationships and rules. The newer institutional developments are providing a set of coherent relationships focusing on national pride, academic excellence, economic growth, and technological diversification.

The drivers for these newer institutional developments are:

1. a desire to foster more basic research;
2. shortages of adequately trained scientists and engineers;
3. difficulty in keeping up to date with developments;
4. gap in new technology transfer, especially when it requires pulling together pure research from different disciplines;
5. a need to fill the gap for diffusion of technology in developing useful commercial products and services by individual companies;
6. increasing international competition; and
7. a determination to diffuse R&D activities across wider geographic areas.

These drivers are taking place within the context of a hypercompetitive environment, where there is need in each community for leadership that reassesses, if not transforms, economic growth. "Hypercompetitive" is a word that connotes the new economy emerging in our American society as a result of intense domestic as well as fierce global competition. Such competition is between states, cities, universities and colleges, industries, sizes of business, as well as between highly industrialized and emerging foreign nations.

At least eight forms of institutional development for commercializing SDI technologies are proposed:

• industrial R&D joint ventures and consortia
• academic/business collaboration
• government/university/industry collaboration
• incubators
• university/industry research and engineering centers of excellence
• small business innovation research programs
• state venture capital funds
• commercialization of university intellectual property

These institutional developments demonstrate the willingness of individuals and institutions to take and share risks in commercializing science and technology. This process provides a means to make and secure the future of local, state, and national economics as well as the future of the participating institutions. Furthermore, the process establishes a newer infrastructure to support entrepreneurship, encourage innovation, and accelerate technology transfer and diffusion.

These eight institutional developments for economic growth and diversification can be directed toward: (1) encouraging emerging industries; (2) providing seed capital for early and start-up entrepreneurial endeavors; and (3) assuring U.S. economic preeminence.

1. *To develop emerging industries.* Institutional relationships involved here are academic and industrial collaborations and industrial R&D consortia. Because the basic research is carried out in the universities and colleges, getting collaborative efforts between academia and industry can accelerate the commercialization of basic research into emerging industries. Industrial joint ventures and consortia are still expanding into newer areas that encompass both high technology and basic industries.

2. *To create seed capital for small and take-off companies.* Some forms of institutional development such as incubators, SBIR programs, and state venture capital funds are providing seed capital for small and take-off companies. They are also pushing regional and local economic diversification through entrepreneurial activities.

3. *To provide for U.S. economic preeminence.* A number of institutional developments are seeking to ensure U.S. economic preeminence. These focus on the creation of National Science Foundation centers of research and engineering excellence, government/business/university collaborative arrangements in technological areas, industrial R&D joint ventures and consortia, and NSF's sponsorship of Industry/University Cooperative Research Centers (IUCR). These are intended to provide a broad-based research program that is too large for any one company to undertake alone.

In conclusion, this landmark volume has recognized the importance of large-scale programs for the comprehensive security of the United States. As a historic large-scale program, SDI has opened up the need for recognizing that undertakings of this magnitude are long-term in nature, can build technology as a resource, require innovative and collaborative policies, and, as a meaningful driver, demand and justify significant investments from both public and private sources. As a large-scale program, it can play an important role in helping to put our nation's economy back into equilibrium and stable growth. The key is to develop multiple uses from our scientific, technological, and human resources through the commercialization process. To do this, we need better mechanisms for technology diffusion that reduce financial and technological risk-taking while expanding risk-sharing across a broader base of recipients.

Perhaps the most counter-intuitive finding of this volume was the recognition that we need people who are multidisciplinary in nature, who can creatively and innovatively transfer technology, and who can successfully link security, profit, and pride in a hypercompetitive domestic/international environment. We do not have such people. Nor are we educating them or deliberately developing cadres through successful experiential learning on the job.

SDI has begun to encompass within its plans the utilization of the newer paradigm for commercializing technology. Through innovative forms of institutional developments, it is creating the infrastructure to accelerate technology transfer. It is certain that as the effort evolves, the SDI program will utilize many of the institutional developments for technology diffusion and commercialization, thereby developing emerging industries and creating small and mid-sized take-off companies.

In the final analysis, the strength of the United States has always been its ability to be scientifically creative, technologically adept, managerially innovative, and entrepreneurially daring. The current SDI program demonstrates the first two abilities. It has the attribute of being scientifically creative and technologically adept. Successful commercialization now depends on being managerially innovative and entrepreneurially daring.

NOTES

1. M. I. Yarymovych, "Leadership Requirements for Large Scale Programs, Large Scale Leadership Short Course," Speech given August 19, 1985, La Jolla, California.
2. Bruce D. Merrifield, "Technology and World Leadership," Speech from "Commercializing Strategic Defense Technologies Conference," Austin, Texas, October, 1985.

APPENDIX

THE SDI OFFICE OF EDUCATIONAL AND CIVIL APPLICATIONS

COLONEL JOSEPH ROUGEAU, USAF
(Retired)

The president's Strategic Defense Initiative is intended to explore the feasibility of enhancing deterrence and reducing the threat of nuclear war through the use of defensive systems. However, national security involves more than the development of military systems and the maintenance of personnel; it requires the maintenance of American economic and intellectual preeminance in today's hypercompetitive global environment.

If the United States cannot compete economically and intellectually with the rest of the world, our national security is diminished no matter which strategic systems we possess.

The Strategic Defense Research effort will require great advances in a number of critical technological areas, discussed in detail in this volume. Because of the tremendous potential for economic benefit to the American people from the fruits of this research, the SDI Office has established the Office of Educational and Civil Applications. This office will encourage the application of results from SDI research across all facets of the economy and society, and will encourage the widest possible use of SDI-related technologies consistent with security considerations. The office will also aid the identification of potential and existing technology applications and techniques that can have economic benefits for the nation.

In developing its program, the office will call upon expertise in the private sector and the universities, as well as the entrepreneurial small businesses known to be vital to job and wealth creation.

The office must also aid in developing the intellectual base at the nation's colleges and universities, as these are the true national resources vital to our future without which no lasting benefits can accrue.

INDEX

Abrahamson, Lt. Gen. James, 35, 171
Accelerator design, 58
Aerospace applications, 34, 45, 58, 70, 71, 96, 98, 159, 171, 174, 175, 191, 199–200, 202; civilian use of space, 166, 174–75; expert system use, 100; financial considerations, 166; free-flying platform module, 174; in-space manufacturing, 34–35, 116–19, 120, 134, 174, 179; launch mechanisms, 146; leading edges, 6; Manned Space Flight Programs, 174; medical research, 161, 162–65, 166, 174; missile nose tips, 6; nose caps, 6; personnel education, 166; research and development, 60; rocket motors, 158; rockets, 158; space boosters, 158; space materials program, 57; space power, 34; space station, 34, 57, 113, 129, 135, 161, 162, 174, 175; space transportation, 34–35, 96; tax benefits, 166; transatmospheric vehicle (TAV), 7, 34, 96. *See also* NASA; Space robotics; Space Shuttle
Agnew, Harold, 21
Air Force Materials Laboratory, 158
Air Force Office of Scientific Research, 47, 56
Aircraft applications, 57–58, 158, 172–73, 219; air traffic control, 33; aircraft design, 55; bombers, 28; breaks, 6, 173; C–5 engine, 172; C–17 cargo transport, 173; guidance, 33; jet engine, 71, 172, 173; jets, 5, 45; J57 engine, 172; jumbo cargo carrier, 58, 173; launch mechanisms, 146; materials, 156, 158; turbofan fan engine, 172–73; turboprop engine, 172. *See also specific aircraft*
Anti-Ballistic Missile (ABM) Treaty, 26, 27, 197, 202; Agreed Statement G, 203; Article IX, 203; technology transfer constraints, 202–4, 207
Antiballistic missiles. *See* Ballistic missiles
Antisubmarine warfare (ASW) technology, 6
Apollo program, 57, 59, 155, 171
Apollo-Soyuz program, 163
Arms control, 10, 12, 27*t.*, 201, 202, 218, 219; illegal missiles, 27
Arms Export Control Act (AECA) [1976], 49, 51
Army Research Office, 47, 56
Artificial intelligence, 7, 96, 99, 135, 139, 150, 152, 199, 200, 214; truth maintenance, 108. *See also* Space robotics

AT&T Bell Laboratories, 71, 172
Atomic accelerators, 19
Atomic energy, 45
Autonomous Land Vehicle (ALV),
135

Ballistic missiles: attack sequence, 29–
30; boost phase, 11, 28, 29, 30;
boost phase intercept, 11, 32, 97;
booster hardening, 33; booster
phase surveillance system (BPSS),
13; bus deployment phase, 28;
chaff, 13, 95; chemical rockets, 18,
28, 30; cost of, 15, 16; decoys, 13,
28, 29, 95; early warning systems,
14; electromagnetic launchers, 30,
31; fast burn boosters, 16; first
warning, 13; flight path of, 28; gun
barrels, 17, 18f., 28, 30, 31; hypervelocity launcher, 32; ICBMs, 24,
45; infrared signature of, 28, 29, 33;
interception of, 11, 13, 14f., 15,
16f., 30; junk, 13; midsource phase,
13–14, 15, 28, 29–30; nuclear-
tipped, 24; penetration aids of, 28;
postboost phase, 28; postboost intercept, 13, 30, 32; production of,
15–16; reentry vehicle, 28, 29–30;
reentry intercept, 13, 15, 30; size
of, 16; space-based launcher, 17,
18f.; terminal phase, 28, 30; terminal intercept, 34; Union of Soviet
Socialist Republics (USSR) defense
system, 26t.; velocity of, 17–18, 32;
war heads of, 28; weight of, 15
Ballistic missile defense (BMD) system, 28, 29f., 95, 202, 203, 204; acquisition, 28, 29, 31f., 95;
antisatellite capabilities, 199; battle
management, 29; during boost
phase, 29, 32; command function,
28–29; control function, 28–29;
damage assessment, 95; destruction, 28; discrimination, 29, 30, 95;
hit-to-kill intercept, 30, 31; interception, 28; kill assessment, 28, 39,
31f.; mobile, 173; during postboost
phase, 32; sensor function, 28, 29–
30; surveillance, 28, 29, 31f.; survivability issues, 199; tracking, 28,
29, 31f., 57, 95; weapon allocation,
28; weapon function, 28, 30, 32
Barlow, Grant, 163
Battle management system, 7, 11, 95,
97, 98, 156, 157; in ballistic missiles
defense system, 29; expert systems
and, 106t.
Bayh-Dole Act (1980), 40
B–52, 219
Bio-Industry Development Center
(Japan), 166
Bioprocessing and Pharmaceutical
Research Center (Philadelphia), 162
Bioprocessing Research Center
(Houston), 162
Biotechnology. See Medical
applications
Black box, 102
Black programs, 64
Boeing 707, 172, 219; 747, 58; 757, 58;
767, 58
Brown and Root, 174
Bucy Report (1976), 51
Business incubators, 90, 188, 220, 221

C³, 97, 98; expert systems and, 106
Capital formation. See Financial
considerationns
Carrier task force system, 28
CAT scan, 6, 34
Center for Electromechanics, Univer-
sity of Texas (CEM-UT), 145, 146,
148
Center for Separation Science (Tuc-
son), 162
Center for Space Policy, Inc., 165
Center for the Utilization of Federal
Technology (CUFT), 48
Cleveland International Research In-
stitute, 129
Comet, 172
Commercial aspects, 33–35, 69, 71,
79, 82–83, 85, 178, 185–89, 197, 199,
211, 217, 218–19, 220, 221, 222;
business dynamics factors of pro-
duction, 83, 84f., 220; commerciali-

zation process, 69; cooperative ventures, 186, 220; of defense technology, 59; institutional developments, 220–21; multidisciplinary research, 56–58; personnel education, 166; personnel involved in, 190; product description, 89; program proposal, 189–91; research and development interface, 4, 6, 7, 69; Sandia National Laboratories (Albuquerque New Mexico and Livermore, California) case study, 193–95; speed of application, 63, 66, 189. *See also* Economy; Financial considerations; Marketing

Commercial products, 5–6; in agriculture, 162, 195, 213; atomic energy, 45; batteries, 194; communication satellites, 5, 33, 195; copier paper-feed mechanism, 119; drills, 148; in electronics, 5, 172, 194–95, 196; encryption technology, 97; expert systems, 99, 100*t.*, 108–11; heat transfer study, 194; high-speed drying, 148; hot gas management, 158; ICBMs, 45; imaging techniques, 34; jeeps, 5; low-density foam, 195; magnetrons, 5; microelectronic component fabrication, 34; microreplication, 34; microwave ovens, 5; miniaturized electronic circuitry, 5; molecular specie discrimination, 34; nonstick frypan, 58; pocket calculator, 172; process control instrumentation, 34; pulse reactor studies, 194; radar, 5, 33; radiation hard microcircuits, 194–95, 196; radiation holography, 34; retinitis pigmentosa goggles, 5; robotics, 115, 129, 131–35; solar terrestrial plasma physics, 56; Sony Walkman, 172; supercomputers, 137–38, 141; Tang, 151; transatmospheric vehicle (TAV), 7; transistor, 172; transportation systems, 34; U.S. Air Defense System (SAGE), 45; weather research, 56; during World War II, 5, 172. *See also* Aero-

space applications; Aircraft applications; Computers; Lasers; Optical technology; Manufacturing applications; Materials; Medical applications

Communication satellites, 5, 33, 57, 71, 95, 96, 97, 155, 158, 195, 214; computers in, 97; COMSAT Corporation, 97; encryption technology, 97; fiber optics, 96, 97; frequency, 96, orbital lifetime, 96; satellite-to-ground links, 97; satellite-to-satellite links, 97; servicing of, 96–97, 113, 119–20; technology, 95–98

Competition, 57, 67, 70, 71, 82, 113, 138, 139, 140, 152, 162, 175, 185, 186, 189, 198, 220

Computers, 11, 13, 14, 57, 63, 71, 95–96, 212, 213, 214; algorithms, 96, 97, 111, 155, 172, 185, 200; benefits of, 102; biochips, 161; in communication satellites, 97; computer simulation, 55; digital gate, 95; firmware, 96; hardware, 11, 71; high-speed, 173; integrated circuits (ICs), 56, 57, 71, 138, 213; logic chips, 139, 140; mainframe, 33, 95; memory chip, 139, 140; microchips, 95; optical, 150, 151, 152; personal computer (PC), 95, 213, 214; programming, 95–96; semiconductors, 14, 140, 155; software, 7, 11, 55, 57, 71, 95–96, 187; Strategic Computing Program, 135; very high speed integrated circuit (VHSIC), 55, 58, 59, 139, 172, 173. *See also* Expert systems; Supercomputers

COMSAT Corporation, 97
Continental Illinois Bank, 180
Control Data Corporation, 138
Coordination Committee (COCOM) [1949], 50, 198, 205, 207
Corporation for Small Business Investment (COSBI), 90
Courier satellite, 5
Cray Research, 138
Cryogenic coolers, 14
CYBER 205, 138

Defense: defensive arms buildup, 12; defensive systems, 24–25, 27, 108, 109*f.*, 199; gross national product and, 4; research and development, 3, 4, 6, 7. *See also* Ballistic missile defense (BMD) system; National security

Defense Advanced Research Projects Agency (DARPA), 7, 47, 139; Autonomous Land Vehicle (ALV), 135; Hypersonic Vehicle, 158; Strategic Computing Program, 135

Defense Logistics Agency, 47; Defense Technical Information Center (DTIC), 47

Defense Production Act (50 U.S.C. App. §§ 1091, 2092, 2161), 180

Deloitte Haskins and Sells, 88

Department of Commerce: Center for the Utilization of Federal Technology (CUFT), 48; Export Administration Act (EAA) [1949], 49, 50–51; National Technical Information Service (NTIS), 47–48; Office of Export Administration, 51; Office of Export Enforcement, 52

Department of Defense (DOD), 57, 58, 64, 96, 134, 139; interest in higher education programs, 58–59. *See also* Technology transfer

Department of State: "International Traffic in Arms Regulation" (ITAR) [1954], 51; Office of Munitions Control, 51

Department of the Treasury: Customs Service, 52

Deterrence policies, 24, 25*t.*, 27

Directed energy technology, 15, 17–19, 21*t.*, 22, 30, 32*f.*, 56, 57, 214; directed energy weapons (DEW), 143

Domenici, Senator, 188

"The Duck," 173

Economic Recovery Tax Act (ERTA) [1981], 41, 43

Economy, 53, 177, 185, 201–2, 211, 213, 214–15, 218, 219, 221; commercialization impact on, 63, 69; jobs

created from new research, 5; in 1920s, 70; in 1930s, 70; research and development impact on, 4–5, 6, 7

Electromagnetic launch (EML) technology, 143–45, applications of, 146, 148; coilgun, 143, 144–45; compulsator, 146, 148; electric power for, 145–46; homopolar generator (HPG), 146, 147*f.*, 148; Lorentz force, 144; pulsed power technology (PPT), 145–46; railgun, 143–44, 146, 148; tactical, 148

Electronics, 5, 34, 172, 194–95, 196, 200, 214

Encryption technology, 97

Energy, 200; atomic, 45; directed, 15, 17–19, 21*t.*, 22, 30, 32*f.*, 56, 57, 214; energy physics, 155; energy programs, 55; energy storage systems, 56; heat transfer study, 194; kinetic, 15*f.*, 16, 17*f.*, 21*t.*, 22, 30, 31*f.*, 56; nuclear power, 71; pulse reactor studies, 194; Sandia National Laboratories (Albuquerque, New Mexico and Livermore, California) program, 193, 194

Enterpreneurship, 69–70, 79, 81–82, 89, 91, 150, 166, 180, 188, 221, 222; enterpreneurial investors, 85–86; increase in, 72 networking, 87, 88; skills for, 81; technology transfer by, 187, 188

ETA Systems, 137, 138

ETA–10, 138

Eureka (European Research Coordination Agency), 197, 199, 200*t.*, 201, 202, 205–7; support of, 206

Expert systems, 99, 111*t.*, 214; advisory knowledge, 105; in aerospace industry, 100; applications of, 101, 103*f.*, 108*t.*; battle management and, 106*t.*, benefits of, 104–5; C³ and, 106; commercialization of, 99, 100*t.*, 108–11; cooperative, 108, 129; in defense systems, 108, 109*f.*; development of, 101; diagnostic knowledge, 105; future system perspective, 107f., 108, 110t., 111; glass box, 102, 104f.; goal of, 102; judgmental knowledge, 100, 105; knowledge acquisition construction, 104; knowledge-based systems, 100, 101f.; knowledge engineer, 104, 105t.; for management systems, 111t.; multiple, 101t., 102; operation of, 100, 101f., 102f.; procedural knowledge, 100; robotics and, 120, 129; small operator interfaces (MMI), 106t.; smart sensor systems, 105t., 106; strategic defense initiative (SDI) and, 105–8; traditional, 100, 102f.; variable processing, 100–101

Export Administration Act (EAA) [1949, 1969, 1979, 1985], 49, 50–51; military critical technologies (MCTL), 51

Export Administration Regulation (EAR), 50–51

Faget, Max, 174
Federal Bureau of Investigation, 52
Federal Laboratory Consortium for Technology Transfer, 48, 187, 188, 190
Federal Reserve System, 180
F–14 fighter, 28
Fiber optics, 96, 97, 157
Financial considerations, 221; accredited individual private placements, 76; business growth characteristics, 74; business plan 89–90; business venture development, 77, 79, 81–84; businesses' financial evolution, 75–76; businesses' goal, 72, 74, 89; capital formation, 72–76, 77, 82f., 83f.; capital gains benefits, 90; commercial bank, 76; commercial paper, 76; common stock, 76; convertible debentures, 76; corporate joint-ventures, 73–74, 76, 77f., 78t., 85, 86–87, 90; Corporation for Small Business Investments (COSBI), 90; direct investment, 86, 87t.; employ-

ment opportunities, 74–75, 79f., 80t., 81f.; entrepreneurial investors, 85, 86; equity financing, 72–73, 74, 86; follow-on deals, 88; foreign investors, 85, 88; future initiatives, 90–91; government grants, 85, 87–88, 90; hurdle rate, 76; initial public offerings (IPO), 72, 73f., 74f., 75f., 76; international placements, 76; investment banking, 72; investment capital, 85; investment grade debt, 76; junk bonds, 76; leasing, 76; leveraged buyouts, 88; line of credit, 86; management team, 77, 79, 81, 89; mezzanine personal resources, 85, 88; minority investment companies (MESBICs), 90; networking, 85, 86, 87, 88; private placements, 76; private financing, 76, 178, 179; R&D funds, 76; R&D partnerships, 76, 86t.; R&D tax credits, 90; risk/return trade-off, 76, 82; royalties, 86; seed financing, 75–76, 90, 221; shareholder wealth creation, 72, 74, 75, 81f., 82f.; small business investment companies (SBICs), 90; for space commerce, 166; for start-up firms, 85–90, 221; state venture capital funds, 220, 221; tax incentives, 86, 90; need for technology investment, 70–72; venture capital, 72, 73, 75, 76f., 88, 89t., 100, 190; venture capital firms, 85, 88–89. *See also* Marketing

Fletcher Study (1984), 9, 21
Focal plane arrays, 29
Fortran, 99
France. *See* Eureka
Freedom of Information Act (Title 5, U.S. Code, Section 552), 49
Funding. *See* Financial considerations

Gallium arsenide (GaAs), 116, 117f., 118f., 119, 156
G. A. Technologies, 194
Genentech, 162
General Electric, 87, 134

General Motors, 87; Crystal Growing program, 174
Goodyear, 173
Government Fluidics Coordinating Committee, 191
Grace, W. R., 87
Great Britain, 205
Gross national product (GNP), defense and, 4
Guns versus butter, 4–5, 6, 7

Harry Diamond Laboratory (HDL), 191
Health care. *See* Medical applications
Homing Overlay Experiment (HOE), 30
Homopolar generator (HPG), 146, 147f., 148
Hypersonic Vehicle, 158

IBM, 87, 119
IBM 360/40 mainframe computer, 95
ICBMs, 24, 45
Industry/ University Cooperative Research Center (IUCR), 221
Infrared sensors, 13, 14, 15, 29, 30
Innovation, 40–41, 43, 44, 63, 69, 70, 82, 186, 187, 188, 189, 221; business incubators, 90, 188, 220, 221; in businesses, 59; commercialization phase, 41; development, 77–78, 79; invention phase, 41; number of years for product production, 40; phases of, 41, 42f.; product phase, 41; risk in, 70; Small Business Innovation Research (SBIR), program, 59, 87–88, 90; Stevenson-Wydler Technology Innovation Act (1980), 48; in Strategic Defense Initiative research, 21, 35. *See also* Technology leadership
Institute for Defense Analysis, 139
International Traffic in Arms Regulation, 52
Invention. *See* Innovation
Investment banking. *See* Financial considerations

Japan, 201, 206, 212; Bio-industry Development Center, 166; Coordination Committee (COCOM) involvement by, 50; cost of capital in, 41; medical research in, 166; supercomputers and, 139, 140, 141; technology use by, 57, 65–66
Jeeps, 5
John Deere Metallurgical, 174
Johnson Space Center (JSC), 163, 174

Kennedy, John F., 70, 179
Kinetic energy technology, 15f., 16, 17f., 21t., 22, 30, 31f., 158; Kinetic Energy Weapons (KEW) program, 143, 146. *See also* Electromagnetic launch (EML) technology
Knowledge systems. *See* Expert systems
Kozmetsky, George, 63

Lasers, 5, 7, 34, 173; chemically powered, 18, 32; free electron, 32; gammaray, 34; ground-based excimer, 18–19, 32; high-power, 71; laser range finders, 5; laser speed indicators, 5; materials for, 157; Mid-Infrared Advanced Chemical Laser (MIRACL), 32–33; mirror system, 18–19, 32; optical, 149–50; research of in Union of Soviet Socialist Republic (USSR), 26; solid state, 148; space-based, 18, 19f., 32; xenon flashlamps, 148
Legal issues, 177–78, 181, 189, 190, 197, 207, 218; Supremacy Clause, 179. *See also* License issues; Patents
Levin, Richard C., 181
License issues, 39, 40, 49, 50–51, 65, 187; general license, 51; validated license, 51
Lilly, Eli, 162
Livermore National Laboratory, 219
Lockheed C–5, 172; C–5A, 58
Los Alamos: Hot Rock Geothermal Energy Program, 190–91; Materials Science and Technology Division, 190; National Laboratory, 219

LTV Hummer, 173
Lubrizol, 87

Magnetrons, 5
Malaria vaccine, 6
Man Tech, 58
Mansfield Amendment, 58
Manufacturing applications, 33, 34,
55, 56, 185; automobile design, 138;
in-space, 34–35, 116–19, 120, 134,
174, 179; optics, 150; in petroleum
industry, 174; processes, 173, 198–
99; space-structure assembly, 120;
supercomputers, 138. *See also*
Materials
Marketing, 81–82, 83; future potential, 82; market conditions, 72–73;
market growth rates, 82; market in-
dentification, 77, 82; market research, 70, 89; market size, 82;
market type, 82; market value equity, 74, 79f., 80t.
Martin Marietta, 119
Maryland (Montgomery County), 188
Materials, 57, 71, 185, 214; for acquisition, 156–57; advanced polymeric
composites, 55, 156; in aircraft,
156, 158; Air Force Materials Laboratory, 158; alloys, 158; aluminum
alloy, 6, 156, 158; amalgams, 156;
for antennas, 157; Beryllium, 33,
157; for cameras, 159; carbon-carbon composites, 6; carbon composites, 158; ceramic matrix
composites, 34; ceramic powders,
146; ceramics, 155, 157–58, 159; for
countermeasures, 156; cryogenic
gas coolant, 158; crystalization of,
174; for detection systems, 156,
157; for engines, 159; fatigue-resistant metal composites, 34; fiber optics, 96, 97, 157; gallium arsenide
(GaAs), 116, 117f., 118f., 119, 156;
for ground-based systems, 157;
heat resistant, 157, 158, 159; hu-
man-made, 56; for icebreakers, 159;
for kinetic vehicles, 158; for lasers,
157; LI900 silica, 157; mercury cadmium (mercad) telluride, 156, 159;
metal matrix, 156; metal powders,
146, 148; metals, 158; molybdenum
mirror, 157; niobium, 158; niobium-
silica alloys, 158; nongrey coatings,
156; for oil drills, 159; in optical
technology, 150, 156, 157; plastics,
58; for radar systems, 159; rapid
solidification metals, 158; for robots, 159; for sensors, 156, 157,
158, 159; for ships, 159; silica, 157;
silica-based ceramics, 158; silicon
carbide mirrors, 157; silicon carbide
whisker-reinforced aluminum, 156;
space materials program, 57; for
strength, 158; for surveillance, 156–
57; for survivability, 156, 157, 158;
synthetic fibers, 63; for targeting
systems, 157; titanium, 5, 158, 159;
for tracking, 156–57; for transportation systems, 158; for weapons,
156, 157–58; for weight reduction,
156, 158
McDonnell Douglas, 163, 164; DC–8,
172; DC–10, 58
Medical applications, 34; acute
trauma care, 6; bioengineering,
163; Bio-Industry Development
Center (Japan), 166; biomedical,
191; bioprocessing, 161, 162, 163t.,
166; Bioprocessing and Pharmaceutical Research Center (Philadelphia), 162; Bioprocessing Research
Center (Houston), 162; bioreactors,
161, 164; biotechnology, 161–62,
166, 188, 213; blood preservation,
6; burn treatments, 6; cancer research, 55, 162, 165; CAT scan, 6,
34; cell cultivation, 161, 162, 163,
164; Center for Separation Science
(Tucson), 162; collaborative research, 162–63; computer biochips,
161; Continuous Flow Electrophoresis System (CFES), 164; diabetes
research, 195; electrophoresis purification system, 163; gene cloning,
161; genetic engineering, 161, 163;
hybridomamonoclonal antibody

production, 161; instrument calibration particles, 165; implantable
insulin pump, 195; insulin, 162; in
Japan, 166; latex microspheres,
164–65; malaria vaccine, 6; maxillofacial surgery, 6; microgravity processing, 163, 164, 165t.; money
from, 162, 165; monoclonal antibody diagnostics, 162; Mycin, 99;
pacemaker, 194; paraplegia, 6;
pharmaceuticals, 56, 161, 163, 164,
174; protein crystals, 165; purification techniques, 161, 162, 163–64,
165; recombinant DNA 6, 161; robotics, 115; space bioprocessing
products, 164t., 165; space research, 161, 162–65, 166; surgery
simulation, 56
Merrifield, D. Bruce, 218
Microelectronics and Computer Tech-
nology Corporation (MCC) [Aus-
tin, Texas], 65, 188
Microwave ovens, 5
Microwave transmissions, 96
Microwave tube, 58
Mid-infrared Advanced Chemical
Laser (MIRACL), 32–33
Military critical technologies (MCTL),
51, 52
Miniaturized electronic circuitry, 5
Minority investment companies
(MESBICs), 90
Minuteman program, 57
Missiles. See specific type
MIT, 188
MITI (Japan), 57
Monsanto, 87
Mycin, 99

NASA, 7, 57, 58, 64, 96, 97, 113, 129,
134, 151, 163, 166, 171, 174; Hyper-
sonic Vehicle, 158; Mars Rover
Project, 134–35; NASAJSC, 164;
NASA Langley, 174; Space Station
Program Office, 113
National Academy of Science Panel
on Scientific Communications and
National Security, 52–53

National Bureau of Standards, 165,
188
National Commission on Space, 166
National Cooperative R&D Act
(1984), 43
National goals, 179
National Institute of Health, 195
National Science Foundation (NSF),
137–38, 139, 221
National security, 52–53, 96, 177,
211–13, 218, 219; comprehensive,
213–14; cultural issues, 214; eco-
nomic issues, 213; educational is-
sues, 214; intellectual issues, 214;
military issues, 213; research and
development for, 5; social/political
issues, 213–14; technology transfer
and, 46. See also Defense
National Security Agency (NSA), 64,
139
National Technical Information Ser-
vice (NTIS), 47–48
NATO, 199, 201, 202
Naval Intelligence, 64
Neuroscience, 56
New Mexico, 188
Night blindness goggles, 5
Nixon, Richard M., 179
North American Aviation, 173
North American Rockwell, 217
Nuclear power, 71

Ocean acoustic tomography, 6
Offensive systems, 25
Office of Naval Research, 47, 56, 63
Office of Research and Technology
Applications (ORTA), 48
Operation Exodus, 52
Optical technology, 14, 18, 20f., 185,
214; astronomy use of, 151; beam
directors, 149, 151; in cameras, 152;
for communication, 152; components, 149, 151; computer engineering, 150, 151, 152; control
devices, 151; fiber optics, 96, 97,
157; image engineering, 149, 150,
151–52; lasers, 149–50; light waves,
149, 150; materials, 150, 156, 157;

mirrors, 151; optical engineering, 149; optical fabrication, 151; optical sensors, 13, 14, 29, 30, 150, 151; phase conjugation processes, 150; quantum engineering, 149–50, 152; robotic sensors, 152; security sensor, 152; switches, 149, 150; trackers, 149, 151, 152

Parallel Market (Amsterdam), 88
Particle beams, 19, 32, 34; research of in Union of Soviet Socialist Republics (USSR), 26
Patents, 40, 43, 59, 181, 189
Phalanx Gun System, 28
Phoenix Missile System, 28
Pratt & Whitney, 172
Pulsed power technology (PPT), 145–46

Radar, 5, 33, 71; imaging, 13, 30; infrared, 159; materials for, 159; sensors, 13, 14
R&D. *See* Research and development
R&D Limited Partnership (RDLP), 41, 86t.
Rapid Solidification Technology, 58
Reagan Ronald: Anti-Ballistic Missile (ABM) Treaty policy, 202; Strategic Defense Initiative (SDI) policy, 9, 23, 36, 202
Research and development (R&D), 70, 220; in aerospace industries, 60; in businesses, 57, 72, 87–88; commercial aspects interface, 4, 6, 7, 69; defense, 3, 4, 6, 7, 58, 66; Department of Defense (DOD), budget, 46; duplication of, 46; economic benefits from, 4–5, 6, 7; goal of, 70; government support of, 71–72, 73–74, 77; growth in, 72; guns versus butter, 4–5, 6, 7; independent R&D (IR&D), 58; jobs created from, 5; joint ventures in, 63, 64, 65; large-scale programs, 217, 221; location limiting, 181; money spent on, 3, 4, 39, 57, 71, 73, 77, 180; National Cooperative R&D Act (1984),

43; for national security, 5; post-World War II, 63; R&D funds, 76; R&D Limited Partnership (RDLP), 41, 86t.; R&D partnerships, 76, 188, 220, 221; R&D tax credits, 90; technology research and, 4, 41; in Union of Soviet Socialist Republics (USSR), 26; zero-sum framework, 4
Retinitis pigmentosa goggles, 5
Riotech, 188
Rockwell Company, 173
Rolls Royce, 172

Safeguard system, 25–26
SAGE (U.S. Air Defense System), 45
Sandia National Laboratories (Albuquerque, New Mexico and Livermore, California), 193–95; energy program, 193; Technology Transfer Officer, 193; weapons program, 193, 194–95
Satellites. *See* Communication satellites
Science, 211, 214, 222; advances in, 6, 211; human progress and, 211; leadership in, 213; moral obligation of scientists, 212; scientific method, 211, 215; transformed into technology, 219–20. *See also* Technology
Score satellite, 5
SDI. *See* Strategic Defense Initiative
Sensors, 13, 14, 29–30, 56, 57, 95, 97, 108, 155, 173; in ballistic missiles defense system, 28, 29, 31f.; during ballistic missiles midcourse phase, 29–30; during ballistic missiles terminal phase, 30; booster phase surveillance system (BPSS), 13; earth sensing systems, 159; homing, 158; infrared, 13, 14, 15, 29, 30; materials for, 156, 157, 158, 169; optical, 13, 14, 29, 30, 150, 151; radar, 13, 14; radar imaging, 13, 30; robotic, 152; security, 152; smart systems, 105t., 106; space-based, 13, 14f., 29; terminal, 158
Shuttle Remote Manipulator System (RMS), 113

Sidewinder missile, 28
Signal processors, 29
Silver market, 180
Small Business Administration, 88
Small Business Innovation Research
(SBIR) program, 59, 87–88, 90; "Re-
quests for Solicitations," 88
Small business investment companies
(SBICs), 90
Solar terrestrial plasma physics, 56
Space applications. See Aerospace
applications
Space Command (Colorado Springs),
98
Space Industries, Inc. (Houston), 174
Space robotics: anomaly reports, 126;
architectural model, 120, 122–29,
135; autonomous robots, 113, 119,
128, 129, 130f., 134–35; Boeing extravehicular robot, 115, 116f.; conceptual framework, 122, 123f.,
124f., contractor reports, 115t.; control execution, 122, 126; control
loops, 122, 126–29; controls, 122,
125, 127; diagnoser, 125, 126, 127;
displays, 122, 125, 127, 134; dumb
robot, 127; effector, 127; executive
control loop, 122, 127, 128; executor, 125, 126, 127; expert systems,
120, 129; fault diagnosis, 129; gallium arsenide (GaAs) production,
116, 117f., 118f., 119; human interface, 134; inferred world state, 126;
in-space manufacturing, 116–19,
120, 134; intelligent robot, 128;
knowledge base, 125, 126, 127;
knowledge-based systems, 129;
knowledge representation, 129; local control loop, 122, 127, 128; manipulator loop, 127, 128f.; meshed
control loops, 127f.; monitor, 125–
26, 127; nominal plan, 125, 126; on-
board monitoring, 120; operator
control loop, 122, 126–27, 128, 134;
operator interface, 122; operator-
systems interface, 115; perceptor,
127; planner, 125, 126, 127; procedural planning, 129; remote manip-

ulation, 115; satellite servicing, 113,
119–20; sensing and perception,
122, 126; simulator, 125, 126, 127;
space-structure assembly, 120;
speech recognition, 134; speech
synthesis, 134; system documentation, 134; studies, 113, 114f., 115–
20, 134, 135; task planning and reasoning, 122, 125–26; technology assessment, 120, 121f.; teleoperator
systems, 113, 122, 127–28, 134
Space Shuttle, 6, 35, 55, 57, 58, 146,
155; commercial use of, 166, 174;
cost of flight of, 166; LI900 silica
tiles, 157; medical research on, 161,
163–64
Sparrow missile, 28
SRI International, 115, 120
Staley, A. E., 87
Stanford University, 99, 188
Stevenson-Wydler Technology Innovation Act (1980), 48, 70–71
Storch, L., 180–81
Strategic Defense Initiative (SDI):
budget, 22, 153; components, 11;
critics of, 171, 175; goal of, 9, 12t.,
25, 36, 71, 185–86, 188, 199, 200,
201; institutional character of, 186,
188; origins of, 9, 23, 24f., 36; rationale for, 23–28; scope of, 28–33;
support of, 178, 201, 206, 218; technology transfer policy, 202, 218
Strategic Defense Initiative Organization, 29, 35, 47; Innovative Science
and Technology Office (ISTO), 56;
Office of Educational and Civil Applications, 35
Strategic Defense Initiative (SDI) research program, 9–22, 23, 26–27,
29; acquisition issues, 13, 155; ally
involvement in, 27–28, 35, 174–75,
181, 200–202, 204–5; architecture,
10, 11; for arms control, 10, 12,
27t., battle management system,
11; competitive bidding, 204–5;
cost-effective factors, 10, 11, 15,
19–20, 21, 25, 34–35, 96, 97, 155,
218; for countermeasures, 9–10, 11–

12, 16, 20, 25; for crisis stability,
10, data fusion, 106; delivery vehicles, 108; diagnostics, 106; directed
energy technology, 15, 17–19, 21,
21*t.*, 56; effectiveness issues, 9, 10;
fail-safe system, 97; Fletcher Study,
9, 21; focal point arrays, 14; identification issues, 155; infrared data,
14; innovation programs, 21, 35;
interception issues, 11, 13, 14*f.*, 15,
16*f.*; interpretation boxes, 106; kill
assessment, 13, 22*t.*, 56; kinetic energy technology, 15*f.*, 16, 17*f.*, 21,
21*t.*, 30, 31*f.*, 56; Kinetic Energy
Weapons (KEW), 143, 146; large
structures development, 97;
launch-vehicle technologies, 96;
midcourse discrimination techniques, 13–14, 15; miniaturization,
97; multitier system, 9, 10, 11; particle beam technology, 19, 26, 32,
34; personnel acquisition, 66, 218;
pointing issues, 33; power supply
issues, 20–21, 34; precision pointing, 173; prediction boxes, 106; requirements for, 10*t.*; support
technologies, 11, 20–21, 22, 34, 56,
106; systems, 56, 57, 95, 108; surveillance issues, 11, 13–14, 21*t.*, 22,
98, 155; survivability issues, 10, 20,
21*t.*, 25, 56, 155; technology issues,
11*t.*, 12, 21, 21*t.*, 34, 71, 171, 185,
195–96, 199, 218; tracking issues,
13, 21*t.*, 33, 155; transportation issues, 155; weight issues, 97. *See
also* Ballistic missiles; Computers;
Materials; Optical technology; Sensors; Weapons
Supercomputers, 7, 55–56, 219; applications of, 138; automobile design,
138; government programs, 139–40,
141; integrated circuits (ICs) design, 138; Japan and, 139, 140, 141;
producers of, 138–39; software,
139; weapons and, 138
Synfuel, 180
Synthetic fibers, 63

Tang, 151
Technology, 198; advances in, 6, 70,
74, 155, 177, 178; goal of, 179, 198;
need for investment in, 70–72, 82;
long-term commitment to, 178–80;
personnel training, 166, 181, 220;
public education in, 178; Rapid Solidification Technology, 58; transformed from science, 219–20; in
Strategic Defense Initiative research, 11*t.*, 12, 21, 21*t.*, 34, 71,
171, 185, 195–96, 199, 218; technical
knowledge, 77; technology assessment movement, 178. *See also*
Science
Technology leadership, 53, 70, 152–
53, 162, 166, 198, 199, 212, 220,
222; antitrust laws, 43; barriers to,
43, 44; Bayh-Dole Act (1980), 40;
capital investment, 41; competition
in, 43; computer-aided design, 43;
computer-aided manufacturing, 43;
cooperative ventures, 43; copyright
laws, 43; cost of capital, 41; Dole
bill S. 1914, 40; Economic Recovery
Tax Act (ERTA) [1981], 41, 43; erosion of in United States, 39–40, 43;
government-owned, contractor-operated (GOCO) laboratories, 40, 47;
government role in, 44; in high-
growth industries, 41, 43; importance of, 41, 43; incentive programs, 40, 41, 43, 44; in industry,
40, 44, 47; manufacturing costs, 43;
National Cooperative R&D Act
(1984), 43; patent laws, 43; number
of patents, 40; R&D Limited Partnership (RDLP), 41, 86*t.*; research
and development and, 4, 41; return
on investment, 40; robotics, 43;
royalties issues, 40; start-up companies, 43; in universities, 40, 44,
47. *See also* Innovation
Technology transfer, 4, 5, 40, 63–67,
77, 79, 81, 83, 171, 175, 185, 199,
202, 219, 221–22; Anti-Ballisitic
Missile (ABM) Treaty and, 202–4,
207; antitrust laws, 207; in busi-

ness, 59–60, 66; controls on, 43, 59–60, 180–81, 189, 190, 198–99, 202; by cooperative initiatives, 66, 187, 188; Coordination Committee (COCOM) and, 207; by entrepreneurship, 187, 188; Federal Laboratory Consortium for Technology Transfer, 48, 187, 188, 190; government's role, 60; impact of, 199–201; by individual initiatives, 187–88; international, 197, 206, 207; licensing, 39, 40, 65, 187; methods of, 171–72, 173, 186–88, 195; mixed, 174; "not invented here" syndrome, 65; by research cooperatives, 188; patents, 59, 189, 207; personnel aquisition, 64; personnel education, 58–59; personnel involved in, 67, 187, 195, 222; plan for, 58–60, 65; procurement cycle, 63–64; by professional communication, 187, 189; proprietary information, 189, 190, 207; quality control and, 66; research results flow, 66, 198, 207, 220; Sandia National Laboratories (Albuquerque, New Mexico and Livermore, California) program, 193; use of special facilities, 187; by staff exchange, 187; Strategic Defense Initiative (SDI) policy, 202, 218; by technical assistance, 187, 189; technology management, 189; time component, 64–67, 189, 221; between unequal programs, 65; by workshops, 187–88

Technology transfer, Department of Defense (DOD) policy, 46; Authorization Act (1984) [P. L. 98–94, Section 1217], 49; bench engineer responsibilities, 48; cargo inspections, 52; through conferences, 47; to contracting agencies, 47; control issues, 49, 50, 51–52; "Dissemination of DOD Technical Information" (Instruction 5200.21), 47; domestic exchange, 47–49, 53; "Freedom of Information Act Program" (Directive 5400.7), 49; inter-

national scope of, 46; large-scale programs, 45; license issues, 49, 50–51; military critical technologies (MCTL), 51, 52; of military technology, 46, 49, 50–51, 52; national security issues, 46, 52–53; on-going programs, 45–46; through open meetings, 47; through publications, 47; "Registration for Scientific and Technical Information Services" (Form 1540), 47; regulations, 47; research and development budget, 46; review process, 46; of scientific and technical information (STI), 47; Scientific and Technical Information Program (STIP) [Directive 3200.12], 47; of space technology, 49; through symposiums, 47; "Technology Application Assessment," 48; technology base, 45, 46; through workshops, 47

Technology Transfer Society, 48–49
Tektronics, 87
Telecommunications. See Communication satellites
3M, 174
Titanium metals, 5
Transatmospheric vehicle (TAV), 7, 34, 96
Truman, Harry S, 179
TRW, 119

Union of Soviet Socialist Republics (USSR): attack structure, 11, 13, 16; ballistic missile defense system, 26t.; research and development programs, 26, 202
United States Air Defense System (SAGE), 45
University of Maryland, 188
University of New Mexico, 194
University of Texas: Center for Electromechanics (CEM-UT), 145, 146, 148
Unlisted Securities Market (London), 88

Very high speed integrated circuits (VHSIC), 55, 58, 59, 139, 172, 173

War, 212; nuclear, 24, 25
Weapons, 63, 98, 155, 158, 213; in
ballistic missiles defense system,
28, 30, 32; cruise missiles, 28; directed energy, 21*t.*, 30, 32*f.*; directed energy weapons (DEW),
143; guns, 144; hypervelocity, 157;
kinetic energy, 16, 17*f.*, 21*t.*, 30,
31*f.*; Kinetic Energy Weapons
(KEW) program, 143, 146; materials
for, 156, 157–58; midcourse, 158;
missiles, 143; nuclear, 33; Phalanx
Gun System, 28; Sandia National
Laboratories (Albuquerque, New

Mexico and Livermore, Caliifornia)
program, 193, 194–95; smart, 15;
supercomputers and, 138; surface-
to-air missiles, 28; tactical, 146, 148;
terminal, 158; thermodynamic gun,
144. *See also* Electromagnetic launch
(EML) technology
Weather research, 56
World War II: Arsenal of Democracy,
177; commercial products from, 5,
172

Yarymovych, Michael I., 217

ABOUT THE CONTRIBUTORS

Bruce Bullock is Vice-President and General Manager of Teknowledge Federal Systems, where he directs the DARPA/RADC Strategic Computing Program Expert Systems Development Effort.

Wayne G. Fox is a Vice-President of Merrill Lynch Capital Markets, Corporate Finance. He is a graduate of the Wharton School of Business, University of Pennsylvania.

George Gamota was former Director of Research in the Department of Defense from 1978 to 1981.

Richard A. Givens is a partner in the firm Botein Hays and Sklar, and Chairman of the Simplification Task Force, New York State Bar Association.

William Gregory retired in 1987 as the Senior Editor of *Aviation Week and Space Technology* for the Northeastern United States. He was formerly the editor in chief of that periodical.

Admiral Bobby R. Inman, USN (retired), was formerly Chairman, President, and CEO of the Micro-electronics and Computer Technology Corporation of Austin, Texas. He was formerly director of the National Security Agency, and Deputy Director of the Central Intelligence Agency. He is currently President of Westmark, Inc., a firm dedicated to commercializing defense technology.

Rodney W. Jones is a Researcher with Science Applications International. He has been a Senior Research Fellow at the Center for Strategic and International Studies at Georgetown University, and a director of Nuclear Policy Studies.

George Kozmetsky is founder and Director of the IC² Institute, President of The Large Scale Programs Institute, founder and Chairman of the RGK Foundation, Executive Assistant for Economic Affairs of The University of Texas System, and the Marion West Chair Professor of Constructive Capitalism. He was the cofounder of Teledyne and the former Dean of the Graduate School of Business of The University of Texas at Austin.

Mark Lancaster is Partner in Charge of International Accounting and Emerging Business for Deloitte Haskins and Sells. He also directs the Emerging Business Services Group that advises entrepreneurs.

Ronald L. Larsen is Assistant Vice-President for Computing, University of Maryland. He formerly managed NASA's research programs in Computer Science, Automation, and Robotics.

Hans Mark is Chancellor of The University of Texas System. He was formerly Deputy Administrator of NASA and Secretary of the Air Force.

John McTague was the Deputy Science Advisor to the President and the Deputy Director of the Office of Science and Technology Policy in Washington, DC. He is now Vice-President for Research at Ford Motor Company.

D. Bruce Merrifield is Assistant Secretary of Commerce for Productivity, Technology, and Innovation. He was formerly Vice-President of Technology and Venture Management for the Venture Group.

Major General Robert R. Rankine, Jr., USAF, was Special Assistant for the Strategic Defense Initiative, U.S. Air Force. He is currently responsible for the Air Force Program in Science and Technology and Space Systems.

Colonel Joseph Rougeau, USAF (retired), was the Director of the Office of Educational and Civil Applications, Strategic Defense Initiative Organization.

Colonel Gilbert Rye, USAF (retired), is Vice President for Government Affairs, COMSAT Corporation. He was formerly National Security Advisor for Space.

Robert R. Shannon is the Director of the Optical Sciences Center of The University of Arizona, and Professor of Optical Sciences.

Eugene E. Stark, Jr. is the Industrial Initiatives Officer at the Los Alamos National Laboratory. He is also the Chairman of the Federal Laboratory Consortium for Technology Transfer.

Robert P. Stromberg is the Technology Transfer Officer for the Sandia National Laboratory.

Gerald D. Sullivan is Deputy Assistant Secretary of Defense for International Programs and Technology Transfer.

Lloyd M. Thorndyke is President and CEO of ETA Systems. He was formerly Senior Vice-President of Technology Development for Control Data Corporation, and has 30 years of experience in the computer business.

Baldwin H. Tom is Associate Director, Bioprocessing Research Center at Houston, University of Texas Health Science Center.

Stanley I. Weiss is Vice-President of the Astronautics Division, Lockheed Missiles and Space Company. He was formerly the NASA Chief Engineer and Associate Administrator for Space Transportation.

William F. Weldon is Director of the Center for Electromechanics at The University of Texas at Austin. He supervises the development of electromagnetic launch technology.

Gerold Yonas is Vice-President, Titan Systems. From 1984 to 1986 he was the Chief Scientist and Deputy Director (acting) of the Strategic Defense Initiative Organization, Office of the Secretary of Defense. He was formerly Director of Pulse Power Sciences, Sandia National Laboratories.

ABOUT THE EDITORS

STEWART NOZETTE

Stewart Nozette is the founding Vice-President of the Large Scale Programs Institute, faculty member of The University of Texas at Austin, Department of Aerospace Engineering and Engineering Mechanics, and IC^2 Institute Senior Research Fellow. He has directed or participated in a number of studies for NASA and the Department of Defense regarding future plans, and he currently supervises research conducted at The University of Texas at Austin, and the Large Scale Programs Institute.

A native of Chicago, Dr. Nozette holds a doctorate from Massachusetts Institute of Technology, where he participated in the NASA Pioneer Venus mission and served as a division scientist at NASA Headquarters in Washington, D.C. Dr. Nozette also heads Macro-Ventures, a California-based consulting and investment firm.

ROBERT LAWRENCE KUHN

Robert Lawrence Kuhn is a strategist, scientist, author, and lecturer specializing in corporate strategy, financial strategy, commercializing high technology, and creative and innovative management. He is an investment banker with expertise in new business formation, venture capital, mergers and acquisitions, and the structuring of innovative financial transactions.

Kuhn is editor-in-chief of McGraw Hill's *Handbook for Creative and Innovative Managers* and Dow Jones-Irwin's *Handbook of Investment Banking* (in press). He is the author of *To Flourish Among Giants: Creative Management for Mid-Sized Firms* and *The Dealmaker* (both from John Wiley & Sons). He has published several books with Praeger, including *Commercializing Defense-Related Technology*.

Dr. Kuhn holds a B.A. in Human Biology from The Johns Hopkins University, a Ph.D. in Neurophysiology from the University of California at Los Angeles, and an M.S. (Sloan Fellow) in Management from the Massachusetts Institute of Technology.

ABOUT THE SPONSORS

Large Scale Programs Institute

The Large Scale Programs Institute (LSPI) was established in 1985 at The University of Texas at Austin to study and stimulate the planning, development, evaluation, management, and implementation of large-scale technological projects and programs. Examples include the space program, the Panama Canal, and selected defense, public works, transportation, and energy projects and programs that require large capital, a long time commitment, and have impact on large human populations. The Institute is a nonprofit corporation involving participation by a consortium of selected universities and industries. The Institute identifies, initiates, and sponsors research conducted in-house and at participating universities, including policy development, methods of cost control, and focused scientific and technological research relevant to a specific project or program. These issues are addressed through focused research, courses, seminars, workshops, conferences, and selected publications.

RGK Foundation

The RGK Foundation was established in 1966 to provide support for medical and educational research. Major emphasis has been placed on the research of connective tissue diseases, particularly scleroderma. The Foundation also supports workshops and conferences at educational institutions through which the role of business in American society is examined. Such conferences have been cosponsored with leading research and academic institutions.

The RGK Foundation Building has a research library and provides research space for scholars in residence. The building's extensive conference facilities have been used to conduct national and international conferences. Conferences at the RGK Foundation are designed not only to enhance information exchange on particular topics but also to maintain an interlinkage among business, academia, community, and government.

IC² Institute

The IC² Institute at The University of Texas at Austin is a major research center for the study of Innovation, Creativity, and Capital (hence IC²). The Institute studies and analyzes information about the enterprise system through an integrated program of research, conferences, and publications.

IC² studies provide frameworks for dealing with current and critical unstructured problems from a private-sector point of view. The key areas of research and study concentration of IC² include: the management of technology; creative and innovative management; measuring the state of society; dynamic business development and entrepreneurship; econometrics, economic analysis, and management sciences; the evaluation of attitudes, opinions, and concerns on key issues.

The Institute generates a strong interaction between scholarly developments and real-world issues by conducting national and international conferences, developing initiatives for private and public-sector consideration, assisting in the establishment of professional organizations and other research institutes and centers, and maintaining collaborative efforts with universities, communities, states, and government agencies.

IC² research is published through monographs, policy papers, technical working papers, research articles, and three major series of books.

Deloitte Haskins & Sells

Deloitte Haskins & Sells is a worldwide accounting and consulting firm of more than 26,000 people from 420 offices in 69 countries. Clientele include leaders in every segment of private and public companies. Among its numerous specialty groups, the firm has professionals in high technology and financial advisory services for entrepreneurs. They provide a full range of integrated services to clients in electronics, medical, high technology manufacturing, and related industries.